SUCH BAD COMPANY

Such Bad Company

The story of Glasgow criminality

George Forbes and Paddy Meehan

Hell is empty and all the devils are here . . .
Shakespeare

PAUL HARRIS PUBLISHING

EDINBURGH

First published 1982
by Paul Harris Publishing
40 York Place
Edinburgh

ISBN 0 86228 042 7

Typeset by Scotprint Limited
Musselburgh
and printed and bound
by Blackwell Press Ltd.

CONTENTS

Introduction

Brendan Behan, the bibulous Irish playwright, once maintained that anyone who has to bother writing an introduction should not have bothered with the book in the first place. But in the present instance, the authors felt justified in stating their credentials at the outset which qualify them to write about the brawling, boisterous, blousy and often sinister history of Glasgow's underworld, especially at a time when the word 'expert' is coming under closer scrutiny with regard to criminal matters.

Who is an expert in this shadowy field? We maintain that a newspaper reporter who has spent more than sixteen years covering crime stories in Glasgow plus a Gorbals criminal of a later generation who has spent his years since childhood in the city's nether regions, and who also received a Royal Pardon for a murder he did not commit, perhaps qualify as a more redoubtable and practical team than any from academic ivory towers.

We also felt that it was about time a proper history of this kind should be undertaken while memories were still fresh, witnesses alive and remnants of an older Glasgow still to be found in haunted nooks and crannies, especially since the city spawned such a rich array of characters, a practice which seems to be on the decline.

SUCH BAD COMPANY

Many histories of Glasgow have been written but these have been dour and respectable and have taken little account of the wide range over the years of its more dubious citizens. Many notorious and fascinating criminal cases involving Glasgow had previously only been dealt with in books either in a superficial manner, almost as a footnote or not at all.

To remedy this situation we interviewed scores of people involved in these cases (which meant many a glass of whisky bought in some low-life surroundings), as well as relying on our own personal involvement in some of them. First hand information from contacts was much more important and detailed than the skimpy information which can be culled from reference books. Court records and newspaper libraries filled in background details. Lawyers, policemen, criminals and journalists all helped furnish information, resulting in what we hope is new insight and some fresh daylight being shed into dark corners.

The contribution has been a mutual one in all chapters and not simply in Chapter 16 which deals with the Meehan case. And we have dealt with cases in chronological order as far as possible.

Obviously it would be impossible to go over all the major crimes committed in a city which was once numbered amongst the world's largest until redevelopment, recession and emigration took their toll.

What we have done is select those cases which are of interest for legal, psychological or historical reasons as well as those which might intrigue the criminologist, amateur or otherwise. As Sherlock Holmes said, "The game's now afoot!" This history of Glasgow is violent but it is to be hoped there are some lessons to be learned.

George Forbes
Paddy Meehan
Glasgow, December, 1981

CHAPTER 1

The Twilight People

It was the Act of Union between Scotland and England in 1707 which vastly increased the trade and industry of the small township of Glasgow and opened the floodgates to the millions of workers who have gathered on the banks of the Clyde and, for better or worse, have helped create the city's glories and despairs ever since.

The name of Glasgow derives from the gaelic 'glas' and 'dhu' meaning a dear, green place and this was an apt description from the time St. Mungo built his church beside the Molendinar Burn in the sixth century up until the 18th century.

The creation of a united kingdom meant that the colonies were now wide open to entrepreneurs in Glasgow and trade with the Americas created the first wealth. Tobacco barons and merchant princes proliferated and no longer was it possible to fish peacefully for salmon in the narrow stream of the Clyde. The channel was widened and deepened, wharves were built, sailing ships plied their trade, the first tall cranes of shipyards pointed skeletal fingers against the sky, warehouses, markets, taverns, town houses, all the accoutrements of a thriving trading port sprouted up to obliterate the grass of the dear, green place. In the eighteenth century the population increased eight times and more than four hundred home based merchantmen plied in and out of the Firth of Clyde carrying away cloth, iron, leather, glass and timber and bringing back tobacco, sugar, rum, limes, lemons and mahogany. The city became the natural outlet for the pulsating industrial energies of the Central Lowlands.

But before all this happened there were those who saw the Act of Union not as a blessing but as a threat and there are still some who share their point of view.

At the time of the Union Glasgow's population was a mere 14,000 but they were a vociferous lot and the town was boastfully called the Capital of the West. The lower orders regarded the Union as a financial sell-out by the aristocracy and there was a full scale riot against it instigated by a patriotic minister, the Rev. James Clark of the Tron Church, who implored "divine deliverance from the impending calamity" and urged his congregation to "be up and valiant for the city of our God!"

Drums were beaten through the back streets and thousands formed a howling, chanting mob. They stormed the house of Provost John Aird, stealing twenty five muskets in the process, and he had to flee to more civilised Edinburgh. A petition signed, or at least marked, by many of the citizens was delivered to the Scottish Parliament declaring their abhorence of the Union with England. The situation gradually calmed down but no sooner had Provost Aird returned than a fresh and worse riot broke out to free some of the ringleaders who had been arrested.

Daniel Defoe, in his *History of the Union,* recounts what happened next, "The Provost went towards his own house; the rabble immediately gathered about him thrusting and abusing him, and not with villainous language only, but with stones and dirt and such like thrown at him. He would have made to his own house but the multitude increasing, and growing furious, he took sanctuary in another house, and running up a staircase lost the rabble for some time — they pursuing him into the wrong rooms; however they searched every apartment to the top of the stair, and came into the very room where he was; but the same hand that smote the men of Sodom with blindness, when they would have rabbled the angels, protected him from this many-headed monster and so blinded them that they could not find him. It is the opinion of many of the soberest and most judicious of the citizens, that if they had found him, their fury was at the time so past all government, that they would have murdered him, and that in a manner barbarous enough; and if they had, as we say of a bulldog, once but tasted blood, who knows where they would have ended. The provost was hid in a bed, which folded up against the wall, and which they never thought of taking down".

Once the mob had gone the quavering provost managed to stay in the shadows until a friend was able to give him a horse and he was able to ride pell-mell for Edinburgh for a second time.

The mob now stormed the tolbooth, seized the town's arms and roamed the streets looting and plundering and stopping people in the streets with the threatening question, "Are you for the Union?" to which there was only one prudent reply.

Deciding to organise itself into an insurrectionary army, the rabble set off on the long walk to disperse the Parliament sitting in Edinburgh because they were deemed traitors. But the ragged band received so little support on the way that they decided to turn back for home.

The Government in the capital now decided a fortnight of this anarchy in the west was enough and despatched a detachment of dragoons and horse grenadiers under Colonel Campbell, uncle to the Duke of Argyll, to quell the rabble.

Realising the town was standing on its own against the might of the United Kingdom, the rioters decided to save their necks and surrendered. The authorities were surprisingly lenient with the ringleaders and they were discharged once the Union had been ratified.

By the time the Jacobite rebellion of 1715 broke out the towns people had been so converted to the benefits of the Union that they lent their support to the Government. But the Old Pretender and his followers never even got as far as their gates and a burlesque

Jacobite song sung in the town's taverns summed up the Glaswegians attitudes to the '15:

There's some say that we wan,
Some say that they wan,
Some say that nane wan at a', man;
But ae thing I'm sure,
That at Sherriffmuir
A battle there was which I saw, man;
And we ran, and they ran,
And they ran, and we ran,
And we ran, and they ran awa, man.

So there such a race was,
As ne'er in that place was,
And as little chase was at a', man;
Frae ither they ran,
Without touk o' drum,
They did not make use o' a paw, man!

However, during the '45 rebellion the city — as Glasgow was fast becoming — and its citizens were unwilling hosts to Bonnie Prince Charlie and his Highland horde on their retreat from Derby.

The staid Lowland trading folk, thriving on the prosperity the expanding commercial empire of Great Britain was bringing to them, were not only pro-Government and Protestant but they could also remember tales of how these wild Gaelic plunderers used to come raiding down from the hills. As a result of their cold "get on your way" reception, the Highlanders wanted to reduce Glasgow with fire and sword. However, Cameron of Lochiel, a more merciful and practical man than most of the angry, dispirited clansmen, swayed Prince Charles Edward to let a ransom of £10,000 be taken from the citizens rather than their homes and lives. As a result the city, after negotiations, was forced to fit out the army with 12,000 shirts and 6,000 coats, pairs of shoes, pairs of stockings, waistcoats and bonnets. The Prince reviewed them in December 1745 and the ladies of the town remarked on what a gallant and dashing body of men they were, considering they were marching to their doom.

The debacle which followed the crushing defeat at Culloden allied to the Highland Clearances helped swell the working population of Glasgow even more and as a result both prison and police conditions had to be overhauled to deal with the tidal wave of crime which follows any population explosion in a growing urban area with poor housing and more demand for jobs than supply.

Glasgow had a tolbooth as far back as 1610 where an archive states that one George Smith was to receive £20 annually to wind up the tolbooth clock for the rest of his life.

The first proper prison was in Duke Street and it later became a women's prison. It was a large, grim, grey building like most prisons and had a clock which never went and a flagpole on which a black flag was hoisted after someone was hanged. The deceased's resting place was inside the prison walls, literally inside, with only his or her initials in the stonework to signify they had ever existed. There was also a Bridewell in College Street and between them these three establishments adapted themselves and tackled the growing problem of prisoners for more than a hundred years.

The Tolbooth, having stood a grim witness to public hangings and scourgings, was eventually only used as a debtors prison and in this age of penal reform and special units it is interesting to note how surprisingly enlightened the authorities were in the 1780's.

In a prison regulation book compiled at this time it states:

When the powerful hand of Providence is laying chastenings upon the sons of men, and for a while afflicts them, it behoves them to submit with humility, and show by their conduct that they are more than ever willing to become good members of society, and improve, as becometh that time of affliction, in the mutual discharge of those duties they reciprocally owe to each other.

No set of men should attend more anxiously to live in a friendly intercourse than those whose similarity of situation bring them together. Persons who are unfortunate, and by unforseen accidents have become by the wise laws subject to be taken from their families and shut up in prison; surely such should comfort and sympathize each other, and ever be ready to ease each others burden. The man who can add distress to distress with an unfeeling heart, should be shunned as the common enemy of mankind, and banished from among the civil, the good and the humane.

Without proper regulations no set of men can live happy, and no place requires a more strict observance of decency and decorum than a prison; for in that place they are deprived of the company of their wives, children and dearest connections who can condole with them.

In order therefore to prevent the horrors of a-jail being multiplied, the following rules are to be most strictly observed.

There then follows a list of twenty five rules for the prisoners, who could walk freely among several rooms on the upper floor of the Tolbooth, to obey, chief of which were:

a) that they could elect their own provost, collector and clerk to supervise and discipline among themselves, with the right to hold their own courts to send troublemakers or unwanted people to separate cells.

b) money the prisoners made or were given by friends was used to help furnish the rooms and supply necessities for all.

c) every prisoner freed was to donate a shillings worth of liquor to the rest remaining and smoking was allowed unless three or more prisoners objected.

d) lights went out at eleven o' clock at weekends and midnight the rest of the week.

As can be seen, in this particular prison the bad old days behind bars were not as bad as has sometimes been painted and enlightenment is not the prerogative of present day reformers. Women are naturally not mentioned in the rules but it would not be difficult to imagine the jailer receiving a bribe to let in some ladies of the town to brighten up the night.

In the Bridewell, too, the enlightened governor in the 1800's was keen to keep his prisoners occupied so that we find the flock under his control being taught such diverse trades as engraving, weaving, tailoring, clock making, shoe making, furniture making, hat making, nail making and even whip making.

An inspector of Scottish prisons in the early nineteenth century waxed eloquent:

The Glasgow prisons present a scene of unflagging and contented industry which it is delightful to look upon. Every apartment is a model of cleanliness; all is lightsome and airy; yet enough of restraint remains to remind the inmates of their position as prisoners. It is, in every sense of the word, a reformatory institution; and many who go in as ignorant and brutalized as "the beasts that perish" come out able to read, write and cypher, and possessed of the hands of expert workmen. From the regular nature of the occupation, and the absence of every injurious stimulant, there are few of the outcasts picked off our streets whose health does not materially improve by a twelve months incarceration; and there are numberless cases of felons going in haggard and attenuated who come out vigorous, plump and rosy. The great want is some intermediate place between the prison and the public; for many who leave the place with a sincere desire to do well, lapse again into the paths of crime, from the urgency of their immediate needs, and the difficulty which they feel in incorporating themselves in the ranks of honest people.

The prison is, in fact, becoming a kind of universal workshop; and the storeroom, fitted up by the present Governor, filled to the ceiling with articles of prison manufacture, is one of the most interesting collections of the kind in the kingdom. There may be purchased a hundred various articles between a pair of braces and an eight day clock. It is a perfect model of a prison store.

An average meal for a prisoner at this time would be eight ounces of oatmeal made into porridge with a pint of buttermilk for breakfast; three pounds of boiled potatoes with salt for lunch; five ounces of oatmeal porridge with one half-pint of buttermilk for tea; all of which cost per prisoner two pence three farthings per day.

But if Glasgow's growing prosperity needed larger and better developed prisons to deal with rising crime it needed even more a strong and properly organised police force to catch the criminals and it took the authorities some time to get round to this.

For centuries a watch and ward system had applied in Glasgow's streets involving night-watchmen who patrolled from dusk till dawn with the wealthy city bailies holding the power of life and death over wrongdoers. The night-watchmen also had to call out the hour — "Twelve o' clock and all's well!" — and also light what street lanterns there were. One of their less pleasant tasks was to sweep the streets and clear them of horse dung.

These night-watchmen were often the butt of practical jokes sprung by drunken young blades during the night. In the 1790's Glasgow had its own Hell Fire Club, a group of debauched local aristocrats who made it their crusade, like their namesakes south of the border, to break society's rules. The night-watchmen were usually impoverished elderly Highlanders, nicknamed 'Charlies', because very few citizens were desperate enough to take the job. The Hell Fire Club used to gather in the East End, put on white nightgowns, cover their horses with white sheets and muffle their hooves, put on white hoods then do the rounds of the watch-men's sentry boxes, terrifying the wits out of the superstitious Charlies. Frequently, they would lay the quivering Charlie on the ground and put his heavy wooden box over him so that he would have to lie there until the blush of morning or until some early morning reveller tripped over the box or heard his muffled cries. For months the Charlies were haunted by fear of the phantom riders until one of them put up a fight and tore some sheets off the 'ghosts'.

On another frolic in February 1793 the Club lived up to its inflamatory name by paying a visit to the session house of the Tron Church which was not only used as a meeting place of the Presbytery but was also the nightly guard house of the Charlies. At three o'clock on the morning of the 15th all was well so the night watchmen carelessly left their headquarters unattended to make a tour of inspection of the outposts throughout the town. The Club members, who were wending their way home from a carousal, burst into the session house and took part in some horseplay. They toyed with the idea of a black mass in the churchyard but decided it was too cold. While toasting themselves at the roaring fire they decided to see who could withstand the longest heat of the flames, especially with the supposed prospect of Hell ahead of them, and to this end they piled on the wood and furniture and panelling and wagers until the flames were licking the ceiling and they had to flee for their lives as not only the session house but also the church went up in a glorious blaze and was totally destroyed. The Charlies who had been absent were dismissed.

Shortly before this inferno the first police force had been officially formed then disbanded. The rising crime rate had forced those in authority to appoint an Inspector of Police along with a number of constables, sergeants and officers under his control. But because of lack of funds, due to stinginess on the part of the merchant classes and gentry, the Inspector resigned and the old night-watchmen system was reintroduced.

It was seven years later in 1788, because the crime rate was reaching crisis point and the propertied class was losing too much property, that another attempt to organize a police force was made. A Bill seeking to assess the city's inhabitants to raise the funds for the upkeep of the police force was presented to Parliament. This Bill proposed that the control of the police force should be in the hands of the magistrates, dean of guild, deacon convener and the heads of the Merchants and Trade's House without permitting the rate-payers any direct voice in the election of those who had control of the police force or the funds. The Bill was heavily defeated. But two years later another Bill was presented and this time, due to the fact that the magistrates and merchants decided to give the citizens a say in the running of the force, the Bill succeeded.

The first Glasgow Police Force was comprised of a Master of Police at a salary of £200 per annum and under him were two sergeants, six officers and sixty eight watchmen or constables. The constables were paid £26 per annum. For a police station the force was given use of the rebuilt Tron session house. On the night of 15th November 1800 the force mustered for the first time. The constables were given a brown greatcoat and a stave. The sergeants and the Master of Police were issued with full uniforms consisting of a blue cloth coat and vest and breeches to match. Both sergeants and officers wore tall hats and were distinguished by braided shoulders. The constables still had to sweep the streets, call out the hour of the night and, in addition, the state of the weather.

The session house was found to be unsuitable and a move was made to a close at the corner of Bell Street and Candleriggs. The new premises took up the ground and first floor and boasted seven cells and two large closets. After three years the Master of Police resigned because he felt the force was not getting the financial support it deserved and he was replaced by a publican who resigned after only two years when he was asked to do patrol work along with the others.

In those days the High Court sat in the spring and autumn in a building behind the Bridewell. The death sentence, flogging and transportation were all common punishments for a large variety of offences, most of which would warrant no more than an admonishment, a fine or probation today. The condemned cell was in the upper story of the building behind the Tolbooth steeple and from its window the hapless prisoner could see the gallows on which he would soon dangle in public.

The Sheriff Court sat on Wednesdays, usually with the Sheriff on the bench drunk, his presence being no more than a figurehead representing the Law. The real business was done by the depute clerk. The Magistrates Courts dealt with what was then called the simple offences but, considering that ten-year-old boys were being hanged for picking pockets, these cases must have been very simple indeed.

Cases which were not at all simple and which plagued the wee sma' hours of the first Glasgow Police Force were those involving Resurrectionists or 'sack-'em-up boys'. These were the names given to bodysnatchers who robbed graves to supply the medical profession with anatomical subjects. Respectable people were caught up in this ghoulish trade and not all of them were dead.

The Burke and Hare crimes of 1827 and '28 were only examples of a more widespread practise than many cared to admit and the two Edinburgh ruffians' notoriety stemmed more from the fact that they circumvented the graveyard and murdered their victims thus being simple murderers rather than bodysnatchers. But the fact that there was a demand for bodies horrified the general public and the fact that an excellent anatomist like Dr. Knox had to flee the country because he gratefully took Burke and Hare's specimens without asking questions was also an example of a general malaise. In fairness to the keen scientific gentlemen it is difficult to see how the furtherance of anatomical studies could be achieved while there was a Kirk inspired ban on touching the dead. Knox's downfall is commemorated in a children's street chant of the time which ran:

Up the close and doon the stair
Ben the hoose wi' Burke and Hare,
Burke's the butcher, Hare's the thief,
Knox the boy who buys the beef.

However, fourteen years earlier a similar fate befell a distinguished Glasgow colleague of Knox's which should have warned him of what to expect when you dabble with shadowy figures bearing sacks at midnight.

Glasgow Cathedral and Ramshorn churchyards were being robbed several times a week and because of the public outcry over the desecration of graves the police decided to act by quietly mounting sentries. On the 13th December, 1813 a wealthy local woman, Mrs. McAllister, was laid to rest in Ramshorn churchyard and later that night taken out again by a group of muffled students cursing in the dark about the intense cold. They were heard by an equally frozen but vigilant policeman who gave chase. He lost them in the dark but said he had last seen the four of them carrying their grisly bundle running in the general direction of the College. Word spread among the already discontented populace who all wanted to be left in peace when they passed away and not interfered with by prying students. An angry crowd gathered outside the College and started smashing windows. The Magistrates decided a search warrant was in order if only to allay the mob and the police duly raided the rooms of the anatomy professors accompanied by Mr. James Alexander, who was a surgeon dentist, and two friends of Mrs. McAllister's. One of the rooms searched was that of Dr. Granville Sharp Pattison who was extremely annoyed at what he regarded as an unwarrantable intrusion. They found nothing and the search party had left when Mr. Alexander remembered they had not examined a bathtub of murky water. They returned, probed the depths and came up with a jawbone with several teeth still attached as well as some fingers and parts of a torso. Mr. Alexander rather promptly said he recognised the teeth as those of Mrs. McAllister and a furious Dr. Pattison and four of his students were taken to jail, having run the gauntlet of the lynch mob outside. After digging up the doctor's floorboards the police uncovered several parts of bodies including what was presumed to be the fresh remains of the much abused Mrs. McAllister. The parts were put in glass receptacles.

On Monday 6th June, 1814 a still indignant Dr. Pattison, three students and a lecturer were tried in Edinburgh because feeling was running so high against them in Glasgow. The indictment only mentioned Mrs. McAllister's body as having been "ruthlessly or feloniously violated by the prisoners and her body taken to their dissecting rooms where it was found and identified". But providence was on the side of the doctor and science, at last. The Defence brought forward expert medical evidence that the portions of body produced could not possibly have been that of Mrs. McAllister. She had been married and borne children; the prosecution productions were portions of a woman who had never given birth. And the doubtful evidence of the teeth was too weak on its own. The result was an acquital but Dr. Pattison had to emigrate to America because of his unpopularity and the threat of further prosecution. He later achieved distinction and honours as a surgeon but ever after would go into a rage whenever Scottish Law or its "ignorant populace" were mentioned.

Heavy stones and elaborate railings were put over graves in the Ramshorn but this did not stop the enterprising students. At the Medical Faculty of Glasgow University they even took to importing corpses from Ireland in sacks irreverantly marked 'potatoes'. This was only discovered one summer at the Broomielaw wharf when one of the imports gave the game away by exhuding an obnoxious odour.

Trap guns were also laid beside graves and around this time a student was shot dead after stumbling over one during a midnight foray. His two colleagues, more terrified that they would be found than taken aback at the fatal accident, tied each of his legs to each of their inside legs and, with him propped between them in the middle, acted drunk and made it safely back to the college past several bored policemen. The student was put to bed and it all ended as an unsolved murder. Poetic justice was done when he was later dissected.

Another two ingenious students having raised a body from the quiet, unguarded village graveyard in Newton Mearns outside the city still had to get it past the keeper of the Gorbals toll house. They wrapped the corpse up in an old suit and overcoat and placed it upright between them on the front seat of their cart. They told the toll keeper their friend was sick and when a light was flashed on the corpse the keeper sighed, "Oh! Puir auld bodie, he looks unco ill in the face; drive cannily hame, lads, drive cannily". And they went on their way.

Sometimes guards were hired by the wealthy to watch over the newly buried and in the High Church burying ground around the time of the Burke and Hare terror an aristocratic lady was interred and two destitute weavers hired to watch over her for at least a week. One night they were sitting by the grave celebrating their employment and keeping out the cold with wine when they saw some shadowy figures begin to dig up another grave. Crouching behind a headstone they watched and listened and it was obvious the group were highly nervous students. Having dug up the body they put it in the customary sack and went off to reconnoitre if the road outside was clear of police or passers-by. The tipsiest of the two weavers, who was somewhat droll in his humour, suggested a practical joke to his friend. The students duly returned and, lifting up their load, made for the road. Once there one of them enquired, "Which way will we take?" From inside the sack boomed the weaver's voice, "Down the Rotten Row, ye scoundrel!" The sack was instantly dropped and the terrified students ran off as fast as their feet could carry them.

The bodysnatcher scare reached the proportions of a full scale riot on the afternoon of Sunday February 17th, 1822. The house of Mr. George Provand, an oil and colour merchant in Clyde Street, was believed to be not only the base of a ring of bodysnatchers but also was reputed to be haunted by those who had been "resurrected". Strange lights, sounds and grey shapes had been noted at the witching hour. This was evidence enough for the wilder elements of the populace and a large crowd stormed and wrecked the house. Police who arrived on the scene were stoned and beaten and had to run for their lives. Mr. Lawrence Craigie, the Chief Magistrate, ran dishevelled and panic stricken to the cavalry barracks in Laurieston while one of his colleagues ran to the infantry barracks in the Gallowgate. Having rallied a troop of bold men Mr. Craigie mounted a dragoon horse and, the occasion having gone to his histrionic head, led a charge sabre in hand at full gallop across the Jamaica Bridge while the infantry with fixed bayonets backed him up in double quick order. The disorganised rioters faced with this onslaught split up and dived up closes, down alleys, some even into the river to avoid the wrath of the authorities.

The next morning Mr. Craigie issued a reward of two hundred guineas to any person who would name the ringleaders. Five were arrested as a result. All were sentenced to be transported to Botany Bay and one, Richard Campbell who was a weaver and a former policeman, was in addition scourged through the city by the hangman, the last whipping of its kind. At high noon on 8th May a strong detatchment of the fourth dragoons paraded in front of the jail and Campbell was bound to a cart. First halt was on the south side of the jail where the hangman gave him twenty lashes with a cat o' nine tails. Next stop was at the foot of Stockwell Street, the third at the top and the fourth at Glasgow Cross — eighty lashes in all with the prisoner groaning and screaming all the while.

Rioting seemed to be an outlet for the fiery Glasgow temperament every so often but the working class which inaugurated them came off second best every time. Certainly some of the troubles were inaugurated on points of principle but inevitably criminal elements took advantage of the lawlessness for their own ends. Considering the squalor of the workers slums during the Industrial Revolution it is a wonder there was not revolution of another kind and this would seem to support the cynical theory that it is better to keep the lower orders under altogether than give them a taste of freedom.

There was that regular defect of capitalism, a trade depression, throughout 1837 when the market slumped and workers were made idle and wages reduced. A spate of strikes were started by cotton spinners who formed a trade union in Glasgow and the colliers and iron miners unions in Lanarkshire followed suit. More than 80,000 men were eventually on strike and, allied to the unemployed, huge bands of ragged men defiantly roamed the streets with banners flying and drums beating. Blacklegs were brutally beaten up when they tried to push through factory gates and the police with a mere 280 men could do little about this. But the situation took a grimmer turn when an organiser of blackleg labour was shot dead in a city street. The bosses, realising the situation was getting rapidly out of hand, held a summit conference and offered a reward of £500 for information about the murderer.

Three days later a couple of informers were met by a Sheriff Alison in a vault under the old college and they told him of a plot to assassinate the new hands and master manufacturers in the city one after another until the demands of the combined workmen had been met. The next meeting of the plotters was to be in the Black Boy Tavern in the Gallowgate on Saturday July 29th.

At nine o'clock on that night the bold Sheriff accompanied by the Procurator Fiscal and Sheriff Officer rendezvoused with twenty policemen outside the close containing the vile den. In the darkness the police silently covered all possible escape routes. The Sheriff, Fiscal, Sheriff Officer and Captain of Police then entered the tavern and went up a ladder, through a trap door and found the plotters, sixteen of them, in session, lit by one gas lamp with the table covered in money. The Sheriff declared, "The game's up! You're surrounded!" They gave in without violence.

On the Monday the cotton spinners met on Glasgow Green and by a large majority voted to go back to work on the masters' terms. The trial of the plotters, most of whom it turned out were cotton spinners, was held at Edinburgh in August and all were given sentences of seven years transportation without any of them naming who had killed the blackleg.

The city was then free of mass trouble until 1848 when another riot took place after a mob of "ill-fed, ill-clad and half armed Chartists", to quote a contemporary account, looted the centre of the city. A local harridan nicknamed Biddy because of her capacity for cheap red wine was one of the ringleaders of the mob who were roused from their East End hovels more at the prospect of booty than for any political ideals. Biddy enterprisingly piled a cart with silver plate and it took the combined forces of the police, the military, special constables and 'merchant princes' to charge the barricades which the rioters had set up. Several people were killed in the ensuing pitched battle in which legitimate guns on the military's side and stolen muskets on the rioters side were widely in use. Any weapon to hand was wielded and many a head was broken by a police baton and the Royal Infirmary was cluttered up with casualties. Order was eventually restored by force of numbers and the rioters fled back to their slumland warrens where it took the police weeks to weed out the main culprits. Biddy was eventually traced and cornered in an old disused malt barn. There was no sign of the silver, however, and it was only a curious constable who found it when he poked his head through the skylight and saw the roof arrayed with the stolen goods which were sparkling in the sun like a sultan's dome. Because of her 'weak mind' Biddy was lucky to get off with a light sentence.

The reasons for these outbursts by the poor and underprivileged are not difficult to find. A survey of the night life in the city centre in the mid 1800's says enough about their social conditions. In less than a sixteenth of a square mile around the Trongate there were two hundred brothels and one hundred shebeens, sometimes every house in a close being given up to these activities. The drinking dens had their pecking order like most things in society. There were the larger, more respectable ones which could cater for up to forty in a big room, a snug for the toffs and an overflow capacity in the kitchen. Then there were smaller ones in the wynds and impromptu portable ones on stairheads where, when gas was invented, the more desperate clientele would bubble the gas through milk thereby creating a potent mixture which in more modern times came to be known as electric soup. Lastly, there were those dens which were a shadowy but raucous combination of shebeen, brothel and thieves' kitchen where stolen goods, illicit hooch and semi-naked whores were the order of the day.

A glance at the prison statistics shows that with the proliferation of commerce and industry on the Clyde and with a growing population of more than half a million in the mid nineteenth century, there was likewise a growth of criminality in the twilight world which the more prosperous elements of society preferred to ignore. To take Duke Street Prison as an example, in 1810 there was an average of 476 inmates per day; in twenty years this had risen to 1,886 and fourteen years after that it stood at 3,414. There were five city centre police courts built in addition to the Sheriff and High Courts whose sittings grew progressively longer. At the Central Police Court alone there were 2,550 offenders sent to prison annually in the mid 1800's. Considering the police had to rely on their feet, their initiative and sheer luck, with none of the modern aids to detection, the true crime rate must have been staggering. The dear green place had certainly come of age.

The ultimate punishment, of course, was hanging and it was widely used without having any noticeable effect of keeping the crime figures down. The hangman was, not unnaturally, an unpopular figure among the criminal classes and often after one of their number had been 'topped' he would have to flee from a howling rabble who were after his blood through narrow alleys and wynds, frequently seeking refuge in the snug of a tavern. There is an old pub called *The Hangman's Rest* to this day off the Candleriggs and it is supposed to have gained its name from this nerve-wracking tradition.

When a Glaswegian used to say "you will die facing the monument" there was nothing complimentary about it. What the phrase meant was that you would end up on the gallows. Public hangings used to take place facing Glasgow Green and the landmark in question was Nelson's Monument.

The last person to be hanged publicly there was Dr. Edward William Pritchard, a tall, balding, bearded, English dandy who went calmly to his fate before an enthusiastic audience in 1865. Estimates of the crowd vary from 30,000 to 100,000 depending on whose account one believes but at any rate everyone agreed it was a record turnout for such an occasion and a 'gate' which any football club would be happy to have nowadays. Front row spectators stayed up all night to be nearest and pie sellers, bible thumpers and pickpockets did a roaring trade.

The centre of attraction had been born forty years previously and had served his apprenticeship as an assistant surgeon in the Royal Navy during which time he met pretty Edinburgh-born Mary Jane Taylor while she was on a visit to Portsmouth. He wooed her ardently and they married and settled down in Filey, Yorkshire, where five children were born to brighten their happy home. He set up practice but was in fact more of a quack than a G.P., although in those days a fluent tongue and a basic knowledge of medicine were all that was necessary to carry off the deception and Dr. Pritchard was nothing if not a natural actor. He was also a popular lecturer (his topics were his travels abroad, most of them made up), a Freemason and an admirer of women. While Mrs. Pritchard had her hands full with the children, the treatment her husband gave some of his more available patients in the privacy of his surgery certainly brought colour back to their cheeks. However, two or three of them started getting silly ideas about falling in love and their husbands started picking up whispers in the town's taverns. Dr. Pritchard also detected rumblings and diagnosed quick discretion in the form of departure would be a suitable remedy. He promptly sold his practice and this time in reality travelled abroad before the ladies knew what was happening.

A year later he settled down with his family at 11 Berkeley Terrace in Glasgow and started practising once more. He applied for the Andersonian chair of Surgery and forged the names of eminent English doctors who had never even heard of him as references. He was severely reprimanded for this but somehow managed by his pleas for clemency to stay a registered doctor.

On the night of May 5th, 1863, while Mrs. Pritchard was out of town, a fire not only wrecked the house in Berkeley Terrace but killed a servant girl in her bed. Dr. Pritchard had escaped out the front door and tearfully claimed he had tried to save the girl, bemoaning the loss of "the bonny lass". A verdict of death by misadventure was returned and the doctor won an insurance claim against a highly suspicious company. The girl had made no attempt to leave the bed which suggests she was unconscious at the time, possibly smothered. In the light of later events it would not be stretching the imagination too much to say the doctor was sleeping with her or trying to seduce her, that she had threatened to talk and that he had decided to get rid of her.

Undeterred by gossips, the bold doctor moved round the corner to a new house in Sauchiehall Street and he was a familiar sight promenading the thoroughfare in the height of fashion with top hat and cane and, instead of business cards, he kept a batch of postcards with his own picture on them to present to any young lady who took his fancy.

The Pritchards employed a gullible 15-year-old Highland servant girl, Mary McCleod, whom the doctor deflowered at the first opportunity following this up after the usual time with an obliging abortion.

Mrs. Pritchard at last found out about her husband's true nature when she found the illicit couple in each others arms in the pantry.

She flew into a rage, there was a scene followed by recriminations and the doctor swore he had just had a brainstorm, that it would never happen again and all would be well. Shortly after this Mrs. Pritchard became strangely ill. The odd thing about it was every time she visited her mother in Edinburgh she got better again. At first it was put down to the allegedly "better" Edinburgh air but gradually the mother became suspicious. Then in December 1864 her daughter did not arrive through as expected. Seventy-year-old Mrs. Taylor and her son, also a doctor, travelled to Glasgow to investigate and found Mrs Pritchard unable to move from her bed. Her suspicions now fully aroused Mrs. Taylor decided to move in to nurse her daughter. That night the guardian mother ate some tapioca, fell ill and died.

Dr. Pritchard took it upon himself to supply the death certificate and put the cause as apoplexy. Meanwhile, he eagerly resumed his affair with the servant girl while ostensibly mournfully nursing his fading wife. He was also a keen buyer of Fleming's Tincture of Aconite which is a distillation of wolf's bane.

On March 17th, 1865 Mrs. Pritchard finally succumbed. When another doctor confirmed death and the sheet was put over the white face Dr. Pritchard, all piety and poison, collapsed weeping, "Come back, my dear Mary Jane. Don't leave your dear Edward!" And when the coffin was about to be taken away he pleaded to have a last look at his wife, the lid was duly unscrewed and he kissed the corpse on its cold lips, shedding copious tears all the while. Again he had been allowed to sign the death certificate. This time it was gastric fever.

However, due to the hunger of their cook, who had filched some of the last meal Mrs Pritchard had eaten, the end was nigh for the doctor. The cook collapsed and, although he later recovered, there was now enough doubts for the bodies of old Mrs. Taylor and freshly buried Mrs. Pritchard to be exhumed. Both contained antimony and aconite.

Dr. Pritchard's trial took place in the High Court in Edinburgh and the defence tried to blame Mary McCleod which Lord Justice Clerk John Inglis dismissed in his summing up to the jury. It took an hour to find the accused guilty.

He insisted upon his innocence until the last day of the final drop when he applied himself to his devotions and confessed, implicating Mary McCleod. It was only at the very last, again with tears (only this time probably real ones) bedewing his eyes, that he contritely admitted that he alone was responsible and we can only assume that this was finally the truth.

As he ascended the gallows to loud catcalls, boos and insults from the large crowd, he was immaculate as ever in his best apparel which included new patent leather boots.

There was a grisly aftermath to his execution. When the new city mortuary was to be built years later it was decided to place it on the unhallowed bare ground beside the High Court where executed people lay buried and uncommemorated. While digging away for the foundations workmen came across the skeleton of Dr. Pritchard and his boots were extremely well preserved. An entrepreneur among the labourers quickly and quietly sold not only the boots but also the skull.

His crimes, domestic poisonings, belong to a definite era when chemicals were freely available, medical science still tottering in its infancy and forensic science unheard of. There must have been many murders committed which were never suspected.

But one suspected murder just seven years previous to Dr. Pritchard's crimes became a *cause célèbre* and will be dealt with in the next chapter.

CHAPTER 2

Mimi

The expression *femme fatale* was never more suitably applied than to vivacious Madeleine Hamilton Smith who shattered the ultra respectable Victorian society of Glasgow with her amours. She was born in the wrong time and her passionate nature contained the seeds of its own destruction. In other eras her sensual nature may have found expression but the constricting conditions she was born in led to frustration, passion and death.

Madeleine was born into a Glasgow which was fast becoming the epitome of Victorian industrial expertise and expansion. More than 80% of the new-fangled steamships built in Britain came from the Clyde and the river was soon to become the largest shipbuilding centre in the world. There was a population explosion with the influx of workers and the city became the fastest growing in Europe, the Lowland lower orders being swollen by Highlanders, Irish, European Jews, Italians and Poles. Expanding iron and coal industries brought new wealth and the banks actually opened their doors to cater for the new, prosperous working class. Glasgow like all industrial centres became a city of stark contrasts. The workers were relegated to their fetid slums in the north, east and south while in the west end and in stately city centre squares the wealthy had their palatial mansions or fine terraced houses, as well as second homes down the Firth of Clyde.

The family to which Madeleine Smith belonged was definitely in the rich, respectable class. She was the eldest of six and her father James was a prosperous architect with a town mansion in Blythswood Square and a country house at Rhu on the Clyde. He was a typical paragon of his age, a self-made, industrious, religious man who was in every sense head of the household and whose word was law. Madeleine by contrast was more wayward, independent and impetuous but she nevertheless stood in awe of her Papa's indomitable presence. There was a strain between her own nature and the constricting disciplines of family life and society.

She was intelligent and well-educated and at the age of nineteen an extremely eligible young lady for the handsome blades of the town who danced with her and her sister Bessie at the numerous balls to which they were invited. However, the family were keeping an eye on her to ensure she did not marry beneath her station.

While out strolling or in her carriage the sisters, chaperoned by Mama, had to acknowledge the courteous bows and admiring glances of gentlemen in the street.

One such who was introduced to Madeleine by a mutual acquaintance was a darkly moustachioed Frenchman named Pierre Emile L'Angelier. Attraction on both sides was there from the first but there was an unbridgeable gap in their social standing for anything overt to take place.

L'Angelier had led a chequered life up to this point. His father had been a nurseryman in Jersey and L'Angelier joined an Edinburgh-based company as a seedsman before joining the National Guard in France during the 1848 revolution, service of which he was always proud. He returned to Scotland at the insistance of a lady from Fife but she eventually became engaged to another, leaving L'Angelier heartbroken and destitute. In the light of later events his emotional response at this time is interesting. He made several gestures at suicide, all of them it would seem calculated to fail. He 'attempted' to jump from a high window but made sure someone else was present to stop him. He seized a knife, wildly gesticulating that he was going to end it all, but he was easily disarmed without injuring himself. He spoke repeatedly about jumping off certain bridges but never did so. Whether all this was caused by a genuine impulse to kill himself because he had been crossed in love or whether it was sheer self pity it would be impossible to say without a detailed analysis of L'Angelier, but his suicide gesture certainly increased in relevance after his eventual demise. At any rate he decided suicide was out for the moment and attained work as a clerk in Glasgow for £50 a year. This bore no comparison to the wealth of the Smith establishment and any form of serious social intercourse was taboo. But L'Angelier was as impulsive as Madeleine and, apart from the physical attraction she held for him, there was the added bonus of possibly improving his position.

In the summer of 1855 the Smiths repaired to their country house on the Clyde but Madeleine and L'Angelier began a secret correspondence. Significantly she prudently destroyed his letters but he, for possible sinister motives, kept hers.

The dashing Frenchman decided it was time to propose and, summoning all her reserves of character, Madeleine approached her father who duly and predictably exploded in rage and said it was out of the question and that she was to have nothing more to do with the impecunious, social climbing foreigner.

Madeleine wrote to her 'dear Emile' saying she was duty bound to obey her father although it was a heavy blow and suggested the correspondence should end, requesting him to burn all her letters.

L'Angelier replied in a tone of moral dudgeon saying that she had deceived him, that he had assumed they were more or less engaged and added a threatening passage, "Think what your father would say if I sent him your letters for a perusal. Do you think he could sanction your breaking your promises. No, Madeleine, I leave your conscience to speak for itself".

The Smiths returned to Glasgow and not only the correspondence but also clandestine meetings started up.

Madeleine's letters now took on a new intensity. She addressed Emile now as "my own darling husband" and signed herself "thy own thy ever fond thy own dear loving wife Mimi", although no formal or legal bond had taken place. They toyed with the idea of elopement but the affair was more sentimental and emotional until the night of 6th June, 1856 when physical consumation took place in the woods at Rhu where the Smiths had once again gone for their holiday break.

In the flush of her physical excitement in the small hours of the morning Madeleine penned in her bedroom a delirious letter to her lover which was half exultant and half remorseful.

My own, my beloved husband, if we did wrong last night it was in the excitement of our love. I did truly love you with all my soul. I was happy. It was a pleasure to be with you. Am I not your wife? Yes, I am. And you may rest assured after what has passed I cannot be the wife of any other but dear, dear Emile. I did not bleed in the least last night but I had a good deal of pain during the night. Tell me, pet, were you angry at me for allowing you to do what you did? Was it very bad of me? We should, I suppose, have waited till we were married. I shall always remember last night. Will we not often talk of our evening meetings after we are married. Adieu again, my husband. God bless you and make you well. And may you yet be very, very happy with your Mimi as your little wife. Kindest love, fond embrace, and kisses from thy own true and ever devoted Mimi, thy faithful wife.

L'Angelier's reply was a wild mixture of hypocrisy, recrimination and sheer bad taste.

My dearest and beloved wife Mimi. Since I saw you I have been wretchedly sad. Would to God we had not met that night — I would have been happier. I am sad at what we did. I regret it very much. Why, Mimi, did you give way after your promises? My pet, it is a pity. We did wrong, God forgive us for it. Mimi, we have loved blindly. It is your parents' fault if shame is the result; they are to blame for it.

I do not understand, my pet, your not bleeding for every woman having her virginity must bleed. You must have done so some other time. Try to remember if you never hurt yourself in washing, etc. I am sorry you felt pain. I hope, pet, you are better. I trust, dearest, you will not be pregnant. Be sure and tell me immediately you are ill next time and if at your regular period. I was not angry at your allowing me, Mimi, but I am sad it happened. You had no resolution. We should indeed have waited till we were married, Mimi. It was very bad indeed.

However, L'Angelier apparently and predictably overcame his alleged squeamishness at the illicit tryst and the two lovers continued with passionate physical intercourse throughout the summer, either among the shelter of the woods or, if the house were empty, in the cosier comfort of Madeleine's bed.

The Smiths returned to their Glasgow house and it was at this point that a third figure entered the drama. He was a staid eligible bachelor, William Harper Minnoch, who lived next door to the Smiths in Blythswood Square. He was an up-and-coming city merchant with an annual income of £4,000. A rather dull, over polite gentleman with no apparent vices who was perfectly in tune with Mr Smith. He started to call on Madeleine and, although at first she was cool towards him, she began to warm to the pleasant young man.

L'Angelier heard rumours of a possible society engagement in the offing and angrily, jealously challenged his Mimi, but at first she said it was idle gossip and that "this Mr. M," was a bore. She continued to see both suitors without either knowing but whereas she discussed aesthetics with Mr. Minnoch in the drawing room over tea it was secret midnight caresses from her basement bedroom window when it came to L'Angelier.

Madeleine's housemaid Christina Haggart was an accomplice at these shadowy, tip-toeing, whispering meetings and several times unlocked the back door to let L'Angelier in and use her bedroom for sex with Madeleine. For his part, L'Angelier bought off the beat policeman who patrolled the Blythswood Square area with a couple of cigars. But usually this creeping about the house at night was too risky and L'Angelier had to be content with talking to and kissing his lover through her bedroom window which was protected by iron bars and below the level of the street in a narrow dry moat between the pavement and the house. If it was a chilly night Madeleine would proffer a cup of steaming hot cocoa through these bars to her lover which he would gratefully drink.

It was now coming close to the time when she would have to choose between the wealthy Mr. Minnoch or the passionate

L'Angelier. Whenever the Frenchman was making love to her there was little doubt in her mind, but as the opportunities for sex lessened and Mr. Minnoch began to press his claim more steadfastly the balance began to change. Her father and family were in no doubt that a Minnoch-Smith match would be ideal whereas a sentimentalised vision of a bohemian life in an attic with "dear Emile" began to pall on her and her letters to her increasingly worried lover became decidedly cooler and shorter. No longer were there any 'husband and 'wife' endearments.

The crunch came on January 28th, 1857 when Mr. Minnoch called and finally, formally proposed. She accepted but said she wanted time to think of a wedding date and that there should be no announcement of the engagement for the moment. Mr. Minnoch was delighted enough at her acceptance to agree to this unusual caution.

It was time to break with L'Angelier and her next letter to him was as marked for its coolness as earlier ones had been for their passion. She wrote that the correspondence should end.

Altogether I think owing to coolness and indifference (nothing else) that we had better for the future consider ourselves as strangers. I trust to your honour as a gentleman that you will not reveal anything that may have passed between us. You may be astonished at this sudden change — but for some time back you must have noticed a coolness in my notes. My love for you has ceased, and that is why I was cool. I did once love you truly, fondly, but for some time back I have lost much of that love. There is no other reason for my conduct, and I think it but fair to let you know this. I might have gone on and become your wife, but I could not have loved you as I ought. My conduct you will condemn but I did at one time love you with heart and soul. It has cost me much to tell you this — sleepless nights, but it is necessary you should know. If you remain in Glasgow or go away, I hope you may succeed in all your endeavours. I know you will never injure the character of one you so fondly loved. No, Emile, I know you have honour and are a gentleman. What has passed you will not mention. I know when I ask you that you will comply. Adieu.

It is to be noted that she made no mention of Mr. Minnoch, probably because she feared the fiery Frenchman's nature might lead him to tell all to her new fiancé.

L'Angelier was shattered by the about face revealed in this letter. With tears in his eyes he told a colleague, "She shall never marry another man as long as I live. It is an infatuation. She shall be the death of me."

It took him a few days to recover and when he next wrote to Madeleine we can judge what his reaction was by her abject reply.

Emile, I have just had your note. Emile, for the love you once had for me do nothing till I see you — for God's sake do not bring your once loved Mimi to an open shame. Emile, write to no-one, to Papa or any other. Oh, do not till I see you on Wednesday at twelve. I shall open my shutter and see you. Oh, Emile, be not harsh to me. I am the most guilty miserable wretch on the face of the earth. Emile, do not drive me to death. When I ceased to love you, believe me, it was not to love another. I am free from all engagement at present. Emile, for God's sake do not send my letters to Papa. Will you not — but I cannot ask forgiveness, I am too guilty for that. Pray for me for a guilty wretch, but do nothing. Oh, Emile, do nothing. I am ill. God knows what I have suffered. My punishment is more than I can bear. Do nothing till I see you, for the love of heaven do nothing. I am mad, I am ill.

However, she was apparently well enough to fabricate an outright lie in this epistle as regards her engagement.

Further pleas followed this one where she wrote of her intense agony of mind over her dear Emile's threat to expose her. She declared: *My father's wrath would kill me; you little know his temper. Emile, for the love you once had for me do not denounce me to my Papa. Emile, if he should read my letters to you he will put me from him, he will hate me as a guilty wretch.*

She reiterated that she had loved him once and had looked forward to marriage but that his picking faults with her had cooled her ardour. She claimed she was not in love with anyone else. She said it was since coming to the city that she had become discontented and ceased to love him. She begged him as her best friend and 'for the love of heaven' to listen to her. She claimed she was ill, mad and her brain was on fire. One letter finished:

I feel as if death would indeed be sweet. Denounce me not. Emile, Emile, think of our once happy days. Pardon me if you can, pray for me as the most wretched, guilty, miserable creature on the earth. I could stand anything but my father's hot displeasure. Emile, you will not cause me death. If he is to get your letters, I can not see him any more. And my poor mother. I will never more kiss her — it would be a shame to them all. Emile, will you not spare me this — hate me, despise me — but do not expose me. I cannot write more. I am too ill tonight. M.

Around this time Madeleine sent the houseboy to buy some prussic acid which she said she wanted for her hands but the chemist refused to supply it without a doctor's certificate.

The lovers now rendezvoused once more and some kind of understanding seems to have been reached although precisely what is not clear. Certainly Madeleine managed to talk L'Angelier out of showing her letters to her father without, however, managing to get him to hand them over to her. The notes she sent him to arrange meetings lost their hysteria without regaining their passion. They were friendly but there was still no 'husband', 'wife' or 'Mimi'.

Nine days after her last pleading 'do not denounce me' letter, Madeleine went with her unofficial fiancé Mr Minnoch to the opera. The performance was of *Lucrezia Borgia,* a melodrama about the notorious fifteenth century Italian aristocrat who rose to power and stayed there by poisoning anyone who was against her.

Their carriage returned to Blythswood Square at 11 p.m., and the couple parted to their separate houses.

The following morning L'Angelier's landlady knocked at his bedroom door and when he called her in she found him sick. He said he had been taken ill on the way home early that morning with searing pains in his bowels and stomach and a great deal of vomiting had only partially eased his agonies. After resting for a couple of days he was able to get up and return to work but he was still badly shaken.

Two days after her night at the opera Madeleine bought an ounce of arsenic from a Sauchiehall Street chemist, charging it on her father's account. She signed a register as required and said it was to be used to kill vermin in her house. In accordance with a statute the arsenic was mixed with soot.

Two days after this L'Angelier had a recurrence of his illness and he was treated for bilious fever, being off work for eight days this time.

He made two significant remarks to a friend while he was

recuperating. Firstly, "I can't think why I was so unwell after getting that coffee and chocolate from her." The friend assumed in the context of their conversation that he was talking of two separate occasions and that the "her" was Madeleine. Secondly, "It is a perfect fascination my attachment to that girl; if she were to poison me I would forgive her."

Around the same time the Smiths went to Bridge of Allan for a few days break. Madeleine wrote to L'Angelier suggesting he go to the South of England for his health's sake but at any rate not to follow her because this would arouse suspicion. L'Angelier, himself still suspicious of Madeleine's faithfulness, said he had no intention of travelling south as his health was too frail but he agreed for her sake not to go to Bridge of Allan and voiced a nagging doubt — was she directly or indirectly engaged to William Minnoch? She denied any involvement.

Before the Smiths left for their break an ex-school friend of Madeleine's visited her and they went for a walk. As they passed the Sauchiehall Street chemist Madeleine said she wanted to make a purchase and the two girls entered the shop where she bought sixpence worth of arsenic, explaining once more it was for rats. This time it was mixed with indigo. Her friend laughed at the idea of a young lady buying arsenic and Madeleine also laughed gaily as they tinkled back out through the door of the shop and into the sunny streets.

Mr. Minnoch visited the Smiths at Bridge of Allan and suggested a date should now be fixed for the wedding and Madeleine agreed. The 18th of June was the date agreed upon. Her note to her bridegroom-to-be a few days later lacks the fire of her letters to her lover. She starts, 'My Dearest William' and continues in warm but courteous and prim terms about how she is looking forward to their new life together, how she will please him and study him and signs herself, 'Yours with affecn., Madeleine.'

A few days after the Smiths returned to Glasgow Madeleine bought another ounce of arsenic telling the chemist the previous dose had killed nine large rats.

At this time L'Angelier went to Bridge of Allan. According to his landlady he seemed distressed at not receiving mail. He returned three days later and around nine o'clock on the evening of March 22nd went out with his pass key which was needed if he was going to be out late. When he returned at 2.30 the following morning he was too ill to use it and had to ring for help. A doctor was called but at eleven o'clock that morning L'Angelier died in agony.

There was no obvious cause of death so a post mortem was held. It showed he had died of arsenic poisoning. Experts reckoned he had swallowed half an ounce or sixty times the fatal dosage.

When Madeleine's letters were found among L'Angelier's effects the Sheriff's Officers started making investigations and a week later she was arrested and charged with her lover's murder.

The trial began in the High Court in Edinburgh on 30th June and Madeleine was fortunate to have a brilliant defence counsel in John Inglis who was Dean of the Faculty of Advocates and who, later in his career, as Lord President, was to pass the death sentence on Dr. Pritchard.

The court was crowded and Madeleine calmly entered the dock "with the air of a belle entering a ballroom" according to one newspaper report. Her parents were not needed as witnesses and they retreated to Rhu and thence to their beds to avoid the publicity.

Medical evidence left no doubt about the taking of arsenic as the cause of death but there was no traces of soot or indigo in the body, both substances being difficult to separate from the poison which is why they were mixed with it as a safety precaution. And the amount consumed would have been difficult to disguise although it was just possible that a thick fluid like cocoa could have served this purpose.

But the crux of the matter was whether the lovers had met just prior to L'Angelier's three bouts of illness. As regards his first attack, which followed the night of Madeleine's visit to the opera, his landlady and friends were too vague about what date he referred to as having seen "the lady" for their evidence to have any weight. There was no proof whatsoever that Madeleine was in possession of poison that night or, indeed, that the illness had been caused by poisoning. Accordingly, the Lord Justice-Clerk directed the jury to find the accused not guilty on this first charge. This was a bad blow for the Crown who were relying on proving a premeditated and persevering design to kill on three occasions.

As regards L'Angelier's second bout of illness Madeleine was definitely in possession of arsenic. But she had changed her story in a statement to the Crown. Now she claimed she had bought the arsenic for a beauty treatment for her skin, having read about it in a magazine, an unusual use for the poison especially mixed with soot. She admitted the story about rats had been a lie because she was shy about admitting using the mixture for cosmetic purposes. There never were any vermin at either of the Smiths houses.

L'Angelier's second illness when he was off work for eight days had taken place in the early hours of February 23rd, a day and a half after Madeleine had bought her unusual cosmetic. In a memorandum book the dead man used for random jottings there are three brief entries relevant to this charge: "Sun. 22nd February saw Mimi in Drawing Room. Promised me French Bible. Taken very ill. Tues. 24th February wrote M. Wed. 25th February M. wrote me." Fortunately, for Madeleine the Judge ruled this memo book out as admissible evidence so it was never put to the jury. If it had been it would strongly have suggested Madeleine, who had poison, met her lover before he became ill with symptoms akin to poisoning (the parents were away which explains why the assignation took place in the living room). And it would have shown that the Frenchman received a letter from his Mimi on the Wednesday. The Crown case was that a letter in which Madeleine refers to his illness and says he "did look bad Sunday night and Monday morning" was written at this time and therefore proved the relevant meeting. But the postmark on the envelope was indecipherable and the Defence claimed it could have been written any time. If the memo book had been allowed as evidence it would greatly have strengthened the Crown case.

As regards the most important charge relating to L'Angelier's last, fatal illness, proving a meeting again was difficult.

There was no doubt Madeleine was once more in possession of arsenic and that L'Angelier was out somewhere in the midnight city prior to his death. The Crown argued that he had hastened back from Bridge of Allan in answer to a fervent summons from his lover which read:

Why my beloved did you not come to me. Oh beloved you are ill. Come to me sweet one. I waited and waited for you but you came not. I shall wait again tomorrow night same hour and arrangement. Do come sweet love my own dear love of a sweetheart. Come beloved and clasp me to your heart. Come and we shall be happy. A kiss fond love. Adieu with tender embraces ever believe me to be your own ever dear fond M.

L'Angelier certainly received this on the day of his return to Glasgow but in her statement Madeleine said no meeting had actually taken place. She said she had wanted to see him to break the news of her pending marriage to Mr. Minnoch but considering the passionate language in which the letter is couched this seems unlikely.

However there were no witnesses to this midnight meeting. Neither the beat policeman or the servants saw L'Angelier or noticed anything unusual that fatal night. From the time he left his landlady until he staggered back to her his whereabouts were unexplained and the Defence went to town on this in the best rhetorical manner.

Mr. Inglis thundered, "The Lord Advocate says it is no doubt a matter of conjecture and inference that in the interval he was in the presence of the prisoner. Good heavens! Inference and conjecture! A matter of inference and conjecture whether, on the night he was poisoned, if he was in the presence of the person who is charged with his murder! I never heard such an expression from the mouth of a Crown prosecutor in a capital charge before. He can ask for a verdict on nothing but a set of unfounded and incredible suspicions and hypotheses."

Mr. Inglis also argued that it was incredible that L'Angelier should take three large successive doses of poison from the hand of a woman he was suspicious of without noticing what he was taking, jumping to certain conclusions or at the last on his deathbed pointing the finger at Madeleine. Yet he had done none of these things.

Mr. Inglis also brought out the history of L'Angelier's suicide gestures years before when his love life had gone awry and suggested that the flamboyant Frenchman had become unhinged once more and had decided to commit suicide in this bizarre fashion.

The Lord Justice-Clerk said the case hinged on whether the alleged meeting took place. It was virtually certain on L'Angelier's return from Bridge of Allan that a meeting had taken place. But the jury would have "to separate firmly — firmly and clearly in their own minds — suspicion from evidence."

The jury retired and on their return silence reigned as the foreman declared the verdict of Not Proven by a majority. Madeleine was dismissed from the bar and one face missing among her congratulators was that of John Inglis who sat slumped and exhausted at counsel's table.

Madeleine was taken out the back entrance where a carriage was waiting for her while a wardress made up to look like her went out the front entrance to face the mixed cheering and jeering mob. Madeleine had not escaped notice, however, because a carriage pursued her and when stopped at a railway station an employee of Madame Tussaud's leapt out and asked for her scarf which was duly handed over with a smile. (When her letters were recently opened up at the Mitchell Library in Glasgow it was discovered there was a distinct scent of Lavender in the air, which she had presumably sprinkled on them and so a small part of Madeleine still physically hovers about to this day.)

The verdict was not greeted with surprise simply because the Crown had not clinched its case and had been outwitted by a superior defence counsel. Madeleine claimed to be disappointed her name had not been cleared entirely.

Certainly the trial did not affect her vivacity or taste for romance or popularity. She received several offers of marriage after the verdict which she ignored. The stunned Mr. Minnoch, who had studiously looked away from the dock when giving evidence despite the calm way she viewed him, understandably saw marriage as totally out of the question for a man of his position.

She moved to London and became a society hostess who also moved in intellectually Bohemian circles. She once dispensed cocoa to George Bernard Shaw (with no after effects) and was the first hostess to introduce table mats on a bare table instead of the customary tablecloth.

She married artist George Wardle, an associate of illustrator

William Morris, and when he died she married an American named Sheehy and settled with him across the Atlantic. After he died a film company approached her asking her to star in a film of her own story. She refused and was threatened with deportation as an undesirable alien, an attempt at removal which failed.

She lived to the ripe old age of 91. On her gravestone are the names Lena Wardle Sheehy, Lena being her sister's pet name for her. Glasgow and Mimi must have seemed a long way away.

CHAPTER 3

That Auld Deevil

In the 1860's Glasgow continued to expand in all directions. Samuel Cunard initiated a mail packet service between Britain and the U.S.A., setting a precedent for other ambitious companies and founding a dynasty which lasted 120 years and produced many great liners, not least the three Queens. Underwater blasting helped deepen and broaden the Clyde estuary. More docks and quays were opened up and the city spread its eveloping mass downriver. The coming of steel ships and Clydeside inventiveness in boilermaking created more prosperity. The opening of the Suez canal and the colonisation of the British Empire meant the creation of new shipping dynasties like the Anchor Line, the Donaldson Line, the Allan Line, the City Line and the Clan Line who plied in every world port and made the words 'Clyde-built' a famous superlative. Emigration accounted for a lot of their traffic across the Atlantic since the Canadian Government had offered 160 acres free to any impoverished Highlander or other hardy Scot willing to build a homestead and settle in the great untamed north-west of America.

Emigration increased when many of the 200,000 workers in Glasgow employed in the cotton trade were put out of work after the American Civil War had reduced cotton imports from 87,000 tons a year to 360 tons.

Pure, clear, Highland water was pumped from Loch Katrine to the city, one of the greatest municipal services ever accomplished in Britain. Many new parks and gardens, some of Glasgow's glories to this day, were created in an attempt to recapture some of the verdure of the 'dear, green place' and the crime ridden darkness was alleviated to some extent by the glimmering introduction of gas lighting.

The first murder case ever investigated by the City of Glasgow Police (Madeleine Smith having been arrested and interviewed by Sheriff's Officers) was one which they bungled to the extent that the wrong person was almost executed while the real and obvious culprit was not even prosecuted.

The mansion house at 17 Sandyford Place in the city centre belonged in 1862 to a Glasgow accountant called John Fleming. He was wealthy and, like Madeleine Smith's father, owned a country house down the coast where he and his family spent their summer holidays and occasional week-ends.

On Friday 4th July of that year Mr. Fleming departed for one of these breaks to the house at Dunoon, leaving behind in his Glasgow home his old grandfather, also called John (or Old Fleming as the neighbours knew him), and a thirty-five-year old buxom attractive servant called Jess McPherson. Despite his years Old Fleming had a passion for the servant.

On the following Monday the accountant returned from his week-end and went straight to his office, returning to Sandyford Place in late afternoon. He was surprised to find himself let into the house by Old Fleming and not by Jess. When asked where she was Old Fleming said she had gone off on the Friday. On investigation the accountant found her room in the basement locked and thinking this curious he opened the door with a spare key.

Jess was lying cold in death on the floor, her head having been chopped up with a meat cleaver. She was semi naked, the lower half of her clothes having been removed. Blood had splashed all over the room but a half hearted attempt had been made to clean up the stains.

The police were called and they quickly established that all the victims best clothes were missing and some plated spoons had also disappeared. They also found a naked bloodstained footprint on the floor.

It took the police three weeks to figure out the answers to the clues available to them and arrest Old Fleming. He spent four hours in front of the examining magistrate denying everything and was committed to prison for further enquiries. On the same day the police were given information which pointed in another direction.

A Glasgow pawnbroker returned from holiday and on reading of the missing clothes and cutlery he remembered similar articles being pawned by a woman on the Saturday after the murder was supposed to have been committed. He went to the police who found the woman had given a false address. And they confirmed the clothes and cutlery were the articles they were looking for.

On checking with everyone who had previous associations with the Fleming house they called upon 28-year-old Jessie McLachlan who stayed at 182 Broomielaw. She had been a servant for two years in the Fleming house. Jessie admitted to being a close friend of the dead woman and was given to visiting her at the Fleming house when the master was away. She also said that she frequently found Old Fleming sitting drinking with Jess on these visits and that the lively grandfather was fond of coming to her own house for friendly chats.

The police made a search of Jessie's home and found some clothing which they later identified as belonging to the murder victim. Jessie said the clothes had been brought to her by a little girl who worked as a scullery maid with the dead woman and that she had been told to take them to a shop for alteration and dyeing. On reading of the murder she claimed she had simply decided to keep them. Then she admitted under pressure that it was indeed she who had visited the pawnbroker but she said Old Fleming had given her the silver cutlery to pawn.

The police took her into custody and an experiment showed that the bloodstained footprint matched with Jessie's right foot. She was charged and Old Fleming was released.

She remarked angrily and bitterly to a cellmate, "The guilty has got out — and the innocent is kept in."

Jessie's trial began in the Old Court at Jail Square on the 17th September 1862, Lord Deas (known by the public as Lord Death because of his penchant for hanging) presiding.

In the witness box Old Fleming gave his age as 87 but he looked a lot younger and being slightly deaf he spoke in a loud voice with a Highland accent. He said that on the Friday when Jess was presumed to have been killed he had gone as usual for a walk in the park after dinner, returning around 8 p.m. He went down to the kitchen to get some heat into his bones and while there Jess made him a cup of tea. He read the paper by the fireside until around 9.30 then retired to bed. He was asleep when he was startled by loud screaming. He leapt out of bed but could hear nothing further and put it down as a dream. He glanced at the clock and saw it was 4 a.m. In the morning he waited for his porridge but when Jess did not bring it up to him as usual he went downstairs to investigate and found her room locked. He had not seen her again from the time he left her on the Friday night.

He admitted he had gone to church three times that week-end without mentioning to anyone that his servant had mysteriously disappeared and he also admitted (previous to the trial he had been denying it) that he knew the accused, Jessie McLachlan. He denied giving her the incriminating cutlery, however.

When defence counsel came to cross-examine Old Fleming he found himself harrassed by the judge who seemed to have already made up his mind that Jessie was guilty.

Under cross examination Old Fleming denied that he had opened the door to a milk boy on the Saturday morning. At one point he was asked, "Why did you not let Jess open the door to the milk boy that Saturday morning?" to which he replied, "Jess — we ken't it wis aw ower wi' Jess afore that!"

When the milk boy gave evidence he swore that at 7.40 on the Saturday morning when he had rang the doorbell at the Fleming household it had been the old man, fully dressed, who had answered.

One witness who had met Old Fleming in church that fatal weekend was asked if he knew anything about the old man's character and he replied that he understood that he had once been up before the Kirk Session.

At this point Lord Deas intervened, "This need not be opened up just now with the witness!"

Defence counsel of course was well within his rights to bring anything known about Old Fleming's character before the court. If the line of questioning had been pursued it would have revealed that Old Fleming had been publicly chastised ten years previously by the Kirk Session for "the sin of fornication with a servant".

Another witness who had been a friend of Jess McPherson said the murdered woman had been unhappy about Old Fleming's advances to her and referred to him as "that auld deevil". She said she had once had to kick him out of her bed.

At the summing up the Crown stressed that it was Jessie McLachlan and not Old Fleming who was on trial while the Defence went for the fact that there was nothing to prove the accused had been in the house at the crucial time.

On the final day of the trial Lord Deas left no-one in doubt about his opinion. He made no attempt to hide the black cap he was carrying and when he sat down he flippantly tossed it onto the bench as if to say, "Let's get this over and done with." His charge to the jury was grossly unfair to the accused and it took them only fifteen minutes to find her guilty by a unanimous verdict, much to his Lordship's satisfaction. He went through the routine of asking the accused if she had anything to say before sentence was passed and was taken aback when the answer was in the affirmative. Jessie said she had prepared a statement and wished her counsel to read it out. Lord Deas reluctantly agreed.

According to this statement, Jessie had gone to the Fleming house to see Jess McPherson, taking with her some rum and when she entered the kitchen she found Old Fleming sitting by the fireside drinking from a bottle of whisky. He poured the visitor a glass but did not give Jess any which annoyed her and Old Fleming told her tetchily, "Ye ken, Jess, we've had twa or three since the afternoon an' the bottle's gettin' gae low". During the ensuing argument Old Fleming told Jess to hold her tongue and he would buy more whisky if Jessie would go out and fetch it. At this he emptied the bottle into a glass and gave it to Jessie along with 1/2d to get a half bottle and Jessie departed in search of a licensed shop but because of the late hour she was unable to find anywhere open. She went back to the house and was let in by Old Fleming. In the passage she heard a moan coming from Jess's bedroom and on entering she found her friend lying on the floor with blood gushing from cuts on her forehead and nose. She was barely concious. When Jessie challenged the old man about what had happened he claimed she had tripped and fallen but some of her clothing had been ripped off and it was obvious the 'auld deevil' had been up to his tricks again. However, the two of them managed to get the injured woman into bed where she partly revived enough to say she did not want a doctor to be called although Jessie felt one was needed. She went on to say that Old Fleming was forever pestering her and that if the master asked her how she came by her injuries, which was almost inevitable since they would not disappear in two days, she would have to tell him the truth. Old Fleming was present when this was said and he was visibly shaken, begging her not to get him into trouble but to make up some story. He turned to Jessie and made the same plea to her and she replied that she would not say anything. But wanting some firm guarantee he fetched the big black family bible and made her swear to keep the secret and he then swore to make it worth both their whiles never to disclose what had happened. Jess gradually became worse and changed her mind about fetching a doctor and Jessie said she would personally attend to it, but when she tried to get out she found all the doors had been locked. Then she heard a scuffling sound and on opening the door was horrified to see Old Fleming, berserk in a drunken rage, battering Jess with a meat cleaver. The old man somehow managed to persuade Jessie to take part in a cover-up, pointing out to her that if she did not go along with him he would implicate her in the deed. Foolishly, she agreed to protect him and he set about trying to clean up the blood. It was his idea to fake a burglary and to this end he got Jessie to take away the clothing and cutlery.

After her statement had been read out, Lord Deas gave it as his opinion that it was "a tissue of falsehoods" and that he heartily concurred with the jury's verdict. Placing his beloved black cap on his head he condemned her to death, ending with "may God have mercy on your soul" to which Jessie shouted, "Mercy! Aye, he'll ha'e mercy for I am innocent."

There was much public unrest over this verdict and meetings were held to protest about it in both Glasgow and Edinburgh. The execution was postponed and a Crown Commissioner appointed to review the case. A report was submitted to the Home Secretary as a result of which the death sentence was commuted to one of penal servitude. One of the remarks in the report stated: 'The prisoner was an accidental and constrained witness of the murder and not an actor in it. She can never be hanged but as she concealed and adopted it she must be severely punished."

Jessie served fifteen years before emigrating to America where she died in 1899. The 'auld deevil' was never prosecuted although the Flemings had to move out of Glasgow because public opinion was so against them. Lord Deas lived to a ripe and respectable old age while the Glasgow police were allowed to treat the case as closed.

CHAPTER 4

The Gully of Fire

The island of Arran lies in the Firth of Clyde between Ayrshire and the Mull of Kintyre. Its scenery is wild, beautiful and rugged, traversed by glens, dotted with grassy banked burns and dominated by the jutting peak of the often snowclad Goatfell. Always a popular holiday resort for Glaswegians upriver, it is an unlikely picturesque setting for the murder which resulted in the longest prison sentence in Scottish history. But that is what happened and the man with the dubious record was named John Watson Laurie.

The Glasgow in which Laurie lived was a hymn to Victorian dynamism and prosperity. In the West End spacious wide streets with grand terraces and squares hedged by high ornate buildings were built: solid, staid embodiments of their owners Presbyterian-fired, profit-inspired respectability. At the University, scientific and medical advances made by the likes of Lord Kelvin and Joseph Lister brought academic distinction to the city. The Boys Brigade was formed in 1833 to keep young ruffians off the streets whilst to transport people along them the tram car made its appearance, those swaying, clanking, colourful vehicles so beloved in the city's folk memory. With 270 miles of double steel tracks down the middle of the cobbled streets Glasgow was one of the great tramway centres of Europe.

And there were some strange ships built on Clydeside in those days, built to cater for the whims of the aristocrat or the new industrial millionaire. The Grand Duke Alexis of Russia, for instance, who once made the monumental gaffe of describing Glasgow as "the centre of intelligence of all England", launched the Czar's royal yacht on the Clyde and was impressed by the number of stabilisers in the ship which allowed billiards to be played, even in rough weather. An American millionaire had a cycle track built on the deck of his yacht while a Glasgow merchant had a full scale pipe organ moved from a church onto his. These vessels were the playthings of the rich and a delightful challenge to the builders who ensured that 'Clyde built' was a guarantee of style as well as reliability throughout the world.

In 1889 the Clyde was thick with pleasure paddle steamers which plied their busy trade between the various newly expanded towns and ports up and down the Firth and West coast. Rivalry among steamship companies was intense (forty steamers a day left the Broomielaw berth in the city centre) and this rivalry often ended with parasolled and top hatted trippers waiting on piers having to run for their lives as speeding ships churned to get to them first. In those days before holidays abroad became commonplace, the working people in the West of Scotland traditionally spent their July holidays flocking merrily and brightly clothed "doon the watter" or down the Clyde coast. Their employers had their own yachts and villas, of course, but for the ordinary folk the crowded decks and sun dappled promenades, with the light breezes wafting across the blue water, was where they forgot for a while their routine lives among the grind and grime.

For twenty-five-year old John Watson Laurie there was more to going "doon the watter" that sweltering July in 1889 than getting away from his job as a pattern maker in the Atlas Locomotive Engine Works in Glasgow's Springburn district (the city was one of the major centres of locomotive building in the world).

The girl he had planned to marry had left him and he believed she was staying with friends in Rothesay on the island of Bute. She had found he had been charged with stealing petty cash and had only escaped prison because the money had been made good by relatives. She knew he was continually on the scrounge and boasting about how one day he would be rich but her fiancé dabbling in theft was an affront and she had determined to find someone better.

Laurie filled his wallet with the small amount he had saved from his wages and boarded the crowded Rothesay steamer at the ever busy Broomielaw where happier travellers thronged around him.

Arriving at his destination he spent a week searching fruitlessly and using up his holiday money in the process. He found the jolly, jostling seaside atmosphere of brass bands, laughing girls, beer froth-bewhiskered fathers and giggling children oppressive — his manly pride and supposed future happiness having been so recently put at risk by his girl. But he did at least make one friend, a cheerfully straightforward Brixton clerk called Edwin Rose who was also holidaying on his own and who was sporting a jaunty yachting cap in keeping with the occasion. Rose was quite taken by the lean stranger with the local knowledge who, unknown to him, had seen gullibility stamped all over the Englishman. Laurie, sensing easy money could be plucked from Rose, had introduced himself as a Mr Annandale and set about planning how to empty his fellow holidaymaker's pockets into his own.

Rose suggested a steamer trip to Arran and Laurie agreed. As the paddles smacked and frothed in the water and the ship's 'band', a violinist and two accordionists, played a selection of the latest music hall tunes, Laurie pointed out the local sites including the towering peak of Goatfell.

On arrival the pair started a tour of the grassy, rocky island and Laurie called at a Mrs. Walker's house in Invercloy village. Using his alias of Annandale he inquired if it was correct that she put up lodgers and had she room for two. She said it was and he could have an outside shed if that was not too spartan for the gentleman. He said it was suitable and Laurie and Rose moved in.

But the amateur confidence man's plans almost went awry when

Rose fell in with two other tourists and introduced them to 'Mr. Annandale.' They apparently were not as naive as Rose and could see there was more to the loud spoken but lean and frayed 'Mr. Annandale' than met the eye. When Rose cheerfully announced he would be climbing Goatfell with 'Mr. Annandale' they advised him against it or at least to be very cautious. However, they had a steamer back to Rothesay to catch and left him, satisfied he had taken their advice. On the third day of their stay on the island the pair set out for the sunlit glories of Goatfell. Rose once more allowed himself to be won over by the breezy, talkative 'Mr. Annandale.'

The following morning Mrs Walker went as usual with a breakfast tray to her lodgers' shed only to find them gone. She was very angry at having lost three days rent and cursed the man she had taken to be a gentleman.

As the days passed towards the end of the month Rose's brother back home became increasingly anxious about his non-return to London, knowing how credulous and even simple he could be sometimes. The police were contacted and inquiries started in Rothesay. His last known whereabouts was traced to Arran and newspapers took up the story as full scale search parties set out to scour the island.

On August 4th searchers scrambled over boulders in a ravine locally known as Coire-na-fuhren — the Gully of Fire — because of the way the red rays of the setting sun could turn the rocks to a burning red. One of the party saw what looked like a hand sticking up from under a loose cairn of rocks and stones. The horrified searchers hurriedly cleared the rubble away to uncover the almost unrecognisable bloodstained body of Rose. His face was badly lacerated and battered and his pockets were empty. Looking up it was easy to see how someone could have pushed him from a ridge high above and then made sure of his demise by bludgeoning him into eternity with a rock.

The body was carried the nine miles to Corrie Village where a macabre ritual took place. The local constables removed Rose's boots and buried them in nearby sand before later digging them up again. This was because of a superstition that the ritual would prevent the dead man's ghost walking after his body and disturbing the peace of the village police station.

The search for 'Mr. Annandale', which had been not only fruitless but desultory since they had been looking for Rose, now began in earnest. His description was circulated, there was a lot of press publicity about the brutal Arran murder and gradually the case against Laurie was built up.

His landlady in Rothesay, recognising the description, came forward and told how Laurie had said he was going to Arran for a few days. He had returned on the same morning that Mrs. Walker, who had also come forward, said she found her lodgers gone. Laurie had also fled Rothesay three days after his return owing his landlady there £3. 3. 8d.

A Glasgow acquaintance of Laurie's who had been on holiday said he had seen him going about with Rose in Rothesay, that they had gone off for a few days and when he next saw Laurie walking along the promenade he was alone and sporting Rose's yachting cap. The acquaintance had thought nothing about it at the time, assuming Rose had handed it over as a parting present. Back in Glasgow when there was beginning to be publicity about Rose being missing the acquaintance had met Laurie in Hope Street and asked him if he knew anything about the mystery. He had prevaricated and gone off as soon as he decently could, disappearing into the crowds.

On the day Rose vanished he had been seen in the hills by other climbers walking with Laurie in the direction of Goatfell. Rose and his companion had been last seen going up the peak heading into the setting sun around 6.30. Laurie was then spotted by a shepherd at 9.30. He was walking alone through the gathering dusk in the direction of Corrie where he arrived at the hotel and had a quiet drink in the bar at ten. Nobody had paid much attention to the quiet stranger in the yachting cap. There were a lot of them around during July.

It is roughly two hours walk from Goatfell to the Corrie Hotel so the time scale in which the murder could take place left ample room. The mystery is why Laurie allowed himself to be seen in the hotel at all, unless he hoped he would be mistaken for Rose and thus fling the police off the murder scent. Another possibility is that he was cocksure the body would never be found and actually wanted a drink.

Meanwhile, realising that the game was up Laurie had disappeared. The hue and cry spread throughout the country. His relatives and his few friends houses were raided and his family were sickened that they had saved him from prison only to have murder committed. Even his ex-girlfriend received a nocturnal visit from the police, an event which required a move of house to live down.

Laurie now began a cat and mouse game by post. He wrote a letter to a national newspaper from Liverpool claiming he had left Rose at the top of Goatfell with two men. He then managed to avoid the combined police forces of the North of England and Scotland ending up in Aberdeen where he sent off another letter stating he had only been in Rothesay looking for the girl who had jilted him, reiterated his innocence and ended by declaring he was going to cut his own throat.

He then turned up days later on the platform at Ferniegair Station where he was awaiting a train for Glasgow. He was recognised by railway staff and the local constable appeared. When he saw the uniform Laurie ran off, leapt a fence and made for a thick wood. Some passing miners coming off duty heard the constable's whistle and joined the chase. Laurie charged into the undergrowth with a dozen men close on his heels. He disappeared into some woodland but was spotted kneeling breathless against a tree. When he was grabbed it was discovered he had been trying to cut his throat with an open razor and had inflicted a superficial wound. A doctor tended him and the bloodstained, bedraggled figure was taken to Glasgow. For Laurie it would probably have been better if his suicide attempt had succeeded.

The trial was heard in Edinburgh High Court in November, 1889. Laurie's defence was that he had left Rose's body at six o'clock.

He claimed his companion had accidentally fallen over the precipice into the Gully of Fire and he had decided, because he was broke, to rob and bury him.

But a witness had seen Rose alive and walking at 6.30 and Laurie did not have a satisfactory explanation as to where he had been between the time of Rose's death and the time of his arrival at the hotel, apart from wandering the hills.

He was found guilty and sentenced to death by Lord Kingsburgh. But Laurie's erratic behaviour throughout the two summer months when he had committed the murder and then been on the run had raised serious doubts about his sanity and well-meaning people in authority and in the legal profession pressed for a reprieve.

It was eventually decided to commute his death sentence to one of life sentence. And for him it really meant life. The reason for the reprieve had been insanity but despite this he was not put in a state hospital but spent his remaining forty one years in prison, mostly in Scotland's toughest, Peterhead.

He made one feeble attempt to run away from an outside party in 1893 but was easily recaptured within 3 hours in a field near Peterhead. Thereafter he took to religion and became precentor in the prison chapel.

He died in 1930 aged 69, having in his final dismal years been transferred to the more relaxed atmosphere of Perth Prison. He was eventually classified as insane and supervised as much for his own sake as that of the general public. The only time he ever hinted at his guilt was when he remarked to an inmate, "Rose hadn't very much, after all."

The Gully of Fire is not haunted.

CHAPTER 5

The Judas Goat

For several days and nights two relatives of 83-year-old Miss Marion Gilchrist had been watching and waiting round her luxurious first floor flat at 14 Queen's Terrace, a sober, grey street in a respectable area off Glasgow's Charing Cross at the west end of Sauchiehall Street. One of the men was a Dr. Charteris, a nephew of the old woman. The other was Austin Birrell, the son of a prominent city businessman. They planned, with the connivance of Miss Gilchrist's maid, who had supplied them with a duplicate set of keys, to break into the rich old woman's house and steal a newly made will which left Miss Gilchrist's considerable fortune to her illegitimate daughter instead of the greedy relatives she despised.

To this end Charteris and Birrell had poisoned the old woman's watchdog but this had only served to put her on the alert.

Since the hard faced, cantankerous Miss Gilchrist kept a lot of jewellery in her house she would never let anyone in until she was doubly certain who they were. The two men would have to be careful about choosing the right moment to get in and out without alerting the fiery, suspicious old woman.

The moment they chose, again with the connivance of the maid, was the evening of Monday 21st December 1908 during the period from 7 p.m. onwards when the maid would be out getting the evening paper and Miss Gilchrist would be resting in her armchair in the dining room after her tea.

They quietly entered, using the duplicate keys and started searching for the casket containing the will in the spare bedroom.

But the ever alert Miss Gilchrist caught them and started shouting a torrent of abuse. Birrell dragged the old woman out of the room and back into the dining room while Charteris continued his search.

Birrell was a young man subject to epileptic fits and while struggling and arguing with the livid Miss Gilchrist he suddenly went berserk and struck her. She fell and her head struck a coal box, alerting neighbours below. Birrell seized a chair and, in a frenzy, bludgeoned the old woman some sixty times with it before the ringing of the front doorbell brought him back to reality. He escaped out a back window and shinned down a drainpipe while Charteris, who had finally found the will, calmly walked past the maid who had opened the door and was standing there with a downstairs neighbour.

Charteris met up with his accomplice in the street outside and the two of them ran off to Charteris' house nearby where they cleaned up, changed their clothes, composed themselves, prepared to be each others' alibi and awaited what they thought would be the imminent arrival of the police.

These were the dramatic facts of the Gilchrist murder. What followed was an even more dramatic miscarriage of justice and one of the most disgraceful episodes in British legal history.

The flat below Miss Gilchrist's was occupied by Mr. Arthur Adams, his mother and five sisters. Miss Gilchrist, ever alert and suspicious, had made an arrangement with the Adams household that in the event of trouble she would knock on the floor. She lived a sedentary existence, her only real interest being her jewellery collection valued in those days at £3,000 and which she spitefully would never let any of her relatives see. Among other precautions she took to protect herself were three locks of three different makes on the front door. On no account would she let strangers in if she were alone.

On the night of Miss Gilchrist's death, her maid, Helen Lambie, left the flat at the usual time to get the evening papers. Around 7 p.m. or shortly after the Adams household heard banging coming from upstairs. Arthur Adams went up the stairs to investigate and noticed in passing that the front door giving access from the street was open. He knocked on Miss Gilchrist's door but, getting no reply, he went back downstairs. However, his sisters insisted that he should go back in case something was wrong and at this point he met Lambie who was returning back up the stairs with the papers. She opened the door of her mistress's flat and noticed that the light had been lit in the spare bedroom. Suddenly a man walked out of this room and sped, "like greased lightning" as Mr. Adams was later to say, downstairs.

Lambie did not seem to be surprised by the man's presence and did not speak to him or try to stop him. Instead, she walked calmly into the kitchen, then to the spare bedroom as if checking the house was empty then finally into the dining room where she saw Miss Gilchrist lying in front of the fire with a rug over her head. She then called Adams, who was rather bemused about what was going on, and when he came in he took a quick glance at the body then ran downstairs to try and catch the man. But he had disappeared.

The description given by Adams and Lambie (who claimed to police she did not know the intruder) was of a man aged 25 to 30, around 5 ft. 8 inches tall, with a dark cap, grey overcoat and clean shaven.

Another witness was 14-year-old passer-by Mary Barrowman who claimed she was almost knocked down by the man running out of the house. She said he was 28 to 30, tall and thin, clean shaven with his nose turned to one side, fawn overcoat, dark trousers, a dark tweed hat of the latest make and brown boots.

Miss Gilchrist's valuable jewellery had not been touched but Helen Lambie claimed that a diamond crescent-shaped brooch was missing.

On Christmas Day the police were informed that a German Jew

known as Oscar Slater, who had lived in the same neighbourhood as Miss Gilchrist, had been trying to dispose of a diamond brooch in a club. When the police called at his house they discovered he had left Glasgow with his mistress to go to America. On investigation they discovered that Slater, who was born Leschzner and also went under the name of Adolph Anderson, had gone to Liverpool where he had taken the *Lusitania* for New York under the name of Otto Sands.

Slater's description bore no resemblance to that of the killer. Slater was thick set, square faced, moustachioed, near to forty years old and of foreign appearance. What is more, the brooch, which was not Miss Gilchrist's, had been in his possession three weeks before the murder. Nevertheless, he was of bad character (a pimp and professional gambler) and there was much public pressure on the police to come up with quick results so they decided to take a chance. They badly needed an arrest and someone of Slater's character fitted the bill whereas the son of a respectable businessman (as Austin Birrell was) did not.

Slater was detained on arrival in New York while Helen Lambie and Mary Barrowman got a free trip over to identify him. In the court house in New York, while Lambie and Barrowman were in the company of a Glasgow detective, Slater was brought along the corridor and the detective pointed to him and said in a whisper, "That's the man!"

Later at an identification parade the two witnesses pointed to Slater as the man they had seen at the scene of the crime. (Lambie and Barrowman maintained years later that the police and the Procurator Fiscal's department had compelled them to make an incorrect identification and that they had been badgered on the voyage over; Lambie of course was too deeply involved in the conspiracy by now to argue whereas all that the teenage Barrowman had meant to say was that Slater was like the man she had seen but was not him).

Slater waived extradition and returned voluntarily to Scotland (he had a naive faith in Scottish justice which received a severe jolt when he was kicked by a hostile crowd upon disembarkation).

Every scrap of evidence pointing to Slater did not stand up to investigation. He had left Glasgow at the invitation of a friend in California. He had asked Thomas Cook and Sons to book his cabin to New York. He had given notice to his maid servant. He had written to withdraw his Post Office savings. He had bid good-bye to his friends in the ordinary way. And this was supposed to be a fugitive from justice.

There was absolutely nothing to connect him with Miss Gilchrist who would never have opened her door to him anyway.

But the police did not release him. They put him on another identification parade, this time with ten other non-Jewish policemen and he was picked out by witnesses, who had seen his photograph in the press, as a man they had seen watching the murder flat. Considering he had stayed nearby, there need have been nothing particularly suspicious about him being in the area of the flat.

A careful search of Slater's former abode revealed nothing. But from his luggage the police removed a small hammer, the type used at that time for breaking toffee. This had no traces of blood on it yet incredibly they came up with experts who claimed it just could have been the murder weapon.

This was enough for the Crown and Slater was brought to trial at Edinburgh High Court on May 3rd, 1909. The Lord Advocate, Mr. Alexander Ure K.C., conducted the prosecution himself and did so with deceit and treachery.

He ranted on about "a flight from justice" and claimed nothing was known of Slater's movements on the evening of the murder until 9.45 p.m. (The evidence of a reliable witness who had seen Slater at his front door at 8.15 p.m. had been deliberately suppressed.) The Lord Advocate claimed that Slater had gone on the run after reading in the press that he was wanted for questioning. This was a downright lie as Slater was out of the country before his name was even mentioned in connection with the case let alone published.

Mr. Ure went on to say Slater had been gasping for money which was also a lie. But the Crown had to get up to all these disgraceful tricks because the indictment was based so shakily on dubious identification.

The weak defence counsel made no attempt to protect their client's character when Mr. Ure attacked Slater's mode of life and declared, "I say without hesitation that the man in the dock is capable of having committed this dastardly outrage!"

Slater was not asked to give evidence.

The jury were absent for over an hour and when they returned found Slater guilty by a majority verdict. As the foreman of the jury sat down, Slater leapt to his feet and yelled, "I know nothing about the affair. You are convicting an innocent man!"

He was sentenced to death. But two days before the execution date he was granted a reprieve and the sentence was commuted to life imprisonment with hard labour. He was taken to Peterhead Prison where he proved troublesome to the prison officers and there were frequent blows exchanged. For weeks on end he was held chained in solitary confinement and remission for good behaviour receded with every outburst. All he had to take his outrage out against were the rocks in Peterhead quarry.

But although Glasgow police and those in the Scottish Establishment might feel smug that they had made certain the case was closed, it simply would not lie down and die.

One man who was very dubious about the way the police had handled the case was a detective involved, Lieutenant John Trench. In 1912 he was sent to Dundee to help the police there on a murder case. A man named Warner was in custody but Trench was able to produce evidence that he was not even in the country at the time despite the fact that five witnesses swore they had seen Warner near the scene of the crime. It was following this revelation about the accuracy of identification that Trench belatedly decided to try and help Slater.

As a police officer it was his duty to let Slater rot but he thought that his duty as a fellow man was more important.

He therefore went to a Glasgow solicitor called David Cook and put his dilemma to him. Trench said he was prepared to divulge what he knew, provided no disciplinary action was taken. He was advised to approach the Prison Commissioners which he did, the Secretary of State was informed and the Sheriff of Lanarkshire was appointed to conduct a secret inquiry. Neither the prisoner nor his agent were allowed to be present. But Trench told the inquiry "I am aware that on the 22nd of December, the day after the murder,

Superintendent Douglas along with Detectives Pyper and Dornan, drove in a taxi cab to the house of Austin Birrell. I am also aware that they did so in view of the information supplied by Helen Lambie, the maidservant. I have endeavoured from time to time to elicit what took place in Austin Birrell's house but I am without information.

"On 23rd December I was instructed by Chief Superintendent Orr to visit and take a statement from Miss Birrell at 19 Blythswood Drive. I had particular instructions to question her with regard to Mr. Birrell as to what Helen Lambie said when she visited her house on the night of the murder. I visited Miss Birrell and from her received the statement word for word as contained in her precognition.

"This said: 'I am a niece of the late Marion Gilchrist. My mother was a sister of the deceased. Miss Gilchrist was not on good terms with her relatives. Few, if any, visited her. I can never forget the night of the murder. Miss Gilchrist's servant, Helen Lambie, came to my door about 7.15 p.m. She was excited. She pulled the bell violently. On the door being opened she rushed into the house and exclaimed: 'Oh, Miss Birrell, Miss Birrell, Miss Gilchrist has been murdered. She is lying dead in the dining room and, Oh Miss Birrell, I saw the man who did it.' I replied, 'My God, Helen, this is awful. Who was it? Do you know him?' Helen replied, 'Oh, Miss Birrell — I think it was Austin! I am sure that it was him!' I said to her, 'My God, Helen, don't say that. Unless you are very sure of it, Helen, don't say that.' She again repeated to me that she was sure it was Austin.'

"The same evening Detectives Pyper and Dornan visited me and I learned from them that she had told them it was Austin Birrell."

Trench went on to state: "On receiving the statement from Miss Birrell I returned to the Central Police Office. I told Superintendent Orr what Miss Birrell had said and he seemed impressed, remarking, 'This is the first real clue we have got.'

"I was instructed to write out the statement. I did so. In handing that statement to Superintendent Orr he said, 'I have just been ringing up Superintendent Douglas and he is convinced that Austin Birrell had nothing to do with it.' "

Trench then described a meeting he had with Helen Lambie on the 3rd of January 1909 when he showed her a sketch of Slater but she failed to identify him and said she did not know him. He mentioned the matter of Austin Birrell to her and she replied, "It's gey funny if it wasn't him."

One suppressed statement which Trench also supplied was from a schoolteacher who had seen not one but two men run from Miss Gilchrist's flat at the time of the murder.

All the police officers involved denied at the inquiry that anyone else apart from Slater had been under suspicion and two months after the end of the proceedings, in answer to a question in the House of Commons, the Secretary of State for Scotland said there were no grounds on which to interfere in the conviction of Slater.

Then came the bombshell for Trench. He was dismissed from the force for communicating with someone outwith the force (in this case the lawyer Cook) confidential information without the permission of his superior officer.

But his former colleagues were not finished with him yet. While serving as a drill instructor with the Royal Scots Fusiliers he was arrested and charged with receiving stolen property and his co-accused was none other than the lawyer Cook. This revolved round a theft from a jewellers and because of Trench's good work the thieves had decided the property was too hot for them and had decided to hand the lot over to the insurance company for a paltry sum compared to what they would have had to pay out if the jewels had gone forever. Trench had approached his Chief Constable for advice and had been told it was up to the insurance company to make their own arrangements. The stolen property was duly returned with Cook acting as go-between and the insurance company wrote a letter to the Chief Constable gratefully acknowledging Trench's good work.

At their trial the evidence against Trench and Cook was so suspect that the judge directed the jury to acquit in these words, "What the accused did was done with an innocent or even meritorious intention. The question is, have these two panels been proved guilty of reset of theft? I think, on the facts, that they have not; and direct you, on the law, that you cannot and ought not to return a verdict of guilty but on the contrary that you should acquit both prisoners of the charge laid against them."

At this there was applause, spontaneous and deserved, from the packed public benches. They knew whose side they were on.

Trench died in 1919, after a distinguished war service, without ever seeing the injustice which had ruined his life corrected. But he was not forgotten. A journalist friend, William Park, wrote a book on the Slater case which raised serious doubts about the investigation and this was published in 1927. The demand for a review of the case grew. Conan Doyle, Marshall Hall and Edgar Wallace all took up Slater's cause and at last the Secretary of State ordered Slater's release.

He had served nineteen years but was never pardoned. The Government had agreed to send the case back to the Court of Appeal and five judges quashed the conviction on the grounds of misdirection in law by Lord Guthrie who had presided over the fiasco all those years before. Apparently, among all the other multifarious errors of that trial, the legal establishment could only find one: that Lord Guthrie had been wrong to deprive Slater of the presumption of innocence in his summing up to the jury.

This further belated cover-up was nineteen years too late for Slater and he was rightly furious that he had not been completely exonerated. To pacify him the Secretary of State granted him an unasked for ex-gratia payment of £6,000.

Strangely enough his relations with Conan Doyle were less than amicable. Slater felt that he was only being used by Doyle for publicity, surely an unjust accusation since the creator of Sherlock Holmes hardly needed extra fame.

Slater married in 1937 and lived in Ayr until his death in 1948, having to suffer the further indignity of internment (ironically because he was both a Jew and a German) during the Second World War.

Writing of the case at the time, Edgar Wallace said of the Scottish legal system, much vaunted north of the border, and its hamfisted bungling of the whole case, "An Old Bailey jury would have stopped the case half way through and dismissed the prisoner. In no other place in the British Empire would such a trial and such a trial be possible. Slater is still in prison. He has served nineteen years for a crime of which anybody but a fool might know he was innocent."

Helen Lambie and all the others concerned went to their graves without ever revealing why the police were involved in such a cover-up. The Birrells were respectable members of society at a time when that really counted for something, making it not only inconceivable to the tunnel-visioned constabulary that such people could be guilty of crime, but also ensuring that their word was respected when they said they had nothing to do with it.

The police have always been the muscular right arm of the Establishment and never more so than in Edwardian Presbyterian Scotland. In addition, it might be said that the Birrell males were leading adepts in Freemasonry as were, and are, many of the top men in the police and there may even have been personal contacts in the case to ensure the cover-up was so complete that there had to be a sacrificial victim, for instance an immigrant Jewish pimp.

If investigative journalism had been then what it is now there may have been the chance of uncovering a lot more. As it was, the press, like the police, passively reflected the prejudices of their day.

One simple fact showed that from the very beginning there was something mysteriously wrong with the handling of the case. A detailed handprint in blood was found on the back of the chair which killed Miss Gilchrist. Fingerprinting had been in existence since the turn of the century and a simple test could have revealed who was and, more importantly, who was not the murderer. This piece of vital evidence was suppressed by the police.

And shortly before Slater's release, when it was obvious he was going to be freed and a gross miscarriage of justice had been perpetrated, the Adams sisters who had been in the flat below Miss Gilchrist at the time of the murder re-entered the saga. By that time they had moved to a village outside Glasgow where they ran a small confectionery shop. But their consciences troubled them even after all those years and they felt compelled to visit their local justice of the peace, a lady with whom they were friendly. They told her about "the man who came over the window". While their brother had gone upstairs to get into Miss Gilchrist's flat this man came down the drain pipe past their sitting room window. They recognised him as Austin Birrell whom they knew from the neighbourhood and who was the son of a prominent businessman. Their statement had been deliberately suppressed by the police and they had been told by them never to speak to anyone about it and they had adhered to this up to now. They added that it would have made little difference to "poor Austin" anyway since he had committed suicide shortly after the murder.

Charteris went on to become a distinguished professor at St. Andrew's University and always denied that he had anything to do with the crime.

CHAPTER 6

Children of the Night

Glasgow is synonymous with gangs just as it is with slums and the first were created by the second. The tradition of the organised gang or team of teenagers or young men, territorially organised into groups who wage war with weapons such as knives, razors and hatchets purely for the violence and the glory, is a phenomenon unusually characteristic of the city and not found in such abundance or historical length anywhere else in Britain.

There are other grim factors unique about the city. According to Alcoholics Anonymous the drink problem is three times as high as anywhere else in Britain, Glasgow being the alcoholic capital of western Europe. Hard boozing has been characteristic of the place for a hundred years. It also has the worst housing in Europe with more overcrowding, more sub-standard and more municipal dwellings than any other comparable city, allied to a 'brain drain' of talent away from areas euphemistically labelled in typical modern jargon as suffering from "multiple urban deprivation" meaning verminous slums riddled with crime and despair. And again this has always been the case since the Industrial Revolution.

During periods of recurrent recession Glasgow has always had the unenviable position of being among the leaders in the unemployment league and recently with the decline of major industries such as shipbuilding and heavy engineering the unemployment rate has been running well ahead of most of the country yet again. It is something the city should be used to by now since there was one in three adult males unemployed in the thirties at a time when Glasgow boasted it was the second biggest city in the British Empire. It also has suffered a high general early death rate and the worst rate of lung cancer and heart disease in Britain, as well as, up until recent years, one of the worst rates of rickets and similar children associated diseases.

It has also been one of the most violent areas in Britain ever since it was designated a city and it has a prison population far above the European average.

With all of these grim records concentrated in the valley of the Clyde it is hardly surprising that other bizarre manifestations have sprung up, among them gangs.

The Celtic temperament common to both Scots and Irish has several broad tendencies: a natural aggression (possibly spawned from an inferiority complex), sentimentality, a belief in man as the hunter and woman as the housewife-cum-mother and a propensity for high spirits in the shape of whisky or whiskey or us'quebaugh as the Gaels called it, meaning 'Water of Life'. They also have a centuries old obsession with religion whether Roman Catholic or Presbyterian. Just as it was Cromwell's transplanting of dour, aggressive Protestant Scots to Northern Ireland which sowed the seeds of Ulster violence, so the influx of Irish Catholics and Orangemen into Clydeside shipyards led to another of Glasgow's unenviable peculiarities, the Rangers — Celtic syndrome.

The Irish Catholic immigrant workers brought over during the Industrial Revolution and the native Protestant Scots of similar religions picked out two rival football teams, for the Protestants the blue shirted Rangers south of the city and for the Catholics the green shirted Celtic in the East End, to symbolise their religious differences on the sporting field and transpose their vigorous theological hatreds from the churches and the chapels to the terracings. Celtic was originally started as a club to provide soup kitchens for the poverty stricken Irish and the early feeling against them was a resentment at the encroachment of these job hungry settlers. But later the anti-Catholic element replaced the ethnic one.

Rangers were formed by Protestant shipyard workers brought over from Ulster to start up a subsidiary of Harland and Woolf's on Clydeside and the bigoted polarisation and rivalry of these two teams supporters became a logical if deplorable extension of their religious differences which regularly erupted into violence.

Every time this century the teams have met in sporting combat the fans, with their banners and war cries, have joined in off-the-field fisticuffs, bottle throwing and general mayhem. This on a grand scale where Chief Constables are still regularly quoted as saying crowds are well behaved when there have been only 200 arrests. It is the same as what happened on a smaller scale in gangland, although in both cases religion, like territory, was and is not so much a reason in itself as an excuse for identifying and belonging to one group to take out animal frustration on another.

The seeds then were there for gangs from the beginning: overcrowded slums, poverty and ignorance, a need to assert oneself, a sudden large influx to the working class which nevertheless was frequently unemployed, and a pronounced tendency for drink also viewed as a test of manliness, all of this peppered with a good dose of religious bigotry.

The first organised groups of brawlers sprang up in the 1880's at street corners and pubs among the city's sprawling tenements in the East End. They started a tradition, followed by their future blood brothers over the years whereby a common fund was set up to pay fines and hence the first Glasgow gang got its name — 'The Penny Mob'. At this time there were frequent encounters with the police and court reports gave the leaders of the packs the rather stuffy title of 'chairmen'.

The Penny Mob bred rivals such as the San Toy Boys from Calton nearer the city centre and the Tim Malloys, the Calton mob's war cry as they charged into street battles being "We are the young San Toys and we can fight the Tim Malloy's!"

The South Side, later to become a notorious breeding ground for the worst or best gangs depending on your viewpoint, came up with the Mealy Boys, the McGlynn Push and the picturesquely-named Gold Dust Gang, although the Gorbals never produced a prospector.

The average age of the gang member was twenty and in some areas it was not only a test of manhood but also advisable for the health to have the support of your local lads when inky nights were dimly punctured by gaslight and eyes could be watching in the dark.

Frequently the drinking dens where the gangs held out and boosted their courage were raided and wrecked by rivals. And passers-by were by no means immune from blows.

Sporadic mayhem continued into this century and even the drain of young men into the mass muddy graves of the First World War seems to have had little effect on gangland manpower. There always seemed to be someone young and eager to fill a hooligan's shoes until he too was marched to the front. There were more than a million inhabitants of the city by 1914 which provided plenty of cannon fodder for strife at home and abroad.

The Redskins took over the East End as their happy hunting ground and fought such worthies as the Calton Black Hand, the Bloodhound Flying Corps, the Hi-Hi's and the Hazel Bells from Mile-End and Bridgeton, the Kelly Boys from Govan and the Baltic Fleet from Baltic Street. The Redskins claimed they 'ruled' their area, the first time the expression was used, and also boasted an organised membership of a thousand who had a loud, quick, tuneless whistle whereby a member could gather fast support to his side should rivals set about him, always assuming he could get the whistle off in time and that a courageous pal was in the neighbourhood to hear it and not run the other way. The Redskins also disdained fists as kids stuff, much preferring a swashbuckling meat cleaver or hammer. They also moved into crime by getting protection money from shopkeepers and tradesmen who were scared they would get their premises wrecked. Pedestrians were attacked and robbed openly in daylight in the street. The police eventually decided the

Redskins should be tamed. They clamped down heavily, made raids and arrests, and cajoled witnesses into speaking and reasserted their particular rule. Among weapons uncovered under beds, in wardrobes and below floorboards were knives, heavily leaded batons of wood and rubber, revolvers, iron bludgeons and steel clubs. A myth has grown up that the old gangs fought only among themselves and while this was generally true it was by no means always the case.

Instead of 'chairmen' gangs now had their 'Kings', an indication of the growth of the pastime. They also had their 'Queens', the wildest and usually most good looking girls in that particular block of slumland. It was quite an honour to hold court and girls were eligible as soon as puberty was reached. The age of consent was not a nicety which bothered the gangs and in true Hollywood tradition, although the cinema had not yet arrived to show them, the molls were as hard talking, brassy and 'gallus', or sharp, as their counterparts while holding their liquor and opening their legs on order. Some of the girls even took part in the fights, probably to prove they were not girls at all, but invariably they ended up at the Royal Infirmary. These girls normally dropped out before their twenty-first birthdays when the inevitable baby came along. They took their place as house-keeper in the male dominated society, taking up the traditional chores of changing the nappies or frying the sausages, or taking the laundry to the 'steamie' and could be seen leaning, like haggard, aproned figureheads with curlers and fags from their windows chatting to neighbours and watching the world go by.

With the end of the Great War (during which shipyard production had reached its all-time peak) and the coming of the twenties, the spectre of unemployment, which always hovered round the corner in Glasgow, crept back to haunt the slum dwellers. The average age group of the gang leaders gradually became older as discontented cloth-capped young men lounging 'on the burroo' at street corners decided to revolt in their own way just like their teenage counterparts. Now with more muscle, more cunning and more bravado amongst the bulky, brawling hooligans, gang battles became more organised, bigger in numbers and more deadly. Throughout the twenties and thirties there were regular pitched battles between rival gangs from north and south sides involving hundreds of screaming, weapon wielding hooligans. There were also more sedate 'fair fights' or 'square goes' between stripped-to-the-waist gang leaders on Glasgow Green without any Queensberry rules, just brute fist and foot smashing where they could, but even these generally degenerated into a free-for-all. Sometimes the police were quite content to stand by and let them knock hell out of each other and then step in and pick up the pieces in the hope that the arrogance would be crushed out of the damaged remains after a spell in hospital and prison. Sometimes this led to the breaking of a gang leader but it also led to others escaping and enhancing their reputation.

The Gorbals, that sprawling district on the south bank of the Clyde, bred the best fighting stock. It also pioneered the use of a new weapon, the open razor, and invented a new phrase 'razor slashing', a particularly ghastly and arbitrary way to slice up a victim. Among other favourite weapons were ghurka knives, bayonets, pokers and broken bottles.

Favourite haunts included the many dance halls dotted throughout the city at this time. The gang members would 'jake up' on potent fortified red wine which they could buy for 3d a gill and show off their girls at 'the jiggin' '. Frequently there were fights between the girls over a particularly virile gang member, hair tearing, face scratching, screaming scraps, casually and laughingly watched by jibing, onlooking males.

Like most Glasgow gangs, serious crime was a peripheral and not an integral part of their activities. Their raison d'etre was simply to bash other people's heads in, cut them and hold onto their district in a primitive machismo-like style which fed stultified egos with a feeling of importance. The more adult and organised the gang the more crime there was, the traditional ones associated with such groups, like extortion and theft. They also organised local shebeens, illegal drinking dens, often just a room and kitchen with a drink laden table where the thirsty could get a drink outside the prohibitive licensing hours if they were willing to pay hefty prices for stolen liquor. Illegal moneylending with extortionate interest rates also became a feature of the more organised gangs of the sixties and this worked hand in pint with the shebeens.

It was a good breeding ground for the lifelong criminals. A man who was handy with his fists when young could be lucratively employed by bigger fish when he was older. But although many of the active members ended their short careers rotting in prison, their bodies prematurely aged through abuse, there were equally many others who lapsed out of their wilder than wild oat days and succumbed to a miserable domesticity and respectability rather than a life of crime. And if they had been lucky enough to escape 'the jailers' they could bring up their children safe in the knowledge that they had no record and in fact had committed no crimes except bash about others as violent as themselves.

In a sub-cultural manner it was the same as junior football teams playing each other except instead of a ball and boots being used to let out youthful animal spirits it was knives and coshes being utilised to ventilate their hatreds. Perhaps this is why gangs gradually changed over the years to calling themselves teams because the former has overtones of big time syndicates while the latter has a more suitable feeling of young recklessness. Although tales of gang warfare became exaggerated by the pint swilling exuberant victors, their exploits rarely rose above an armed clash in the street, sometimes organised, sometimes accidental.

In the thirties the Bee Hive gang were the Kingpins in the Gorbals but it was a near run thing holding their ground against such battalions as the Billy Boys, Stickit Boys and Derry Boys from Bridgeton, the Antique Mob from Shettleston, the Black Diamond Boys, the Hammer Boys and the Dirty Dozen from the South Side, the Romeo Boys from the East End and the Kelly-bow from Govan.

The Bee Hive's territory was the Cumberland Street area of the Gorbals. It's leader was a man named Peter Williamson who, because of his prowess as a fist fighter, became a legend in his own day.

The Bee Hive was a bigger threat to the citizenry than most gangs of that era because its members concentrated on money making ventures like shop-breaking and safe-blowing. This did not mean that they were averse to doing battle with any other Glasgow gang. When the necessity arose to settle differences with some other gang then Peter Williamson would send a message to the leader of the gang involved, inviting him to single combat. If the other leader accepted the challenge then he and Peter, accompanied by their seconds, would meet at some secluded spot on Glasgow Green. There they would fight it out, and afterwards shake hands and go off to the nearest pub or shebeen for a restorative drink.

With the outbreak of the Second World War, the Bee Hive gang broke up. Petter Williamson went off to the army where he was soon promoted to the rank of sergeant. After the war Peter went back to safe blowing for which he was to serve a couple of sentences at Peterhead Prison.

Around 1930 religious bigotry spread its fiery torch through the city with the rise in the East End of the Billy Boys who were rabid Orangemen (they took their name from 'King Billy', the Prince of Orange). Their arch Catholic enemies were the Norman Conquerors (known better as the Norman Conks) whose H.Q. was in Norman Street.

In 1935 on all Catholic Saints and Holy Days the Billy Boys Drum and Flute Band, led off by their prancing, pirouetting, 'pipe major' leader Billy Fullerton, would march down Norman Street playing rousing Orange tunes. Each time this happened the Conks let fly from their windows and roofs a hail of bottles, bricks, pickshafts and buckets of excreta down on the immaculately sashed musicians who would continue to make their haphazard, out-of-tune way to church where, instead of going in, they would simply disband. So much for religious feelings. The chaotic marches were finally and truly disbanded and the flutes silenced by a full-scale charge of mounted police who scattered the Orangemen and dealt baton blows from their horses to the nearest Billy Boys. One of the gang, Elijah Cooper the big drum player, escaped injury by diving into his instrument and, using it as a shield, rolling away from the thundering hooves of the police.

The Billy Boys had kept up the tradition of the Penny Mob because each of the eight hundred men commanded by Fullerton carried membership cards on which a weekly 2d payment had to be marked up. At one stage there was more than £1,200 in their local bank lodged under three names and it was used for fines and keeping wives whose breadwinners had been jailed. Some local shopkeepers were also 'asked' to contribute. It was Fullerton's brainwave to lift six hundred pounds to form the flute band as a way of emphasising their contempt of the Conks.

No Billy Boys wedding was complete without a certain robustness. On one occasion, fearing a Conks intervention while one of the Billy's lieutenants was getting married, Fullerton arranged for the bridegroom to be at the altar with a sword concealed in his morning dress, the best man with a gun in his pocket, a guard of honour holding razors instead of swords and finally, seeing there was to be no battle after all, the ritual smashing of champagne bottles took place on the pavement outside the church.

Fullerton was a member of the blackshirted Fascist Mosleyite movement and was an admirer of Hitler, his gangs being ready to use their strong-arm methods in true storm-trooper style should the need arise. They had their political and religious ideologies mixed up, however, and instead of beating up Jews they would beat up Catholics which shows that their belief in a superior race was only another excuse for a show of power.

To his credit Fullerton also organised youth clubs of a sort and kept his boys fit and interested in sports but, of course, another motive for keeping his gang in the gym rather than the pub was to ensure their fitness in the pitched battles. Truces were called at New Year when there would be a spate of pub break-ins and drunken, naked 'Queens' would perform at parties for anyone who asked. On these occasions the leader of the Parlour Boys, James Dalziel or 'Razzle Dazzle' as he was colloquially known, only danced with other large male members of his gang, deeming it effeminate to dance with girls.

But even gang members and their molls have sentimentally long memories for at Fullerton's funeral in 1962 there were more than 300 mourners which, considering he was very much a spent force by that time, was a remarkable turn-out, the Orange Order being amply represented.

The ordinary policemen who had to control all this mayhem had their hands full. A typical example was Constable Roddie Gillies of the city's Eastern Division who, years later, described what one of those riotous occasions was like. "On the last Sunday in May each year the children in the East End became members of the Sacred Heart Chapel in Old Dalmarnock Road and the inauguration was celebrated by a procession of the children led by a junior pipe band from a Catholic school.

"On one of these occasions we were ordered to turn out in force in squad cars to Bridgeton Cross. When I got there the Cross was a battlefield. There was fighting everywhere and policemen were being chased onto tramcars.

"The juvenile pipe band was being escorted by men from Maryhill or the west end who had no experience of gang warfare and as they were being attacked by at least 500 Billy Boys they never had a chance.

"The first act of violence had been a brick through the big drum and this scattered the young band. My colleagues could not keep them together and had to run for their lives themselves.

"Just as I arrived Sergeant Robertson jumped out of another car and, as the Billies turned to attack us, we drew our batons and shoulder to shoulder we charged the gang and, despite their weapons, we laid out at least a dozen and the rest took to their heels when two police vans appeared.

"We rallied the pipe band and escorted them down to the chapel and then took the prisoners back to the police station where they were locked up.

"After they were locked up Inspector McPherson arrived and called me over.

" 'I'm just back from Bridgeton Cross. It's really simmering and there is going to be a lot more trouble. Get a colleague and go there.'

"I got an older policeman, Hugh Jarvie, and we went back to the Cross. The place was indeed really simmering and so we had to be on our toes.

"We had not been there very long when a woman appeared with what she said was a stray child. She didn't really convince me but Hugh decided to take the little girl to the office.

"He wasn't far away when the trouble started. A double-decker bus was making its way slowly through the crowd from Dalmarnock towards London Road on its way to town. It had an open stairway to the top-deck, and it had not got clear when I heard a scream and saw a man running for his life after the bus with dozens of Billy Boys chasing him, all carrying knives or hatchets or some kind of offensive weapon.

"The leading gangster was carrying a butcher's knife and he was close to the man who made the bus but instead of diving inside he ran up the stair.

"His attacker did a hand balance on the rail and drove the knife into his back.

"I had been struggling through the crowd who were very obstructive and I only got there after the knife had been withdrawn. I laid the ned out and the knife fell out of his hand and was picked up before I could reach it.

"I went on one knee to stick the handcuffs on him, one of the gang gave the most vicious kick in the small of my back, it straightened me up and I saw his reflection in a mirror in the window opposite. He then tried to get past me to the bus but I laid him out and handcuffed him to his pal.

"I got them on to their feet and saw that the crowd were attacking the bus, throwing bricks through the windows.

"I shouted to the conductress to get away and take the injured man to hospital. They forced their way through the crowd and got away.

"I had a prisoner in each hand and started backing along London Road towards Tobago Street police station. The mob were throwing stones and bricks at me.

"When I was nearly opposite the part of Abercromby Street, I heard a voice, an Irish one, say, 'Can we help you, sir?' I turned around and saw two Irish boys as big as myself. 'Yes, you can help me,' I said. 'Take these two and I'll hold the mob back.' We got to the foot of Tobago Street when we met a rescue party from the office. A woman had ran there and told them I was in big trouble.

"When we got to the office there was a call from Duke Street Hospital giving the name of the man who had been taken there by the bus driver and saying his condition was serious but he was expected to live.

"I charged the two neds with forming part of a riotous and disorderly crowd, with waving knives and bayonets and with assault.

"They were locked up and eventually appeared at the High Court where they were sentenced to two years hard labour.

"The sequel to the story as far as I was concerned came when I collapsed in the street all of two months later and couldn't get up. The large muscle that had been kicked that Sunday had jumped out of place and was pressing against my lung.

"When I came round in the Royal Infirmary I was told I would never walk again but would be on full pay for the rest of my life.

"I was eventually put into plaster and kept on my back for some weeks.

"The muscle healed back into place and I was back on duty in three months.

"When I had first regained conciousness a Sergeant at the Infirmary read a commendation from the Chief for bravery. 'They must have thought I was going to die,' I said. 'They weren't the only ones,' the Infirmary doctor said."

Those were certainly tough days in which to be a policeman in Glasgow and the gang situation was getting so out of hand that successful crimebuster Sir Percy Sillitoe was brought from Sheffield to smash them. His methods were robust but worked. Using the roughest, toughest men of the force he would secrete them in furniture vans, converge on fights and let them have a free hand with whatever force they cared to use. This was in the days before such niceties as the Council for Civil Liberties and, even if the hooligans had understood their rights, the heavy squad, as they bludgeoned into them with fists, boots and batons, would not have been inclined to take much notice. Injuries sustained to accused hooligans were in court accredited to other gang members. Sillitoe was nicknamed 'Hitler' by his victims (which was ironic coming from Fuhrer worshipper Fullerton). But the fact remains that the gangs feared him because he was fighting them on their own terms and his methods were partially successful in that they forced gang warfare into decline and put offenders behind bars without, however, obliterating the problem. No great detective work was needed for these louts, simply brute force.

Sillitoe at the time he was Chief Constable (from 1931 to 1943) was idolised as the perfect policeman by the city's respectable citizenry. As well as gang busting, he brought in the fingerprint department, police boxes, diced police caps because they are easier to recognise in the dark and he introduced Glasgow's first marriage guidance council. He also started an intelligence force called the 'C' Specials, introduced radio cars and formed a river patrol. A dedicated Chief, hard but fair and a stern disciplinarian, he frequently dressed up as a workman and went round the city to check up on his own men. But he also went to the funerals of down and outs and paid for meals and drinks for those who turned up for the service without revealing who he was. His opinion of the gangs was succinct, "We are determined to fight gangsters with the utmost ferocity. These hooligans are merely unemployable louts. They find their courage in numbers. They are craven-hearted rats when alone. We are out to teach them that they must take heed of the law."

However, certain members of Glasgow Corporation lived to regret inviting him into the city. After he was finished smashing up organised hooliganism and imprisoning the violent leaders, Sillitoe turned his attention to graft rings within the Corporation. His plain clothes 'C' Specials eavesdropped on conversations in the back rooms of pubs where contractors gave over wads of notes to councillors in the building committees involved in carving up, demolishing and redeveloping the sprawling city. Several councillors ended up behind bars alongside the gangsters. But like gang warfare Sillitoe was not able to stamp out graft which has plagued the city up to the present day. Old boy networks and corruption flourish just as easily among so-called socialist friends of the people, who have dominated the City Chambers for years, as among anyone else.

The first Chief Constable of Glasgow to be knighted, Sillitoe went on to become head of M15 and died in 1962. But he always claimed his years as Glasgow's Chief were the happiest of his life, the most rewarding and most satisfying.

While Sillitoe was smashing the gangs someone else was making them immortal in a book. It is sad but typical that the best known, some would say notorious, and most read book about Glasgow is not a great work of art about beauty and nobility but is instead an arguably poorly written treatise on squalor and violence. The subject of *No Mean City* by A. McArthur and H. Kingsley Long is the razor gangs of the Gorbals and the characters, most of them exaggerated, are nevertheless based on real life. The conditions of massive overcrowding in evil smelling ghettoes are certainly not exaggerated. Written in suitably arid style by Mr. McArthur, a Gorbals grocer, when the longhand manuscript arrived on the desk of his publishers they were impressed by the book's power but appalled at its lack of literacy which is why a second writer, H. Kingsley Long, had to be brought in. The book became a best-seller, topping the million mark following its publication in 1956. Up to now it has sold more than 17 million copies.

It is sad but typical that Mr. McArthur gained little from this. He tried to write a sequel, *No Bad Money,* which would be a similar success (again with a co-writer) but it was a poor reflection of his first book. He subsequently took to drink because his confidence in any writing ability he might have had was shattered. He was finally found dead on the banks of the Clyde full of methylated spirits.

To add to the city's bad image, it is at least unfortunate that the picture conjured up by the name Glasgow was for many years abroad based on the brilliant caricature of a drunken, bunnetted Scottish working man portrayed by Will Fyffe leaning on a lamp-post, bawling and slurring,

Ah belang tae Glesca, dear auld Glesca toon,
But there's somethin' the ma'er wi' Glesca
Fur it's goin' roon' an' roon',
Ah'm only a common old workin' chap
As anyone here can see
But when Ah get a couple o' drinks on a Setterday
Glasgow belongs to me!

Will Fyffe, a Dundonian, paid only a few shillings for the song to an impoverished writer and then proceeded to make his fortune.

Sillitoe's ongoing campaign to clean up Glasgow was interrupted by the Second World War which helped his task enormously because it channelled the young Scots natural aggression into killing Germans instead of his fellow countrymen, just as the Great War had done.

The Jocks have always had a proud military reputation since the

Napoleonic Wars and they were among the foremost in every campaign against the Nazis. Robert Graves was a trifle unkind when he said the Jock was the first soldier to run into battle and the first to run out, because many a commander was grateful he had the Scottish regiments to fling into the line where others wavered. Among the military cemeteries scattered throughout the world there are lying many who undoubtedly would have made up the ranks of armed gangs and come to a bad end. It was William Pitt the Younger's idea to channel the aggressiveness of the clan system, with its feuds and territorial squabbling and raiding, into organised regiments and it is interesting to note that an old clan map of Scotland resembles on a grand scale what a Glasgow gang map represents on a smaller scale. Perhaps history has only changed on the surface and the city has become a microcosm for a national tendency of banding together for mutual defence and attack.

Be that as it may, not even World War could wipe out the Glasgow gangs, as had previously been shown in 1914, and the domestic warfare continued uninterrupted although on a much reduced scale than in its heyday. The blackout was great fun for the teenagers not yet called up. The temptations of bombed or derelict houses where there could be cash, the tripping up and baiting of drunks in the black streets, the thrill of escaping down moonlit alleys, the real fireworks on Clydeside with the bombs blitzing the shipyards and the world gone mad with violence, and all of this with Dad away at the wars and Mum too busy coping with rationing and no discipline anywhere except from exasperated policemen with inefficient torches stabbing through the darkness.

After 1945 many young men had had their glut of violence. Many had their eyes and aspirations opened and widened to the world, thanks to military service. With horizons broadened and senses they never knew they possessed newly stimulated they were not prepared simply to slide back into the narrow, claustrophobic jungle of the closes where the next district could be the other side of the moon. Some simply emigrated, some decided to make a new kind of life for themselves well away from the threat of a criminal life. Most felt there was a social change in the air and there was. The huge, gaunt ghettoes were to be a thing of the past and the socialist brothers in the City Chambers were to bring in a New Order. Needless to say, it did not happen quite as envisioned.

Their good intentions cannot be doubted but that was not enough. The Labour-controlled Corporation idea was that because of the appalling slumlands choking up the city like cancer, an affront to modern man and a strangling grip on civilised development, there should be no less than a bulldozing blitzkrieg on these old areas and the inmates should be lifted and deposited en bloc in brand new dormitory estates on the virgin green fields fringing the city. The project and cost was colossal (as was the graft) and the estates were huge, cut off except for poor bus services from the city centre and virtually townships on their own. But townships without a heart.

While the Corporation were flinging up hundreds of miles of lookalike three storey, balconied rows of houses, admittedly cleaner than the slums and with indoor toilets and the luxury of baths, the planners forgot basic amenities which make society en masse tolerable. The new inhabitants of Easterhouse, Drumchapel, Pollok and Castlemilk in the East, North, West and Southern fringes found it even difficult to find nearby shops. And as for any form of entertainment or sport or public relaxation of any kind, a resolution of 1890 forbidding this on municipal housing estates put a real damper on the spirits of the people. There was no money to build places of entertainment anyway because the first priority was always houses, houses, houses. Glasgow was to be dragged screaming into the mid-twentieth century world of concrete and chrome by eager architects whether it squealed about it or not.

As word filtered through to the beleaguered areas to be demolished that all was not exactly paradise in the new estates, panic spread and inhabitants who loved the old areas in which they had been reared fought councillors, contractors, sometimes even police before being taken from their tenements, in some cases on the same day they were demolished. For with all their obvious faults, the tenements were built in districts which had themselves been villages before being swallowed up by the city and they did have a community atmosphere. Everyone knew their neighbours, took their turn washing the stairs, cared for people when they were ill, went to the same weddings, parties, funerals, the same churches or chapels, the same schools, cinemas, pubs, dance halls, laundries or 'steamies', swimming baths, shops, football grounds, bookies. Doors were often left unlatched throughout the day for families and kids to come in and out at will. And yet those in authority made little attempt to keep this community spirit intact. Possibly many middle class professionals were not even aware it existed. People were only statistics and flung to the four winds regardless of friends, relatives or neighbours, leaving behind decimated or demolished areas with only the wind tip-toeing over what for all the world resembled bomb sites. What the Luftwaffe could not do the planners did with a vengeance. Throughout the late forties, fifties and early sixties this furious rehousing to far flung new schemes continued apace.

But even the misplaced enthusiasm of the planners could not cope with the problem. More than 80,000 new municipal houses were built between 1945 and 1968. And in the decade alone from 1958 more than 17,000 families were rehoused completely outwith the city boundary whereas more than 36,500 were given new homes in the 27 redevelopment schemes earmarked within the city. And yet one house in three was considered sub-standard by the mid-sixties. It has been a case of staggering from crisis to crisis with still no solution in sight. In the late sixties it was estimated Easterhouse had a population of more than 45,000 and Drumchapel only slightly less. Both had an unusually high number of teenagers, around 16% of the total population, who were aged between fifteen and nineteen and ripe for trouble.

The effect on street gang warfare of this upheaval was not at first apparent. Internecine fighting had continued since the thirties like a low grumbling volcano. Sons whose fathers and grandfathers had been tearaways could hardly be expected to turn into angels, although many did manage to improve themselves at the onset of what was briefly to be known as the affluent society. But apart from occasional eruptions the fighting was not an unusual phenomena and was one that could be contained.

It was with the widespread rehousing projects and the massive drifts in population within a restricted area that gang violence gradually began to increase. If youngsters felt it necessary to assert their individuality and identify themselves with a gang in an environment where they had amenities and where their parents were reasonably contented with their lot, how much more likely that they would feel the need to ventilate their aggression collectively in the housing deserts they now found themselves transported to and where there was nothing else to do but hang about and grumble, where the atmosphere, even at home, was one of boredom, depression and frustration.

And in the areas nearer the city that they left behind, the disruption and demolition turned communities into shell shocked ruins, where occasional tenements stood like giant dolls houses or where soulless high rise flats reared up like vast concrete tombs and where bitterness took once more to the streets, fed by the appalling ugliness and deprivation all around.

And so it was that in the late fifties the old Glasgow tradition of street gang violence, omnipresent and ever dormant, came back with a vengeance.

On the police charge sheets it read 'group disorders' but it was mass gangs fighting in the streets with greater viciousness, with more knives and weapons allied to a ruthless disregard for life or property.

At one stage the situation deteriorated to such an extent that the Royal Infirmary was running out of blood with which to transfuse victims.

One top surgeon let the public know exactly what was going on by stating that during one summer nine hundred and fifty cases of assault were dealt with by the casualty department and said his staff had also coped with 42 serious stabbings, the knife now having taken over from the razor as the weapon among the hoodlums who were mostly in their late teens or early twenties.

Newspaper reports of stabbings and gang fights, mostly at weekends, rose alarmingly throughout the early sixties and new gang names began to appear. The Tongs from Townhead, the Fleet from Maryhill, the Shamrock from Blackhill, the Cumbie from the inevitable Gorbals, the Govan Team, the Buck and the Drummie from Drumchapel, the Toi and the Young Team from Castlemilk, and a veritable vipers nest from Easterhouse including the Bal Toi, the Bar L (named after Barlinnie Prison), the Torran Toi and so on.

One even more alarming aspect was the indiscriminate use of violence, not just against rivals but against society as a whole. In the past if an innocent passer-by was assaulted by a gang it was normally in the furtherance of theft. But now pedestrians were being felled in the streets simply because they were there. Even girls standing looking in shop windows ran the risk of being literally stabbed in the back and it became a common occurrence for gangs high on cheap wine and pep pills to go running amok during the city streets at night, slashing out at anything that moved. These were truly children of the new schemes.

A typical case which thankfully ended in a prison sentence was that of the leader of the Tongs who was sitting in a cafe in Parliamentary Road near Dundas Street Bus Station in the city centre when he boasted for a bet that he would leap on the first bus to come along and stab the first person he came across. He was as good as his word and the fact that the victim who died was an elderly cripple who had just been visiting his sister in hospital was irrelevant as far as the sacrificial act of killing for ego was concerned.

The gangs varied from groups of kids trying to act tough right through to real killers with little conscience and a hatred of society. One thing was certain, there were a great many more gangs and they were on the increase. A certain amount of affluence in the sixties which made them more independent of their parents was a contributory factor but basically it was the old aggression in a more virulent form.

Of course the more wild and outrageous the deeds the more the thugs laid themselves open to prosecution and the High Court dock began to fill up with the 'most mental' ones, those with the worst reputations, those who verged on the psychotic but who were looked up to with awe by the disturbed members of their teams. The judges were not at all in awe and led by Lord Cameron the sentences meted out became more swingeing.

However, there seemed to be more hooligans than police and Easter 1967 went into the annals as 'Bloody Easter' because there were twenty two stabbings in the city on the Friday and Saturday nights alone.

The tenants of Easterhouse wanted to form vigilante groups but were warned off this shortcut to anarchy by the senior magistrate. There were the parrot calls for bringing back capital and corporal punishment with the usual politicians jumping on the bandwagon. Shopkeepers and businessmen petitioned M.P.s for protection from vandalism. Figures revealed that in 1965 more than 850 people had been arrested for carrying offensive weapons and that more than 1500 were arrested for breach of the peace and almost the same amount again for disorderly behaviour in connection with gang fights. To ease public alarm an anti-teenage gang committee was formed headed by the Lord Provost and Chief Constable.

In 1968 gang violence in Easterhouse hit the national headlines through an unusual source. Popular singer Frankie Vaughan who had done much to help boys clubs in England was asked by desperate locals in the East End if he would come to try and save the situation in Easterhouse. He made several flying visits and launched 'the Easterhouse Project', gaining much free publicity in the process. There was a weapons armistice for a day and an assortment of knives and bayonets were actually handed in by teenagers, but not as many as stayed in private hands and, anyway, they were replaceable. There were press conferences, lectures to schoolchildren, discussions with police, social workers and prison officers but at the end of it all the 'Easterhouse Project' deteriorated down to two rainlashed and slogan sprayed nisson huts on a piece of waste ground used sporadically by teenagers. But many youth leaders poured a lot of energy into keeping their flock out of trouble and it aroused a lot of interest at the time although one cynical television comedian, remarking on a current spectacular Army action by Colonel Colin 'Mad Mitch' Mitchell against terrorists in Aden, suggested the Argyll and Sutherland Highlanders be parachuted into Easterhouse.

Several of the toughest gang members as they matured in the criminal fraternity left street fighting behind to go into organised crime, not just in their native city but throughout Britain. They were a respected lot and the favourite hirelings of mobs in London who knew they could be counted on to mix it with the most notorious.

The Kray twins used several specially flown-in criminals but even they were sometimes dismayed by the lack of sophistication and misplaced enthusiasm used to persuade victims when instead of ending in fear or bruising or cuts as well as cash the situation culminated in an unremunerative death. But other mobs and other cities had their quotas of Glaswegians who had decided to move on to other hunting grounds.

Thanks to the police once more getting tough, using flying support units to converge on battles, more sophisticated techniques in radioing for help, heavy sentences from the courts and, not least, the stupidity and reckless bravado of the gang members themselves in committing acts for which they were bound to get caught, the menace of the gangs controlling the streets was held at bay and once more subsided to a tolerable level. But it did not go away and just like the past hundred years there is no sign that it will do so.

There has been one dramatic change in the seventies and eighties compared to the past and that is one for the worse. The number of murders and serious assaults committed by gang members has increased. The reason for this is the indiscriminate, callous use of the knife in attacks rather than the use of the traditional, less lethal razors and bludgeons of the past. Ghastly as it is, a razor will disfigure before it will kill whereas once a knife has punctured a vital organ it results in death.

Although the scrap may not have started out as lethal, once it is all over a bloodied corpse can be lying in the gutter. It is ironic that while the actual number of weapon wielding gangs roaming the streets have decreased from "the slashing sixties", when attacks occur now they are much more deadly because they involve knives being wielded by a hard core of potential murderers. It has always been an argument of the police force as regards stop and search powers that apart from any potential infringement of human rights they would possibly be saving a human life.

A thug who pockets a knife before going out on the streets is well aware he could kill so why not take it off him before he gets the chance is the way the argument runs — it is a perfectly valid one although it implies having trust in the police doing the searching.

Murders committed by gang members, outside any they might commit inside their family circle, are in two categories: firstly, against another hoodlum in a gang brawl and, secondly, against a complete outsider.

Two examples in the early summer of 1977 will illustrate them both. In Easterhouse yet again there was an arranged Friday night pitched battle between two drunken rival gangs using knives, swords and hatchets. One thug was isolated from his mates in the melee and blows were rained down on him by surrounding rivals. The battle was still going on when the ambulance arrived but it could not get through to the assaulted youth because his attackers had not finished their work.

The ambulance was attacked, its windows were smashed, the crew threatened and they had to beat a retreat, urgently summoning help by radio. By the time another ambulance and a squad car arrived the youth was dying from multiple stab wounds. This led to Easterhouse residents resurrecting plans for vigilante groups because of the breakdown of law and order, a situation not helped by Government spending cuts on the police. Periodic bus curfews against outlying districts as a protest against assaults on crews did not help matters either. This is a typical situation of lawlessness in the street leading to arbitrary death of a gang member.

The second totally callous type of murder can be exemplified by a case where a uniformed primary schoolboy and his pal were sitting in a park in Bishopbriggs, a middle class burgh outwith the city, drinking lemonade on their way back from school. Two older louts from a more low-life area passing by started some horseplay and one of the boys was forced to drink vodka before being stabbed once and fatally. Killer and victim never met before.

When the two thugs were finally traced one blamed the other and when the accused was found guilty and sentenced he shouted his gang slogan "Bison!" and gave a defiant salute. He no doubt thought he had proved himself a hard man to go down in the violent folklore of his area.

It is completely motiveless murders like this which led yet again to demands for the reintroduction of the death penalty and yet another committee, this timed formed by the Scottish Tory Party, looked once more into the whole question of law and order without coming up with anything original.

Apart from the traditional historical elements in the Glasgow hooligans character there must be added the more modern ones of dehumanisation, isolation and lack of identification. The young Easterhouse dweller has no cultural background to fall back on at times of stress except the call of the blood which says stand your ground against your enemy and hit back where you can. The youth who becomes a gang member is basically weak because he is controlled by circumstances. He is born in a straitjacketed working class environment barren of opportunity because of decades of poverty and bad planning and, political radicals would argue, a basic flaw in the structure of society as a whole. His methods of escape are limited, be they legitimate or otherwise. The one instinctive way of rebellion for a crude Glaswegian, other than being a Red Clydesider, a chronic drunk or a rabid religious bigot or football fan, is to prove oneself in physical combat and this, ever since the dark spires of the tall cranes rose above the Clyde, has always been the case and it may be too late to change now.

Slums and gangs are synonymous with the city and also interlinked. It is ironic that now the new slums of the outlying estates, less than thirty years old, are to be partly knocked down. The mistakes have been learned too late. Young people have left the city altogether because of the threats of poor social conditions allied to the grim prospect of ending up in one of the giant housing estates. The policy is now to rebuild those areas nearer the city which were demolished in the post war frenzy of rehousing in a desperate attempt to repopulate the ravaged inner city.

Current housing estimates make appalling reading, as they always have. There are 150,000 substandard and 53,500 "intolerable" dwellings in the city. But there are more than 13,000 unwanted surplus empty houses because in schemes like Easterhouse more than 25% of tenants apply for transfers out each year, a trend which if continued would lead to 20,000 empty houses by the mid-1980s, hence the need to demolish.

One final irony which may not be unconnected with the way young people grow up to view authority in Glasgow: some of those who unwillingly went to the peripheral schemes but have managed to settle down will have to be compulsorily evacuated because the streets around them are emptying of tenants and 'selective demolition' is now the order of the day. They could also end up back in the inner city area they were forced to leave in the first place.

CHAPTER 7

The Two Trial Man

Patrick Carraher was the archetypal Glasgow slumland killer: alcoholic, ruthless, arrogant and short tempered with no real concern for the consequences of his actions and no clear conception of right and wrong. Brought up in the Gorbals during that area's most notorious period, he was a razor slasher, a thief and housebreaker, a double murderer who yet remained outside the organised gangs, preferring the solitude of his own violent daydreams.

He was born into a poor working class tenement environment in 1906. His mother died when he was four and his father remarried. However, young Carraher did not get on well with his stepmother who disliked his dour, sullen moods and his failure to respond to any kind of discipline from even a very early age. His stepmother kept complaining about him to his father as a result of which he received many severe beatings. Carraher took to sleeping out of the house in closes and derelict sites to get away from the tense, violent atmosphere at home. It was around this time that he fell in with the shadowy underworld of the slums where children and teenagers led an Artful Dodger-like existence amidst the tall, dank tenements and the labyrinthine back courts.

He left school at 14, having been of average intelligence. He was never in regular employment except for very short periods and took up a life of crime as naturally as any other school leaver might take up a more respectable apprenticeship.

His first sentence was 14 days imprisonment for theft and assault when he was only 16 and there then followed a long string of offences, mostly for housebreaking. In 1934 he was sentenced to two years hard labour for housebreaking plus possession of explosives and after the sentence was delivered he tried to cut his throat in prison but was saved in time by an alert prison officer.

A later medical report on Carraher while he was awaiting trial on a murder charge gave some idea of the man's mental make-up:

During my examination of the accused I failed to elicit any symptoms of mental disease in the ordinary sense of the term, but, in my opinion, the accused cannot be regarded as normal. Throughout his life he has shown a gross lack of moral sense, and a complete lack of any social responsibility. He has shown himself to be emotionally unstable, and at times violent in his behaviour, and with very little capacity to control his actions.

During my examination of him he failed to show any signs of normal appreciation of the seriousness of his present position. His chief concern when I saw him seemed to be not the consequences to him of the charge against him, but the fact that he is under close supervision in the prison. This he resents strongly, and he complained to me about it, saying that he was sane, and yet he was being treated as a person of unsound mind, and he appealed to me to put an end to what he considers to be an injustice to him.

The accused is sane and fit to plead, but, in my opinion, he is not a normal person, in as much as that throughout his life he has shown a lack of regard for his own safety or for the safety and well-being of others. These characteristics lead me to regard him as a psychopathic personality, which is a recognized clinical condition, in which are included those persons who from childhood or early youth show gross abnormality in their social behaviour and emotional reactions, but who do not as a rule show a degree of abnormality amounting to certifiable insanity.

When he came out of prison in 1936 Carraher was even more

bitter and twisted. He continued in his life of crime and started drinking constantly, eating sparingly, and going around in a miasma in which imaginary fears and suspicions took on the form of reality. He began to develop a persecution complex and felt that people were constantly looking at him, talking about him, even following him. He was always looking in cupboards and wardrobes and opening doors to see if anyone was eavesdropping on him.

Detective Chief Inspector John Johnston of the Central Division, who was to play a major part in Carraher's downfall, described him thus:

"He was like a human time bomb, set to explode in all directions, but no one could gauge just when. That depended on Carraher. But, when the moment came, he was lethal. He always looked ready for trouble. In fact, he was the sort of man who couldn't avoid it — and wouldn't if he could. He would go out looking for trouble, regardless."

Physically, Carraher was 5 feet 6½ inches tall, sharp featured with sandy fair hair thinning above the temples, thin lips and heavy-lidded, hooded eyes which gave the impression that they were peering at you piercingly. Almost everyone who met him later remarked on the chilling effect of Carraher's eyes. He suffered from a weak chest and a bad stomach which gave him a Grade 4 rating when it came to a medical examination by an Army board who decided he was unfit for national service. But although he was no muscle man and his frame was continually being debilitated by alcoholic abuse, Carraher was fond of a fight and made up for his weaknesses with speed and ferocity, not to mention sharp, lethal weapons.

The events leading up to his first callous, off-hand killing began on the evening of Saturday 13th August 1938, at Gorbals Cross. A teenage girl had arranged to meet her window cleaning boyfriend, James Durie, at the Cross at around 11.15 p.m. It was a humid, clear summer's night as the girl waited for her boy friend. But first to appear by her side was Carraher whom she knew in the neighbourhood and who was under the influence as usual. He asked her to act as an intermediary with one of his old girlfriends who had fallen out with him. The girl told him she had better things to do and ran to Durie whom she saw approaching. But Carraher was not to be put off and followed her, grabbing her by the arm and pulling her away from her boyfriend. The two men then struggled over the girl who broke free and Carraher then grabbed the lapels of Durie's jacket with his left hand and threatened him with an open knife in his right.

Durie broke free and ran off and away from the Cross with his girl. He went up to his older brother's house and the two Duries then decided for the sake of family honour that Carraher had to be taught a lesson. A crowd at the Cross had witnessed young Durie's humiliation and such an event could not go unpunished according to the clannish laws of the slums.

When they spotted Carraher they stopped him in the street and suggested to him that there should be a fair fight with bare fists with one of them. But Carraher was having none of this and said he was in no condition to fight. A heated argument began, the noise of which drew the attention of a regular soldier home on leave, 23-year-old James Shaw, who was wending his way home after a celebration. He stuck his belligerent nose into the argument and asked if anyone could join in. Language, insults and swearing became more heated and the soldier accused Carraher of "speaking like an Englishman" — a remark not likely to endear him to any Scotsman let alone a drunken psychopath with his temper already riled.

A police constable, hearing the noise, moved the group along but Carraher and Shaw continued to sling insults at each other as they walked along the street. Suddenly a blade flashed in the gaslight and Private Shaw collapsed on the pavement, clutching his throat as spurts of blood came from between his fingers. Carraher darted into the sheltering darkness like a black cat.

Shaw managed to stagger 150 yards and into the arms of the nearby constable. An ambulance was summoned and passers-by offered hankerchiefs to staunch the flow of blood but Shaw died shortly after being admitted to hospital. His jugular vein had been severed.

During the early morning hours the Gorbals grapevine hummed with the news of the murder. At one stage an innocent passer-by was taken in for questioning and Carraher, who was still out on the streets curious to know how things were developing, told a female acquaintance of his casually that he, Carraher, had stabbed Shaw When she asked why, Carraher said the soldier had been too cheeky. When she asked how he did it, he said with a knife which he then produced from his pocket. When the girl said the police had the wrong man, Carraher smirked with an air of bravado that they would let him out because he would give himself up since he did not want an innocent man to swing for it. As he cocked his cloth cap at a jaunty angle and set off for a nearby bridge to fling the knife in the Clyde, Carraher could have been acting out a role from the Warner Brothers gangster movies to which he was addicted.

It took the police only a few hours to pinpoint the perpetrator of the crime and Carraher in a very subdued mood was taken into custody, from a Gorbals flat by Detective Chief Inspector Johnston. His trial took place at Glasgow High Court in September and Carraher was well served by his counsel who went on to become Lords Cameron and Wheatley. They ferociously cross-examined every witness and in the summing-up stressed one vital aspect of the case: there were no witnesses to the murder. No-one had seen Carraher or anyone else in the darkened street inflict the fatal blow. They cast very grave doubts in the jury's mind, always reminding them that a guilty verdict would mean the scaffold.

Lord Pitman was punctilious in his summing up and told the jury: "I am bound to say I have never heard of a case in which there has been so little evidence of provocation, and it is usually provocation which results in an intention to do bodily harm.

"It is tragic almost to think that a man should have lost his life merely because he intervened in an altercation between two brothers and a drunk man as to whether he should have agreed to have what they called a straight fight. The intervener, James Shaw, butts in, so to speak, and remarks that the drunk man speaks like an Englishman.

"You may take the view, and you are entitled to, that the only explanation of such a happening was the fact that the accused was intoxicated. If you do, I must tell you that it has been laid down by the Courts in this country that the fact of intoxication may be taken into view in considering whether an act was done with full malicious intent or only with culpable recklessness in a minor degree.

"The degree of intoxication is of course the determining factor. If it is such as to preclude the possibility of malicious intent to do serious injury then a verdict of culpable homicide is justified. But you must apply your mind to that question, and as best you can make up your mind to what extent the accused was really capable of appreciating what he was doing or really had the intention to do serious bodily injury.

"I think it comes to this. You are entitled on one view of the evidence to acquit a murderer, being of course satisfied that the hand was the hand of the accused, and return a verdict of culpable homicide.

"On the other hand, if you think that the accused deliberately brought the knife into play to settle his dispute, regardless of the consequences, and killed Shaw, it is your duty to return a verdict of murder, a duty from which you should not flinch if that is your view of the evidence."

The jury went out for two hours and then returned to ask the Judge what constituted aggravated assault as a possible verdict.

Lord Pitman said he did not understand their question but said that when an assault took place which resulted in death there could only be two charges, either murder or culpable homicide. Mere assault, of whatever kind, did not count.

The jury then took only minutes to bring back a majority verdict of culpable homicide.

Lord Pitman told Carraher as he stood in the dock "The jury have taken a lenient view of this case because I think their verdict means that they were satisfied that because you were under the influence of drink you had not the deliberate intention that is required in a case of murder. Drink can be founded on in a case of that kind to modify a conviction or a charge, but drink is no excuse whatever for assault resulting in death. The crime of culpable homicide is a very serious one, and the very least punishment that I can inflict is penal servitude for three years."

There was much discussion in letters to the press following this verdict as to whether the newly introduced mixed juries should sit on murder cases. It was generally felt among the protective males who made up the stalwarts of society that the weaker sex baulked at finding accused people guilty if they were going to be hanged and therefore there was the danger of people literally getting away with murder. This was long before the days of any feminist movement, of course, but after a few hangings it was eventually realised that women did indeed have a stomach for punishment and the controversy subsided.

While Carraher was serving his sentence, Glasgow along with the rest of the country prepared itself for war. Apart from black-outs, food restrictions and the transport of the young and elderly to the countryside, the city provided 150,000 people for the armed services, including many of Carraher's fellow toughs from the slums. Convoys sailed weekly from the Clyde and shipyards and engineering firms were working at full capacity. In the spring of 1941 there were massive air raids on the river's lower reaches with thousands of casualties. But the city still managed to maintain a rip-roaring social life at night, becoming known as the dance capital of Britain because of the proliferation of nightspots where bands blared the blues away. When the United States entered the war, the Scottish west coast was often the first sight they had of Britain and Glasgow was so popular that 90% of all American troops on leave converged on it.

By the time Carraher came out there was a perfect atmosphere in the city for criminality. There was a flourishing black market, deserters on the run, a depleted police force, money to be made in illicit alcohol and, above all, the pitch darkness at sundown in which all sorts of evil deeds could be perpetrated without fear of discovery.

Carraher moved his base of operations from his native Gorbals across the river to the Townhead area of the city where he set up house with his girlfriend Sarah Bonnar and her brother Daniel who became his partner in crime. His new operational territory was even older than the Gorbals and included such landmarks as Glasgow Cathedral and the City Chambers but its outstanding characteristics were steep winding lanes and alleys lined with gloomy slum tenements. There were dingy, dangerous pubs at every crossroads and the whole atmosphere of dark, furtive deeds in the overcrowded houses was one in which Carraher the convicted killer revelled.

His activities climaxed in a pub when he slashed a customer in a pub brawl with a razor "to his severe injury", as the indictment later put it, and his sidekick Bonnar pole-axed a barmaid with a beer bottle. As charges quaintly put it, they "had put the lieges in a state of alarm" and after a trial on 11th May 1943 Carraher was jailed for three years.

On his release it was obvious to both the police and his cronies that imprisonment had made no improvement to his dour, aggressive mentality and he simply went back to his old ways. If he had cared at all he should have been able to read the runes of his reckless life and foretell that only disaster lay ahead if he continued along his reckless path but he apparently made no effort to change anything, probably because his character was incapable of change although the Christian doctrine might say otherwise. Possibly he knew subconsciously that he was doomed anyway and simply did not care.

His downfall came about with an almost casual brutality. One Friday in November 1945, Carraher and Bonnar had been spending the end of the week as they always did, getting drunk. By around 8.45 p.m., they decided they had tired of the local pubs and decided to go home for a party taking a local drunk known as 'Wee Watt' with them. Having reached their tenement flat they then discovered there was not enough drink and Bonnar was dispatched to get some more. On his way he ran into a rival gang, known as the Gordon Clan, debouching from a pub. They vociferously declared their intention to clear the street of lesser men and Bonnar promptly and defiantly doffed his jacket, put it on the pavement and raised his fists ready to take on all comers. The challenge seems to have been heartily accepted by all concerned and a skirmish with flailing knuckles ensued which only ended when the outnumbered Bonnar had to beat a hasty retreat down a lane and seek sanctuary in his sister's house. He paused only long enough to draw breath and stop some bleeding before arming himself with a hatchet and putting on his sisters costume jacket before storming back out into the night to seek revenge.

Meanwhile, a woman cleaning her windows had set the bush

telegraph of the slums into operation and word was passed to Carraher that his brother in arms was in trouble. Not hesitating for a moment, Carraher recruited 'Wee Watt' and went racing down the stairhead steps to the rescue. He ran into the quaintly attired Bonnar in the street and they set off scouring the dark neighbourhood for the Gordons, eventually confronting them at an ill-lit corner. Battle was joined and again half way through Bonnar decided to retreat, this time being chased by some of his opponents. Carraher was left with John Gordon, the latter ending up alone in the gutter with blood pouring from a wound at the back of the neck. Passers-by took him by taxi to the nearby Royal Infirmary where he died a minute after the doctor on duty at the gatehouse had made a superficial examination of his injuries.

The police converged on the Townhead district in droves and sealed it off with road blocks. Since the murder was the talk of Townhead and the drama had been more or less played out in public it did not take the police long to rope in all the participants in the fray including Bonnar and Carraher who had made no attempt to escape their tenement hovel.

Once more it was Detective Inspector Johnston who tracked Carraher to his lair, entering it at 5 o'clock on a chilly November morning, shining a torch into the startled face of Carraher as he slept in a bed recess with his arms round Sarah Bonnar.

As they trudged round the prison yard at Barlinnie, Carraher kept reassuring his partner that there was insufficient evidence against them and that he, Carraher, had got off under similar circumstances from a murder charge. All they had to do was keep their mouths shut. But the pressure was beginning to tell on Bonnar who had done little except take part in a bit of Friday night horseplay and had no intention of swinging for the sake of his wild partner in crime.

Bonnar's loyalty ended one morning as they trudged once more round the yard. He was called away on his own by a prison officer and Carraher instinctively knew that this was an ominous sign. A deal was struck and Bonnar was released back to the slums just down the road, having agreed to turn King's evidence against Carraher. Soon the betrayal was being whispered about all over

Barlinnie and Carraher when he heard it went wild in his cell and had to be restrained in solitary.

He stood trial alone at Glasgow High Court on February 28th, 1946, charged with murdering John Gordon. Throughout the three days of proceedings he remained glum and subdued, wrapped in upon himself, his penetrating eyes hooded and looking at no-one as if he sensed it was all over.

There were four witnesses to the fatal fray, none of whom could say for sure if Carraher had struck the fatal blow. But when Bonnar took the stand the fate of Carraher was sealed. Bonnar told how he had fled from the fight (his testimony being corroborated by the surviving Gordons) which meant that only Carraher was there to commit the murder. Bonnar went on to say a taxi driver had appeared at their flat shortly after the fight and told them Gordon was dead. Carraher had then said, 'I gave one of them a jag and ran away!' He then gave the taxi driver a woodcarver's chisel and told him to 'chuck it away'. Carraher wiped blood from the blade onto a towel before handing the weapon over. The taxi driver who lived on the opposite side of the street dropped the weapon down a drain as he fled home, terrified of the wild eyed killer. This good neighbour verified all Bonnar's testimony. The chisel had also been recovered.

Then it was the turn of 'Wee Watt' to go into the witness box. He told how when they had gone looking for the Gordons it was Carraher who took the chisel from his breast pocket, ran his thumb along it and said, "This is the very tool for them!"

And later when they were back in the Bonnar household after the fight but before anyone else arrived, Carraher demonstrated how he had dealt with Gordon. The trial Judge Lord Russell, asked 'Wee Watt' in turn to give a demonstration of the demonstration and the witness in the box started dancing on tip-toe like a boxer, swinging his arms and then suddenly lunging downwards with clenched but empty fist at where a man's neck might be in a grotesque pantomime of the deed. The jury sat staring throughout this silent show and never had Carraher been more alone.

Apart from trying to discredit witnesses, all that Carraher's defence could do was bring in some medical opinion to say that

Carraher was a psychopath who did not know what he had been doing and that the verdict should be the new and unfamiliar one of diminished responsibility. Two medical experts testified that although Carraher was not insane he was extremely abnormal. They said that he was responsible to the extent that he knew intellectually the difference between right and wrong and knew that if he did something wrong he ran the risk of punishment. But he had no moral sense, had no appreciation of social responsibility, was incapable of resisting what to him were temptations and could not control his actions. He also repeatedly did things which were detrimental to himself without learning from his errors. He was also an alcoholic which made him even more incapable of controlling the primal passions which raged inside. He was impulsive and if he wanted something or wanted to do something he just went ahead and did it, regardless. He had no feelings with regards to conscience and in talking over the events which had led to his trial had displayed a jaunty attitude to psychiatrists who interviewed him, treating the fatal fight almost as a frolic. To sum up, he was a psychopath.

Lord Russell in his summing up to the jury pointed out to them that, if they had decided it was indeed Carraher who had killed Gordon, it was entirely up to them to make up their minds whether he suffered from diminished responsibility. The judge pointed out to them, "It will not suffice in law for the purpose of this defence of diminished responsibility merely to show that the accused person has a very short temper or is unusually excitable and lacking in self-control. The world would be a very convenient place for criminals and a very dangerous place for other people if that were the law".

He went on to say there were four criteria which had to be met if a verdict of diminished responsibility were brought in. These were aberration or weakness of mind, mental unsoundness, partial insanity and great peculiarity of mind. Lord Russell also tellingly pointed out that, as opposed to psychiatrists who had only examined Carraher on a few occasions, the prison doctor at Barlinnie who had been in contact with him daily said in evidence that he gave no countenance to the suggestion of diminished responsibility.

As it turned out, the jury apparently were not too interested in going into the nuances of Carraher's psychological make-up. They took only twenty minutes to find him guilty of murder by a unanimous verdict.

Lord Russell then put on the black cap and staring at the impassive Carraher said, "Patrick Carraher, in respect of the verdict of the jury the law leaves me no alternative but to pronounce the sentence which I now pronounce.

"In respect of the verdict of guilty of murder as libelled just received, I decern and adjudge you, Patrick Carraher, panel, to be carried from the Bar to the Prison of Barlinnie, Glasgow, therein to be detained till the twenty third day of March current, and upon that day, between the hours of eight and ten o'clock forenoon within the walls of the said prison, by the hands of the common executioner, to be hanged by the neck upon a gibbet until you be dead, and your body thereafter to be buried within the walls of the said prison, and ordain your whole moveable goods and gear to be escheat and inbrought to His Majesty's use; which is pronounced for Doom."

When they came to take him to the gallows some beast awoke in the up till then impassive Carraher. He fought all the way, screaming in terror and rage, his yells echoing along the silent corridors where the other prisoners locked in their cells shivered in horror. Four prison officers had to drag him to the trap door and restrain him, only stepping back at the last minute as the lever was pulled. The bang of the trap door could be heard throughout the prison. Then there was an eerie silence. There was none of the usual shouting and clanging of bars by other prisoners in sympathy. And outside there was only a small crowd to see the notice of execution pinned up on the prison gates. Among them was one red-eyed woman, Sarah Bonnar. If Carraher had cared for her a bit more it could all have been so different.

CHAPTER 8

The Patriotic Cracksman

Great escaper, expert safeblower, decorated undercover agent, folk hero, athlete, rebel, villain — 'Gentle Johnny' Ramensky was all of these and one of the most colourful characters ever to emerge from the shadows of Glasgow's underworld. Throughout his long criminal career he was many things to many people while always remaining his 'own man'.

He was of a breed now virtually extinct: a criminal whom the public liked. As opposed to the anonymous hooligans dealt with in the sixth chapter, he was every inch an individualist, one of those people who by some of their daring, often ridiculous, exploits bring some light and human warmth into the darkest of corners.

Johnny was born in Glenboig on the outskirts of Glasgow in 1905 the son of Lithuanian immigrants. His father, a coal miner, died when he was a child and his mother, who had lost an arm in an accident, had to bring up Johnny and his two sisters in a gloomy row of cottages where poverty was rife and the day's meal a crisis to be considered with every dawn. Johnny was left very much to his own devices and loved to get out into the country fields, away from the restrictions of home, where he excelled himself among his mates at athletics and football. His high spirited fitness marked him out as different from what he considered the grubby, rough company around him.

He left school at fourteen and, following the tradition of coalfields everywhere, took up his father's job down the mines. But the sparkling twenties somehow did not reach Lanarkshire where the depression struck early and miners were laid off or had their wages cut. The Ramensky family decided work prospects might be better in the city and moved into the Gorbals where many of their fellow Lithuanians and their descendants had settled to await the good life which was always just around the corner out of reach.

But un-employment in Glasgow was running at 30% at this time. Heavy industries had been the first to be hit by a worldwide recession and, as well as coalfields contracting, shipyards and factories were closing. The city stopped growing. The unemployed took to the streets, socialist agitators addressed mass gatherings and the army and police had to disperse crowds of up to a hundred thousand.

The more passive unemployed spent their time playing dominoes in public halls or church halls or took part in organised country walks and hill climbs or in the reading rooms of public libraries or sitting about public parks. Johnny Ramensky was neither political nor passive so, like many others, he made a conscious decision. He looked around him, felt the holes in his pockets and decided if he could not make it to the top legitimately he would get there up the back stairs. He took to a life of crime.

By the time he was eighteen Johnny had come several times in contact with the law because of petty thieving. After two court appearances within a short space of time he was committed to Polmont Borstal near Falkirk. Pending his removal there he was required by statute to spend two months in solitary confinement at Barlinnie Prison which he loathed with all his heart and soul. But he found Polmont even worse. In those days it was the only borstal in Scotland and was staffed by officious, uniformed thugs who believed in putting in the boot and baton first and asking no questions at all. It toughened up young Johnny and he found nervous release in the compulsory physical fitness regime in the gym. He took out his frustration and anger in stretching his body's energies to the limit. Within months he was a keep-fit fanatic, a passion that was to remain with him throughout his life.

Five feet seven inches tall, he had extremely strong muscle-bound arms and was stockily built with fair hair and a hardened, bitter face. His keep-fit regime meant no smoking and throughout his life he never drank spirits although he enjoyed an occasional stout.

When he came out of the Polmont breeding ground of young prematurely hardened criminals Johnny returned to his tenement home in the Gorbals but conditions were no better and now, with the added burden of a criminal record, he found it impossible to get work. Along with another borstal boy named Tommy whom he had befriended in Polmont, he decided it was the moment to move into the big time. They became safe blowers.

An incentive for Johnny to make money quickly had come from the realms of romance. He had fallen in love with a pert, lively neighbourhood girl called Daisy McManus and after a brief, passionate courtship they became engaged.

In the late twenties and early thirties there were very few expert safe blowers in Britain, probably not more than ten. Of these the majority were from Glasgow and the surrounding area. Johnny, with his early apprenticeship in explosives down the pits, became a quick learner and even taught some of the older hands a few tricks. Tommy was also an adept cracksman, having learned at the hands of the top man, 'Scotch Jimmy', who he had shared a cell with in Barlinnie.

Johnny and Tommy roamed far and wide and the pickings were good for in those days a few hundred pounds was a fortune. They became known as a good team in the underworld and inevitably the police got to hear.

On his illicit earnings Johnny married his Daisy and for a while it was all wine and roses. But one night the police raided their happy home and Johnny was arrested after one of his safe cracking sorties and jailed for several years.

It was while he was in Peterhead Prison in 1934 that Johnny was summoned to the Governor's office and told that criminal life's harsh realities had taken their toll of his bright bride and that she had collapsed and died of a heart attack. Shattered, Johnny immediately applied for permission to attend the funeral. This was refused. The model prisoner up until then, he now decided to escape, if only to stand at the plot where Daisy was buried and say a quiet prayer.

One night shortly after midnight he dipped a small wire he had filched into the door lock of the hospital wing where he had been put because of chronic depression, stole across the courtyard and, using his physical fitness to the full, scaled the high, crenelated prison gate and hung by his fingertips on the other side before dropping to freedom.

But once clear of the prison there was still 170 miles to Glasgow and no previous escaper had ever succeeded in getting south of the River Don Bridge at Aberdeen some thirty miles from the prison. Indeed few escapers had ever succeeded in getting south of the bridge at Ellon, only some fifteen miles from the prison. Anyone going south had to cross these two bridges above treacherous and fast flowing rivers and it was naturally at these points that the police always set up their road blocks.

Such was the case on the occasion of Johnny's first escape and shortly after daybreak he was caught trying to cross the bridge at Ellon in the back of a lorry. On being returned to prison he was placed in the punishment block where he was shackled to the cell wall like Oscar Slater years before. The news that he was being held in chains reached the outside world and an M.P. travelled to the prison to protest at such barbarity. As a result the chains were removed and Johnny had the dubious distinction of being the last prisoner in Scotland to be shackled.

On his eventual release, Johnny returned to his old haunts and now, with Daisy gone (he had promised her he would go straight when he got out), there was no compunction to give up his life of crime. He and his pal Tommy returned to safe blowing.

But by the time the Second World War broke out Johnny was back in Peterhead serving five years for blowing an Aberdeen baker's safe.

It was in 1942, two months before his sentence was due to expire, that Johnny received a mysterious visitor, one who had come all the way from the War Office in London to talk about safe blowing. Johnny was taken under military escort to Whitehall where in a subterranean room he was told his criminal expertise was to be used in the fight against Nazi Germany.

After signing a document agreeing to join the armed forces, Johnny was escorted back to Peterhead because the law had to be obeyed first — war or no war — and he impatiently sat out the remaining weeks of his sentence.

On his release he was met by a jeep at the prison gates and taken to a special training camp where he was put through a tough commando course, a fitness test which Johnny revelled in, tuning his body like tempered steel and taking on the toughest tests with comparative ease. He was taught how to use more sophisticated explosives and, much to his amusement, was requisitioned a number of safes to practise with. When his special training was complete Private Johnny Ramensky in red beret and uniform, was promoted to the rank of sergeant and assigned to a crack commando unit.

Much of his wartime activity is shrouded in mystery but several facts are known. He was parachuted several times behind enemy lines in order to get into designated enemy premises and blow safes to acquire secret papers and military plans. After D-Day Johnny and his unit took over enemy army posts far in advance of the front line and Johnny would crack safes while his comrades held off the enemy until reinforcements arrived. When the Allies invaded Rome it was his unit which took over the foreign embassies and on one day alone Johnny blew fourteen safes. It was also in Italy that he was a witness to an atrocity when his unit over-ran an S.S. outpost. The young Aryans with the death's head insignia were separated from the Wehrmacht soldiers, taken outside and cursorily shot. Johnny was asked if he wanted to take part but, detesting bloodshed, declined. When the Allies stormed Reichsmarshal Goering's palatial estate at Karinhall in the Schorfhleide it was Johnny who blew the pompous, bewildered drug addict's safes.

When hostilities ended Johnny was given the Military Medal for his war services and found himself with an ill-fitting suit of clothes back in civvy street. But after his heady days with the commandoes, he found it difficult to adjust to what he considered dull normality. He met up with Tommy again and before long they were back at their old trade, Johnny having gained additional expertise due to his war services.

In the North of England they were caught in the act after a particularly loud explosion and Tommy was given seven years whereas Johnny, because of his outstanding war record, was let off with five. He was returned to the familiar grey walls of Peterhead and after serving three years and four months he was released. But not for long. Soon he was back emptying safes, again he was caught and again the High Court decided to be lenient — five years.

During his brief spell of liberty Johnny had met and fallen in love with an attractive widow from the Gorbals, Mrs. Lilly Mulholland, and once more he started to entertain thoughts of going straight.

But like most of his kind Johnny's idea of going straight was something you did after the 'Big Haul'. Money, quickly achieved and enough of it, was the criteria when it came to building a new future. During his spell in prison he hit on the idea that maybe he could earn enough legitimately by writing his memoirs. This was easier said than done because prison rules forbid the writing of autobiographies. But Johnny had the solution — he would write the outline of his memoirs secretly then escape to find a publisher. In 1952 with the manuscript of his life story tucked inside his shirt Johnny once more went over the wall at Peterhead.

This escape made front page news and, again because of his war record, the editorials were more sympathetic than condemnatory. The public was beginning to adopt him as an unlikely folk hero who was challenging the oppressive post war authorities and Johnny was rather inappropriately compared to Errol Flynn acrobatically escaping from the Sheriff of Nottingham's castle.

His second escape ended like the first and, still clutching the school excercise books which contained his life story, he was recaptured at the Bridge of Ellon by the same police officer who had caught him at the same spot previously. The news of his capture served to increase public sympathy and in the punishment block at

Peterhead Johnny was swamped by letters from well wishers including an offer of marriage from a lady of means who offered him a life of ease and security. Although attracted by such an offer, Johnny wrote a polite refusal. His heart was with Lilly in her Gorbals flat.

In 1955 the gates of Peterhead were once again opened to allow him to walk free. On returning to Glasgow he and Lilly were married. Johnny typed his memoirs out but his literary plans came to nothing because his wartime exploits were covered by the Official Secrets Act and the Ministry of Defence refused to allow publication. This was a serious setback for Johnny's plans to go straight and he began to dream of that elusive 'Big Haul' once more, the big safe whose contents would set him and Lilly up for life. And he almost pulled it off.

In the summer of 1955 Johnny and two other Glasgow criminals raided the British Linen Bank at Oban. They blew open the strongroom and two inner safes. They got away with £8,000 of the Bank's money plus deposit boxes and jewellery. His share of the booty would have been enough to set him up in business but within only a few months enough of it had gone to make this impossible. Johnny's greed and the desire to double the money had ruined his plans and fattened the wallets of several bookmakers.

Within weeks of this the public was reading press reports that Johnny Ramensky was once more in custody, this time for a raid on a bank in Rutherglen. Lilly, the bride of only a few months, was, like her predecessor, shattered when a policewoman appeared at her door to tell her the news.

Once again Johnny stood up in the dock at Glasgow High Court. The judge was Lord Carmont, notorious for the severe sentences he handed down. Johnny, conscious of the terrible pain he had caused Lilly, literally got down on his knees in the dock to plead for mercy but Lord Carmont was not the sort of man to fall for that kind of stuff.

He frowned sternly down at Johnny and declared, "You have been given chance after chance because of your war record. This time there will be no mercy. You will go to prison for ten years".

To Johnny this was totally unacceptable. He was serving the same sentence as a murderer or child rapist. For him it simply was not on. The public was not at all taken aback when once again the Press blazoned the news in 1958 that once more 'Gentle Johnny' had escaped from Peterhead. Twice more during the same year he succeeded in getting over the wall and always the result was predictably the same — recapture at the Bridge of Ellon, although he nearly made it clear the third time with a bit of inside help.

This plan of escape was not his own. It was thought up by another prisoner, 'Darky' Davidson, who worked as the cleaner in the prison hospital. 'Darky' had an interest in locks through his profession of burglary and by a process of trial and error he succeeded in making a replica of a prison master key. Then he rolled back the heavy carpet in the doctor's office and prised up a couple of floorboards and showed Johnny where there was enough space for a full grown man to hide comfortably. This was the great escaper's domicile for the next few days. When the appointed time came, Johnny disappeared from the exercise yard. The alarm was raised and all prisoners ordered to their cells. There was no sign of Johnny. Up went the police cordons in the surrounding area and a special watch was kept on the Bridge of Ellon where the wife of one of the policemen, assuming the predictable, prepared a hot meal for Johnny.

As day followed day with no sign of Johnny, public interest, kept alive by press reports, intensified and bets were placed in Glasgow as to whether he had finally made it or not. Johnny, of course, had not even left the prison. Every day 'Darky' would raise the carpet in the doctor's office and pass down food and drink and an empty bottle. The idea was for him to remain there until the situation cooled and the road blocks were lifted so that he could walk out at midnight one night using the master key and make his escape knowing the police were not looking for him in the immediate area. But Johnny in his cramped space was too impatient. After only a few days he went over the wall. This time he did not even get as far as the Bridge of Ellon. He was following the road south when a bus full of passengers went by and, because of the press publicity, he was recognised. The driver of the bus flagged down a police car and Johnny was recaptured once more. He offered no resistance thus living up to his nickname 'Gentle Johnny'. After his usual cup of tea at the police station he was returned to prison.

The general public feeling for him led to the actor Roddy McMillan writing a song *Set Ramensky Free* and this was recorded and sold well while Labour M.P. Norman Buchan jumped on the bandwagon by writing *The Ballad of Johnny Ramensky* which also became popular.

But despite all this sentimentality it was 1964 before Johnny was eventually released and by then he was almost sixty. Promises of employment made to him by businessmen while he was inside came to nothing on his release. He took a job as a labourer but within months of his release he stood in Paisley Sheriff Court and admitted breaking into Woolworth's Store in the town's High Street and attempting to blow a safe. He was only given two years and this surprised him so much that he staggered and said to the Sheriff, "Thank you very much, Sir, thank you."

But he was now at a stage in life where giving him a chance meant nothing. He was too old to make a fresh start. No sooner was he released than he was in trouble again.

On the night of January 3rd 1967, two constables patrolling in Rutherglen to the south of the city were blown onto their backs by a blast from a bank in the Main Street which also shattered several windows. Surprised and a bit stunned they picked themselves up and, after investigating, they saw a shadowy figure drop nimbly from the bank roof and race off. They gave chase but it took them all their time, a rugby tackle and some fisticuffs to catch and hold the figure who turned out to be Johnny.

It turned out that not only had he used a ludicrously excessive amount of gelignite on the safe (which was empty) but in the process had contrived to ignore a drawer at his side which contained £80,000.

At the subsequent trial Johnny willingly pleaded guilty to the safeblowing charge but stubbornly refused on principle to plead guilty to a lesser charge of police assault. He protested angrily that he had never assaulted anyone in his life, hence the nickname 'Gentle', and had only been defending himself against two over-enthusiastic young constables. The jury believed him and he was quite delighted that his reputation remained untarnished on this point, even although he was given four years on the safe blowing charge.

By the end of that time he was nothing like the athlete he had once been. His age and the years in prison had worn him down to a shell of his former robust self and he was now a sad caricature, snowy haired and deeply furrowed. But he would never acknowledge that he was finished.

On one nocturnal foray into an office building, he shouted to his accomplice that he was having great difficulty trying to get a safe open using welding equipment. Johnny was on a lower floor of the building while his accomplice was rifling a safe upstairs. The second man eventually became fed up with Johnny's complaints and decided to have a look for himself. He found the cracksman had been trying to open the boiler used for heating the building.

In July 1970 he was again in court, this time for trying to blow the strongroom of the Burgh factors in Stirling. In making his way over the roof of the building he had slipped and fallen into the street where he could only lie suffering from severe injuries which only helped emphasise he was not the Ramensky of old. He was in hospital for fourteen weeks and on his discharge was sentenced to two years.

On his release he was shortly after charged with being on the roof of a shop in Ayr at midnight and given twelve months. It was to be his final sentence for while serving it Johnny made his final escape — in a wooden box. He collapsed in Perth Prison and died shortly afterwards in hospital.

Hundreds attended his funeral in St. Francis Chapel in the Gorbals, including all the notable characters of the underworld not in prison, a send-off befitting a villain who, for all his misdeeds, had captured the public imagination.

CHAPTER 9

Wolf At The Door

Scotland's worst murderer was — like Patrick Carraher — a loner, an enigma to most people who knew him, a creature who roamed on nights of the full moon creating in the confines of his egocentric personality a sense of power and omnipotence, a feeling that he could toy with peoples lives and deaths. He was highly intelligent but always self centred and boastful. He was good-looking and graceful with a slim but strong body, wicked eyes which could freeze over like the black marble of tombstones, an aquiline face with jet-black, brushed-back hair. He was a criminal who was yet never really part of that shadowy fraternity because there was always something icy about him deep down which could not merge with his fellows and it was the underworld which helped to eventually put him down. He was attractive to women yet was humiliatingly impotent at the crucial moment and could lapse into fearful outbursts of temper or sullen moods and at such times he was as unfathomable as the dark waters of a still loch. He took a psychotic delight in the phallic handling of guns which enhanced his powers of destructiveness. His name was Peter Thomas Anthony Manuel.

He was born in Manhattan, New York in 1927. The family who had emigrated decided the New World was not up to their expectations and returned to the old country in 1932 where they went back to Motherwell, Lanarkshire, before moving to Coventry. It was here that the rebellious adolescent who never could do what he was told first broke the law at the age of twelve. He was put on probation for burglary and only five weeks later, having sneeringly turned his back on this warning, was sent to an approved school for an identical offence. Here he was nothing if not dedicated in his determination to get out — eleven times he escaped and was recaptured in three years. While on the run he invariably committed more thefts to keep himself in funds and on one housebreaking expedition he assaulted an occupant with a hammer. Just before Christmas 1942 he robbed and indecently assaulted the wife of a school employee. In March 1943 he ended up in borstal, which he did not escape from, and on his release two years later he rejoined his family in Viewpark, Uddingston, Lanarkshire, where they had moved following the Coventry Blitz. On a visit to Blackpool he was acquitted on a charge of burglary.

The important years of puberty and adolescence had therefore been spent in hard, oppressive, all male institutions or on the run where self reliance and survival and his own considerable resourcefulness were the priorities of the day. There was no stabilising influence of home, no love, no guidance, no reassurance, no praise, no encouragement. He was a public enemy from very early on and he knew it and revelled in it. As far as he was concerned he was the underdog who was going to become top wolf.

And on his return to Lanarkshire from Blackpool he was involved in a series of incidents which were to seal his fate.

It began on the night of 3rd of March 1946. A Mrs. K. was walking along a quiet, deserted footpath between Mount Vernon Avenue and North Carrick Drive on the eastern outskirts of Glasgow verging on Lanarkshire. She had her three-year-old daughter with her as she stepped through the unlit dark. Suddenly a shadowy figure sprang at her from some bushes and dragged her down an embankment. But she screamed and fought off her attacker who scrambled up the embankment and ran off.

The woman later gave a vague description to the police and, because of this and his record and the fact that he was local, suspicion fell on Manuel. They called at his home the next day but he had gone away.

Four nights later in the same area a young nurse returning from the local hospital was attacked. She was carrying a suitcase and walking along a lonely, dark road when a figure sprang on her and hauled her into a hedge. But her screams were heard by a motorcyclist who was passing and he stopped his machine. The attacker once more took to his heels with his business unfinished. The brief description the nurse could give to the police again fitted Manuel.

The following night at around the same time — 9.30 — the third victim was attacked in the same area. A Mrs. M. was on her way home along a deserted road when she was pounced upon from behind. The assailant first beat her then forced her in a state of shock to walk along the road towards an overhead railway bridge where he forced her through a barbed wire fence and down an embankment. He tore off her dress and raped her.

Later Mrs. M. struggled back up to the road where, in a distaught state of collapse, she met a pedestrian. Again the description of the attacker fitted Manuel but it was a vague one as in the two previous cases.

The next day Manuel was taken into custody and an identification parade was held at which all three women attended. The young nurse and Mrs. K. picked out Manuel but Mrs M. who was the only one who had actually been raped and who had spent the longest time with her attacker, failed to pick him out.

At the time of the attacks Manuel was on £60 bail after being charged with a break-in at a bungalow the previous month. This was the first time he had been charged in Scotland and shortly after the identification parade he was found guilty of this break-in and fourteen other similar offences for which he was given a sentence of twelve months. With their suspect safely locked up the police, and more particularly the forensic department, meticulously investigated the rape of Mrs. M. The evidence they came up with was the cast of a shoe heel found at the scene which matched a pair of shoes belonging to Manuel and specks of dust and red sandstone from the ground in the area of the attack matched particles found on his clothing. And although Mrs. M. had failed to pick him out her description of the attacker was still similar to Manuel.

The Procurator Fiscal decided not to bring Manuel to trial for all three attacks but only for the one where, ironically, the victim had failed to identify him. His subsequent conviction was due almost entirely to forensic evidence and he was sentenced to eight years.

In his defence it must be said that there was nothing unusual about his shoes or their size and that particles of dust and red sandstone are common throughout the whole of Lanarkshire.

Throughout these long years in prison Manuel brooded and kept very much to himself. Any conversation with fellow prisoners inevitably led to him reiterating time and again that he was entirely innocent of the rape charge. He boasted he would get the police back for what they had done to him and spent long hours dreaming up schemes of revenge.

His anger and frustration took itself out on the only form of uniformed authority around — the 'screws'. As a newly sentenced prisoner he was required to spend the first three days in solitary. This was so that the staff could keep him under strict observation and report to the prison medical officer if he was showing signs of mental disorder or suicidal tendencies. During this period he was not allowed cigarettes. One prison officer on looking through the judas hole of Manuel's cell saw him puffing away arrogantly. On opening the cell door to demand that he give up the cigarette, the officer saw Manuel flick it under his bed. Foolishly the officer stooped to retrieve it and Manuel aimed a savage kick in his face, the officer fell in a heap and Manuel put the boot in with a vengeance. Screams brought reinforcements, the prisoner was overpowered and that night received the beating of his life from Barlinnie's 'batter squad'. Twelve months was added to his sentence.

At Peterhead he again attacked a prison officer, this time with a steel food tray. He was sent to the segregation top security unit, known as the 'snake pit'.

As the years passed he wrote to lawyers about his innocence but no-one would take on his case. All appeals to authority came to nothing. Whether he was innocent of the rape is something that will never be known. What is fact is that shortly after he gave up the fight to clear his name he set out on a course that was to cost lives and cause a great deal of embarrassment, bafflement and consternation to the police who had sent him away. That he should have committed so many crimes in that particular area certainly strengthens the theory held by many criminals that his atrocities were his psychotic way of hitting back at the police. If he was in fact innocent of the rape charge the stigma attached to this would have been doubly hard to bear if, even at that stage of his life, he suffered the impotency of his later years and was incapable of raping anyone. The psychological wound throughout these dark years behind bars would have deepened and festered and have become such an ineradicable part of his vicious soul as to be virtually incurable. To say he was simply a psychopath with no regard for human life is too facile an explanation for the unusual nature of his crimes.

One of his first moves after his release was to go to Superintendent James Hendry of Lanarkshire Police to whom he strenuously claimed that he was innocent of the rape and he accused certain police officers of framing him but his allegations were cursorily dismissed.

He now mapped out in his head a very clear plan of where his hunting ground would be, his very own topography of terror, where he would stalk and seek his prey in a macabre act of revenge against the police, against society, against life itself. His county of murder, Lanarkshire, had to be narrowed down to heighten the terror. His hunting ground was to stretch from Mount Vernon, a salubrious suburb on the south eastern outskirts of Glasgow to nearby residential Burnside and from there to the town of East Kilbride and back to his base headquarters in Uddingston, an area of a few square miles of dark lanes, rows of villas and bungalows and pockets of miners cottages with open woodlands or moorlands and derelict industrial waste ground never too far away, the night sky sometimes glaring from open hearth steelworks, split by the occasional shrill whistle of passing trains, with the winking city lights always bejeweling the horizon.

Shortly after his release he took up with a pretty bus conductress from Carluke, Anne O'Hara, and after a few months courtship they became engaged and the wedding was fixed for July 1955. Then, because he could not keep up with the sexual side of the relationship, Manuel had second thoughts. But instead of simply breaking off the engagement he perversely penned an 'anonymous' letter to his fiancé detailing his criminal past and Ann took the initiative in promptly calling the whole thing off.

Again perversely, on July 30th — the date when he had planned to marry — Manuel terrorised a woman with a knife.

Towards midnight the screams of a woman were heard to come from Lucie Brae near Birkenshaw. It was a quiet, warm summer night and several people heard the screams, two patrolling constables among them. They made a quick search of the area but found nothing suspicious. While this was going on a young woman named Mary McLauchlan, a 29-year-old weaver who came from Birkenshaw, was lying in a field with a knife pointed at her throat. She had been returning from a dance in Blantyre when she had been attacked by the man who now lay over her. The man detained her in the field all night but made no attempt to rape her. At one point, when he lit a cigarette, the woman recognised him in the sudden flare of the match although she did not know his name. She had seen him on the bus when she went to work in the mornings sitting chatting to an older man.

Next day the woman went to the police and later picked out Manuel's photograph. He was arrested within twenty-four-hours.

The trial was in October of that year at Airdrie Sheriff Court and Manuel the showman came into his own. He successfully defended himself, showing an adroitness and expertise in legal matters which enforced the opinion that many people always had of him that his quicksilver brain and eloquent talents were wasted in the world of criminality and, with the proper dedication and psychological outlook, could have been successfully channelled into another profession than that of violence. Certainly Manuel knew he was a cut above the ordinary crook and his success as a barrack room lawyer enhanced his already swollen ego.

The jury at Airdrie brought in a verdict of 'Not Proven'. In his defence Manuel had claimed that he and the woman had been courting and that the incident took place at noon not midnight. He claimed he had struck her earlier and that afterwards they had gone to the field accompanied by his Alsatian dog and that he had thrown the knife at the dog when it had gone too near the railway lines. He had failed to find the knife after this. The story was a blatant lie but the jury, not knowing of his record, decided to take the easy way out and Manuel walked free.

Cocksure of himself, Manuel now set off on a grim trail. On the afternoon of January 4th 1956 a labourer named George Gribbon was on the golf course at East Kilbride looking for lost golf balls when he saw in a hollow what appeared to be the body of a woman lying face down. He thought it might be a drunk woman taking a nap or sleeping it off but as he got nearer he saw that the skull had been badly injured and that she appeared to be dead. Mr. Gribbon hurried to find help and came upon three men working on a new road. When he told them what he had seen they seemed to think he was joking or mistaken and told him to shove off. Mr. Gribbon then hurried to nearby Calderglen Farm and the police were phoned. Meanwhile the three sceptical roadworkers had second thoughts about the matter and went to look for the body. When they found it they dropped their picks and shovels in horror and rushed to a nearby house and once more the police were telephoned.

The dead girl, seventeen-year-old Anne Knielands, had suffered a terrible death. Her skull had been smashed into fifteen pieces. She had been murdered on the night of January 2nd and her body had lain undiscovered in the hollow until the 4th. The signs found at the scene of the crime suggested that she had tried to run from her attacker. Her body had been lacerated with barbed wire in a frantic dash to escape. On the night she died a Mr. Hugh Marshall, out walking his dogs, heard a cry around 8.30 p.m. He later described it as a squealing kind of cry.

The dead girl's knickers had been ripped off, her clothes were in disarray and one of her nylons was also missing but there was no sign of any sexual attack.

Manuel came into this case at the beginning and in a very strange way. Police Constable Marr, one of the first officers to arrive on the scene, was despatched to trace Mr. Gribbon. On the way to Calderglen Farm, P.C. Marr spoke to a man who was in charge of a group of gas board workers. This man, Mr. Corrins, was in the company of Manuel at that moment. From Mr. Corrins P.C. Marr obtained a description of Mr. Gribbon who had passed them by. In the course of the conversation Manuel said to P.C. Marr, "What if this Gribbon doesn't want to come along? Can we punch him on the nose?" P.C. Marr, who did not know Manuel, noticed he had a number of scratches on his nose and right cheek.

Ten days after the murder, Manuel was interviewed by his old adversary Superintendent Hendry as were his parents. His alibi was simple: he had never left home on the night of the murder. As for the scratches, he had received them in a fight in Glasgow but he could give no details about the man he had fought with and as for the scratches being inconsistent with a fight he said he found that highly debatable.

The murder investigation came to nothing and Manuel remained on the prowl until the night of March 23rd of that year. The police, acting on a tip-off, waited at Hamilton Colliery to capture two men who intended to break into the canteen. When they appeared around midnight one was captured on the spot. The other, Manuel, outran the police but he had been recognised and was arrested at home in the early hours of the morning. When he appeared in court he was granted bail and his trial was fixed for October.

But the threat of imprisonment did not deter him. On July 28th the police at Uddingston received a call that two men were acting suspiciously at the rear of a house and when squad cars converged two men were seen to jump from a wall and run off. One got away and one was caught. The first was Manuel and the second, his accomplice, Joe Brannan. Despite hours in the interview room Joe kept his mouth shut about who had been with him which raised him in Manuel's eyes to a position of trustworthiness. This was to have important repercussions later on.

But it was two weeks before his trial that Manuel really showed his teeth once more. The plan was to break into the house of Mr. William Watt at number 5 Fennsbank Avenue, Burnside, where Manuel and a second villain hoped to steal a large sum of money after tying up the occupants. The accomplice was not aware of what Manuel's other intention was but the two agreed they would break into number 18 before raiding the Watt home.

A few days previously Mr. Watt had gone off on a fishing holiday taking with him his black labrador, Queenie. Mrs. Watt was not in good health and suffered from a heart complaint. On the night of the break-in her sister, Margaret Brown, came to the house to spend a night or two with her. Around 11.30 that night the Watt's daughter, sixteen-year-old Vivienne, came in from the house next door where she had been with her friend Deanne Valente.

From the house at number 18, which they knew would be empty, Manuel and his accomplice had a modest haul: a few rings, some clothing and some cash. In the early hours the pair made their way to number 5. Entry was gained by breaking a pane of glass in the front door and inserting a hand to turn the lock in the inside.

Both men entered the dark house and crept along the hallway. Manuel went first and disappeared into the room where Mrs. Watt and her sister were asleep. The accomplice moved towards the room where Vivienne was sleeping. As he turned the door handle he heard a loud bang come from the other room. He froze. Then there was another bang. At this Vivienne appeared at the door and, in an instinctive panic, the man punched her, connecting with the left side of her chin. Vivienne slumped unconcious to the floor. The man picked her up and placed her on the bed then ran into the room where the two bangs had come from. Manuel stood with a smoking revolver at the bedside, grinning. When the horrified accomplice saw the two women lying dead on their pillows, mouths agape, the blood trickling onto their nightdresses, he turned without a word and fled out of the house and the district as fast as his legs could carry him.

Manuel entered Vivienne's room and as she started to come round calmly shot her in the head as he had the two other women. But the girl did not die immediately. She was to linger on as if waiting to be discovered so that she could say something.

The nightdresses of the three were disturbed and they were placed in humiliating positions with their legs open but there were no signs of sexual molestation.

Not knowing if his accomplice might go to the police, Manuel decided to leave the house rather than search it for money or valuables. But he did pause for a few minutes to revel in the feeling of power the shootings had given him.

Mrs. Watt had a home help who was first to arrive on the scene but despite knocking on doors and windows she could not get in. It was the postman who realised something was seriously wrong when he saw the smashed panel. He used the same method of entry as the intruders and he was the first to discover the horror. Vivienne, who was still moaning when the postman found her, died as the ambulance was on its way. She had not managed to utter a word.

Forensic experts found a fairly fresh cigarette end and a spent match on the carpet of Vivienne's bedroom and the police quickly established that nothing had been stolen. The break-in at number 18 was discovered by a neighbour. It was found the place had been ransacked, someone had been lying on one of the beds with dirty boots and a tin of tomato soup had been spilled on one of the carpets.

In the small hours of the following morning detectives raided the Manuel house and despite an intensive search and lengthy interviews not only with Manuel but with the whole family they drew a blank. They did not press their enquiries because they felt they had a better suspect — Mr. Watt.

However, one man who was certain Manuel was the culprit was Chief Inspector Muncie of the Lanarkshire force. On the day the murders had been discovered he had received a telephone call from one of his contacts in the underworld. The informant said that the previous evening he had been in Manuel's company drinking in a hotel. Manuel had told him that on that very night he was going to a wealthy house to rob it of a stack of money and, tapping his pocket where there was something bulky, he had added that he had the right thing for anyone who caught him at it. The informant had assumed he was talking about a gun. In the course of this conversation Manuel had boasted that he had tested the gun by shooting a cow dead in a field. He had shot it up the nostril. By a curious coincidence this rang a bell with Muncie. While on top of a bus in the Viewpark area he had seen a cow lying dead in a field. As a senior officer in the county force he was also an Inspector under the Diseases of Animals Act and had ensured that the cow had been examined for anthrax. The vet reported that there was no sign of anthrax but while he thought the animal might have died from stomach staggers he had noted bleeding from one of the nostrils and now agreed that the animal might have been shot although it had not crossed his mind at the time. It was now a race against time to try and trace the carcass and find the bullet. But the police were out of luck. The carcass was by this time in the local abattoir inside a boiling vat. But even here the police, in their determination to nail Manuel, did not give up. It took them four days to empty and search the vat but again they drew a blank.

Another informant told them that Manuel had also tested the gun by firing it into a tree near his home. The police methodically examined all the trees in the Viewpark area but again luck was with the killer and no bullet was found.

In checking out all the recent break-ins in the area Muncie found that one house had been broken into the night before the Watt murders. This was at Douglas Drive in Bothwell. The housebreaker had opened a tin of pears, drunk the juice and scattered the pears on the carpet similar to what had happened to the tomato soup at Fennsbank Avenue the following night. Curiously enough not much of value had been stolen but, among the articles that were, an unusual type of electric razor stood out as identifiable. Another curious aspect was that a mattress had been slashed and a watch belonging to one of the occupants inserted into it for no apparent reason. Closer investigation would have found a much smaller object — a spent bullet. Manuel had broken in and fired his gun into the mattress to rehearse the slaughter scheduled for the following night. Tragically, the bullet was not discovered until nineteen months had elapsed.

The police, under daily public pressure, now tried to build up their case against Mr. Watt. Unlike the other suspect, Manuel, who they were now — with one or two exceptions — inclined to eliminate from their inquiries, Mr. Watt had no record and was a prosperous and decent member of society. He was a master baker who owned a string of shops, was a respected Freemason and had a distinguished record in the Police War Reserve. But eleven days after the murders he was arrested and charged with having committed them.

There is no doubt that Mr. Watt, who was totally innocent, came perilously close to being hanged. Again doubtful identification played its part.

A week before the murders he and his dog had gone to the Cairnbaan Hotel in Lochgilphead for a fishing holiday. He had motored down the Loch Lomond Road, a distance of ninety miles. There was nothing unusual about this holiday. There had been similar ones several times before and he had stayed at the same hotel. Each night he telephoned his wife and on the eve of the murders he told her he was enjoying the rest and wanted to have an extra few days if that was okay with her and she agreed. He then sat and had a drink with the proprietor of the hotel who was an old friend, letting Queenie the labrador out for a run around midnight. On retiring for the night he said he would be getting up at 5.30 a.m. to go fishing and to this end borrowed an alarm clock. But it was not until 7.30 that he got up and to fill in the time till breakfast he had gone out to have a look at the water. At 8.30 a.m. he returned to the hotel, had breakfast and set out to do a days fishing. Two and a half hours later there was a telephone call from his brother. On returning to the hotel and being told the news, he collapsed, weeping. He was in such a state that it was agreed that a friend should go with him as far as Alexandria where Sergeant William Mitchell, an officer of the Lanarkshire force, was to pick him up. On the way to Alexandria Mr. Watt managed to pull himself together. He had once been a member of the police force himself and wanted to show a dignified, manly front. He even managed to pull a brave smile when he met the sergeant. It would have been better for him if he had remained weeping. Mitchell was later to state, "I went to Alexandria thinking I was bringing back a bereaved and broken man. What did I find? A man with a smirk on his face and without a tear."

In all their investigations the police heard from numerous people, barmen, hoteliers and friends of the family as well as business partners, that Mr. Watt had been devoted to his family. But he had to admit to being unfaithful to his wife on several occasions which, considering his wife's weak condition, was no heinous sin for a man still with healthy appetites. But at no time was a mistress found. There was no-one special in the background.

The police theory was that Mr. Watt had crept surreptitiously out of the hotel with his dog without disturbing anyone in the early hours, drove to Glasgow, murdered his family then drove back to the hotel for 7.30.

Long distance lorry drivers were interviewed and all garages were checked to see if he had filled up with petrol, without success. Then the alarm clock took on a sinister significance. The bell on the clock only rang for a couple of seconds before shutting itself off but the theory was that if he had been in his room as he said then this should have wakened him up. But a middle aged man who had been out in the fresh air a lot and had also been drinking could easily sleep through a two second alarm and, even if he had woken up, could easily have gone back to sleep again.

The time taken to do the Lochgilphead-Glasgow trip was checked. Mr. Watt said that at night, especially along the notoriously tortuous and winding Loch Lomondside road, it usually took him at least two and a half hours. A police driver showed at breakneck speed and with expert driving it could be done in two hours four minutes.

But the trump card for the police was what came to be known as 'the Ferrymaster's story'. The route which Mr. Watt was alleged to have taken to have committed the murders would have involved him crossing the Clyde on the Renfrew Ferry. In the early hours of the relevant day the Ferrymaster, Mr. John Taylor, said that around 3 a.m., a man drove his car on to the boat and was taken from the north side (the Lochgilphead end) to the south (the side the Watt house was on). He was not sure in the darkness of the make or colour of the car but he noted there were two occupants, the man and a large black dog sitting beside him. He gave a description which roughly fitted that of Mr. Watt (and countless other men). Photographs of Mr. Watt, his car and even his dog had been splashed on the front pages of every newspaper, it was the talk on everyone's lips and there were regular bulletins on the radio detailing the progress of the case. Mr. Taylor, an elderly man, knew all the details of the investigations long before he attended an identification parade and picked out Mr. Watt and long before he said the dog 'could' have been a black labrador.

The Crown Office decided to proceed and the distraught widower now faced the nightmare of being charged with the callous murders.

Things began to look up for the police when a Mr. Morrison suddenly decided it was his duty to step forward. He had been driving with his wife and two sons along the Loch Lomondside road around 2.30 a.m., on the relevant date when he saw a fast moving car approach along the lochside. He saw its headlights suddenly go out and wondered if it had landed in the loch but further on they came upon it parked off the road with no lights on. Thinking something might be wrong Mr. Morrison pulled up. There was a man in the car smoking with his hand half across his face. As Mr. Morrison got out, the car suddenly started up and sped off. He was not sure of the car's make and had seen no dog. Despite this fleeting glimpse in the dark Mr. Morrison managed to pick out Mr. Watt at an identification parade.

While all this was going on Manuel was languishing in Barlinnie, having been jailed for 18 months for the Hamilton Colliery canteen break-in. But all the talk and publicity centering on Mr. Watt was annoying him and he now decided it was about time he stole a bit of the limelight and if he could sicken the police at the same time so much the better. The fact that Mr. Watt and he were now both in the same prison added piquancy to the drama as far as he was concerned.

Manuel wrote to Mr. Watt's solicitor, Laurie Dowdall, saying he wanted to see him about his client and that it would be to their mutual advantage.

Mr. Dowdall later described what happened during the macabre interview, "He said Mr. Watt was innocent. So I said, "Well how do you know Mr. Watt is innocent? And his answer was, 'Because I know the man who did it'.

"So then I said to him, 'Well if you know the man who did it, why don't you go to the police?' He indicated in a few sentences that he regarded the police with some disapproval.

"I then said, 'Well, what was the name of the man?' and he didn't give me any name. So I said, 'Well, you had better tell me something about it'. He then told me that on the night before the Watts were murdered — and he made it clear that by the Watts he included Mrs. Brown — that a man had come to him and he had a gun in his possession, a revolver, and he wanted Mr. Manuel to go with him on a housebreaking expedition in Burnside.

"Mr. Manuel told me that he would not go with the man and that he did not go with him. He then said that he had read about the murders of these people in the paper and on the night that he had read about these murders the man came back to see him. This man he described as being in the horrors and he had a gun with him — the same gun. And he told Manuel that he had broken into the house at Fennsbank Avenue, number 18 I think he said, and then had gone down and broken into 5 Fennsbank Avenue and there he had shot three women. He wanted Manuel to get rid of the gun for him. Manuel said he took the gun from the man and the man also gave him a couple of rings. Now he described these rings to me and he said that each ring was an old fashioned type. One had had three stones, a diamond flanked by two rubies. The other he also described.

"I told Manuel that he might be pulling my leg. I asked him how I could be sure that he was telling me the truth. So he said, 'Well, I can give you information about the Watt house.' He then told me about the position of certain articles of furniture in the house and he described the position of the doors and in particular he described the door of what he called the girl's 'room. All this was something I would be able to check so I told him I would make some enquiries and come back. I left the establishment and telephoned Detective Superintendent Hendry who had charge of the investigation and told him I would like to see the interior of the Watt house. There I found that the description given by Manuel was an accurate one and I was quite satisfied that he had information which could be of interest to me in the defence of my client. So I went back to see him in the prison on a second occasion. I told him that I had verified the information but I said to him that I hadn't read or seen all the newspapers and you might have got this information from the press. So then he said, 'I can give you information on how the man got into the house'.

"According to Manuel the man entered by breaking the panel. He went into the bedroom on the left and shot the two women dead. One woman was shot twice in the head. He left that room and, as he left, the girl came out of another room. He struck her on the chin with his fist and knocked her out. He then tied the girl's hands behind her back and placed her on the bed. He left her there and then went round the house ransacking it and examining articles. On returning to the bedroom he saw the girl had come to, so he shot her through the head."

Mr. Dowdall left Barlinnie to check out this information and found out that one woman had indeed been shot twice so he went back for his third interview which he later described, "I asked him some more questions about the gun and I think it was at this meeting that he told me the man to whom he had referred had on some occasion prior to the Watt murders been in a house somewhere in the outskirts of Glasgow and he was there with a woman and it had been a housebreaking expedition and apparently there had been some kind of quarrel and the gun, which had been used in the Watt murders, had been fired and the bullet had gone into the bed.

"I then said to Manuel, 'Do you mean to tell me that the man who committed these horrible murders came to you and told you such unnecessary, piffling information as the disposition of articles of furniture in the house?' Manuel replied, 'Well, he did'. So I said, 'Well, that leads me to only one conclusion. I don't believe that and therefore you must know something more about this than you are telling me. Why don't you go to the police about it?' Again he indicated that he did not wish to go to the police and that he did not trust them.

"I said, 'Look Manuel, information such as you have and the suggestion that the man who committed these murders would start and tell you the piffling information about the furniture leads me to one conclusion — that you were there'. He said, 'Oh no, I wasn't there'. He insisted on this so that was the end of that conversation.

"At one of the meetings he sketched me a revolver and he told me that particular gun was a Webley Markiv."

Mr. Dowdall also received confidential information from another source. Another client and fellow prisoner told how Manuel had boasted that when the police searched his house after the Watt murders there had in fact been revolvers in a secret drawer.

And information reached the ears of the police from another source other than Manuel. An informer said a man named 'Scout' O'Neil had provided Manuel with a Webley revolver for a cash sum a week before the Watt murders. When interviewed about this O'Neil (his full name being James Tinney O'Neil) maintained the crooks unwritten code of silence and lyingly denied all knowledge of the deal.

A small army of police officers now descended on Manuel's house once more, to Manuel Senior's accusations of harassment, and went over it with a fine toothcomb and once more found nothing.

Despite these frustrating setbacks the authorities finally realised they were holding the wrong man and on December 3rd Mr. Watt was allowed to walk free from Barlinnie. He had been in prison 67 days, an ordeal from which he never fully recovered. And even after Manuel was dead and gone the spiteful mutterings of the small minded claiming to be in the know continued to haunt him and up to his own death he was never completely free of the false gossip that he had something to do with the murders.

On November 30th 1957, Manuel was released from his eighteen months sentence and could not resist some more goulish pranks at the expense of Mr. Watt. He asked to meet him through Mr. Dowdall and the bizarre confrontation took place over many hours at the Whitehall Restaurant, at Jackson's Bar in Glasgow and at the home of Mr. Watt's brother. The sense of the absurd and the melodramatic once more tickled Manuel and he loved manipulating Mr. Watt as a dog plays with a bone it has chewed. At one of these meetings Manuel, being the centre of attention where he always wanted to be, named the murderer as one Charles Tallis and involved with him indirectly was a man called Martin Hart and Tallis's girlfriend, a woman named Mrs. Bowes. The tale Manuel spun was that Tallis, Hart and Mrs. Bowes had gone to 18 Fennsbank Avenue and broken in. They had afterwards gone along to identify the Valente house next door to the Watt house because Hart had told them that a large sum of money was in a safe there. But seeing Deanne Valente in the Watt house, as indeed she had been that night, they had mistaken the Watt house for the Valente house. In the early hours they returned, Tallis had broken the front panel of glass and they had gone in. The plan was to shoot everyone in the house except one who would be forced to disclose where the safe was and the key then the last one would also be shot.

Manuel again went into great detail about the things in the house. He told Mr. Watt that he had thrown Tallis's gun into the Clyde. He also told him the story about the bullet being fired into the bed of the house in Bothwell.

All of this reached the ears of the police but they had no concrete evidence on which to base a conviction since Manuel was bound to deny everything and say it was a frame-up and, besides, he was notorious as a liar, bluffer and boaster, always trying to be Mr. Big. (When the Burgess and McLean spy scandal broke Manuel claimed to have inside information and was actually flown to London by the police for questioning. He, in fact, knew nothing. But this was his style, always wanting to be centre stage in a big public drama. He could also put on a convincing American accent and say he was born in Manhattan, which was true, and that he had been a henchman of Al Capone, which was not.)

Within days of his last meeting with Mr. Watt, Manuel went off to Newcastle where he applied for a job on December 6th at the British Electrical Repairs factory in Shields Road where the transport manager later recalled the incident. The following day his movements are unknown but he was seen in the evening by a taxi driver in a cafe at the railway station. On December 8th he took a taxi at 4.30 a.m., and headed for Edmondbyers, County Durham. The taxi driver was a bachelor named Sydney Dunn, aged 36. His mates at the station later identified Manuel because they recalled him ordering Mr. Dunn to take him to Edinburgh and they remembered remarking that Sydney had "knocked it off".

The following day Mr. Dunn's body was found 140 yards from his cab on the moors near Edmondbyers. Manuel had shot him in the back of the head and cut his throat because he had taken the wrong road. He had then in a fit of temper smashed all the windows and lights and left the cab looking like an abandoned wreck. On the 28th

July the following year a Coroner's inquest found that Manuel had murdered Mr. Dunn.

The next incident occurred that same month on Christmas Day and it was back on home territory.

A house occupied by the Reverend Alexander Houston and his wife at 66 Wester Road, Mount Vernon, was broken into. The minister and his wife were fortunately visiting friends at the time. Entry had been made by breaking a panel in the kitchenette door. The front sitting room had been ransacked. Missing were a pair of sheepskin gloves, a Kodak camera and £2 in mixed coins. This break-in was to prove vital in the case against Manuel.

He gave the sheepskin gloves to his father and the camera to his sister Teresa as Christmas presents.

Three days later, midway between the Yuletide festivities and the New Year celebrations, the killer whose bloodlust was now rampant singled out 17-year-old pretty, dark haired, grey-eyed Isabelle Cooke as his next sacrificial victim. She lived with her parents and three younger brothers at 5 Carrick Drive, North Mount Vernon.

In the afternoon the parents left the house and did not return until eight in the evening by which time Isabelle had left to go to a dance at Uddingston. The parents went to bed but lay awake listening for Isabelle to return. When she had not done so by 12.30 a.m., this was so out of character that Mr. Cooke got out of bed, got dressed and with a torch went out to look for her. Fifty yards from the house was a path by a works railway, an unlit short cut which led to Mount Vernon Avenue and the bus stop. He knew his daughter was in the habit of taking this path, the same one on which, eleven years previously, Mrs. K. had been attacked.

Mr. Cooke flashed his torch around in the darkness but saw nothing and eventually returned home. Their telephone was out of order and they assumed Isabelle must have decided to spend the night with a girl friend but had been unable to let them know.

However, by ten in the morning with still no word they went to the police. At teatime a constable called at their house and showed the distraught parents a small cosmetic bag which had been found: it was Isabelle's. Later they returned with other articles which had been found on waste ground, all belonging to the missing girl: a vanity case, a short raincoat, a fan and a spray of imitation flowers.

A murder squad was formed under the charge of Detective Inspector John Rae. (Supt. Hendry had coincidentally retired on the very day of Isabelle's disappearance.)

It had been a cold, pitch black night and she had been supposed to meet her boyfriend at a bus stop in Uddingston. When she had failed to turn up he had gone on to the dance alone, assuming she had done the same.

In the case of Isabelle — as in that of Anne Knielands — someone had heard a cry in the night. A woman and her dog had been in their back garden which was beside the unlit path Isabelle had to walk along. Suddenly, somewhere in the darkness, a feminine voice cried out in fear. The dog heard it too and began to bark. But the woman, straining her ears into the night wind, heard nothing further and took no action.

A full scale search of the area was launched and some of her clothing was found in the River Calder while a handbag was found in a disused colliery air shaft.

It was while Supt. Muncie was searching round the shaft that the county's Chief Constable John Wilson appeared to inform him that three people had been found shot dead in their bungalow in Uddingston. The date was January 6th 1958 and the family had been dead for six days.

They were forty-five-year old Peter Smart, his wife Doris and their 11-year-old son Michael. They had been shot in the head as they lay in their beds in the early hours of New Year's Day while parties had been going on in bungalows all around them. (Manuel must have entered their home sometime after 6 a.m. because he was at his parents house celebrating New Year up till then; but having committed the murders he also spent around four hours in the house admiring his handiwork and relaxing in the comfort of the luxury bungalow as if this in itself was a symbolic form of rape and defiance combined.)

Four nights after this a Mr. and Mrs. McMunn were asleep in their home near the Smarts when they awoke with a start. Something had disturbed them and when Mr. McMunn switched on the light and saw a man's face at the bedroom door he shouted to his startled wife, "Where's the gun?" (There was no gun; he was wisely bluffing.) The man then ran off down the stairs, out of the house and away. The McMunns were lucky. Manuel had by this time flung his tell-tale gun into the Clyde off the King George V bridge.

Detectives investigating the Smart murders found that the dead civil engineer's Austin 35 had been found abandoned in Florence Street, Gorbals, but enquiries in that area did not turn up anything.

Lanarkshire was now living in a state of fear verging on panic. All the paraphernalia of security-locks of every description, alarm bells, peep holes, bolts, door chains and guard dogs were in terrific demand and neighbours made pacts to keep their eyes open and make regular telephone calls to each other.

A few hours after he had committed the Smart murders Manuel had gone to his old pal Joe Brannan's house and said he had a lot of money. Asked where he got it, he replied that he had gone into Glasgow and collected £30 and more at the Gordon Club in connection with the Watt murders. He said there had been some difficulty but he had got the money in the end. But it was money spent by Manuel which was his undoing.

After the Smart murders it was belatedly decided to call in the help of Glasgow C.I.D., and Detective Superintendent Alex Brown and Detective Inspector Tom Goodall joined the hunt. It was decided to enlist the help of a member of the underworld and the obvious choice was Joe Brannan, Manuel's true and trusted friend, the one who had refused to name him as the accomplice all those years ago, the one Manuel went to after the Smart murders. Detective Inspector Robert McNeill was the one selected to approach Joe, a villain who like other notable underworld figures, was horrified at what was going on, not simply out of decent basic human feelings but also because the heat was on every man with a record as the combined police forces of central Scotland got more desperate to catch the killer.

Manuel's style upset the Glasgow underworld. Where he wanted to be flamboyant and in the limelight they preferred the anonymous shadows, committing crimes without getting their names known at all. For Manuel being well-known was a vital part of the game.

For these reasons it had been decided among Glasgow's criminal fraternity that Manuel had to go and, therefore, Joe Brannan agreed to help trap him and began to hang around with him, buying plenty of drink courtesy of police funds. It was unofficial liason between the jacks and knaves which helped close the case. Every night around midnight Joe met a police officer and reported to him on the evening's conversation and what Manuel had let slip.

From Joe they learned where Manuel had spent his New Year's Day money and they checked the specified pubs to see if the money tallied with the new notes Mr. Smart had obtained from the bank. These were Commercial Bank of Scotland notes and some of them were still traceable, although there were only hours before they would have been in circulation among customers. The money Manuel had spent in the first fortnight of January matched with money taken from the Smart house. The net was beginning to close and the murder squad decided to swoop on Manuel's house once more. They arrived at 6.45 in the morning and removed his clothing for forensic examination to the usual remonstrations about harassment from his father. They found nothing to connect with the Smart murders in the house but they did find a pair of sheepskin gloves and a Kodak camera which were the property of the Reverend Houston. Teresa told how the camera was a Christmas gift from Peter. And Sam, the father, told how the gloves were also a gift from his thoughtful son.

Sam was taken to Bellshill Police Station and locked up, the charge being possession of stolen property. He was then further charged with breaking into the Houston house along with his son Peter.

At Hamilton Police Headquarters the following day Manuel was put on an identification parade for the money he had passed in pubs and hotels and numerous people picked him out. Manuel then asked to see Supt. Brown and told him that the notes he had in his possession had been given him by Samuel 'Dandy' McKay of the Gordon Club. Manuel claimed he had met 'Dandy' between 10 and 10.30 on the morning of New Year's Day which was an unfortunate time to choose because a local shopkeeper in Uddingston had seen Manuel near his home at that time. Manuel claimed he had met

'Dandy' near the Airport Bus terminal in St. Enoch's Square in Glasgow and said he had sat in 'Dandy's' car and received from him £50, of which 30 were in £5 notes and 20 in blue £1 notes. The money had allegedly been paid for showing 'Dandy' around the Sheepburn Road area where he was supposed to be going to break into a bookmaker's house.

But Manuel could not have chosen a worse figure than 'Dandy' to implicate because he was a popular, flamboyant, gregarious character with a reputation as a clean type of villain. The idea that he would break into a house and kill in cold blood was out of the question and detectives knew this. In response to a police request 'Dandy' called at Hamilton Police Station, the H.Q. of Manuel's much hated Lanarkshire force, on the evening of January 14th and was deliberately confronted with Manuel who told him nervously. "Sammy, I'm sorry I had to tell them about the money you gave me."

'Dandy' made a move to approach Manuel but was gently restrained. He glared at the killer and snapped, "You've made the biggest mistake of your life — you're going to swing!"

Manuel, white faced and visibly shaken, was led away.

In the eyes of his friends in the criminal fraternity where he wielded a great deal of influence 'Dandy' was and always had been completely trustworthy when it came to his fellow villains but now he felt no loyalty towards a creature who would shoot innocent defenceless people, especially children, in their beds and then try to frame him for such diabolical crimes. This infuriated him and he decided to help the police put Manuel out of the way forever. He told senior detectives that he knew Manuel was in possession of a Beretta on December 19th. He had given Manuel a lift to a house in Florence Street (where Mr. Smart's car had later been found abandoned) where a brown paper parcel was to be collected. This turned out to be a gun which Manuel showed off to 'Dandy' who had no idea the horrible use to which it was to be put. He had been told it was only for self protection. 'Dandy' continued to elaborate on all he knew about Manuel, which was quite a lot, and the detectives listened with growing interest.

That same evening an identification parade was held and Mrs.

McMunn picked out Manuel as the man who had peered in at the bedroom door and 'Dandy' also officially picked out Manuel as the possessor of the Beretta.

At 11.10 that night the police charged Manuel with the Smart murders as well as breaking into the minister's house and the McMunn's house.

The following day Manuel asked to speak to Inspector McNeil but the detective kept the killer waiting several hours to keep his nerves frayed before, along with Inspector Goodall, he went to see him. Manuel said he wanted to clear up certain unsolved crimes in the area but before he would say any more he wanted to see his mother and father. At this point he said, "Bring my mother and father here and I will speak to them with you present and once I have told them myself and made a clean breast of it you can take them away and I will clear up everything for you and I will take you to where the girl Cooke is buried."

He was asked if he wanted a solicitor but replied, "I want to do this myself. I will write something out for you."

He was given paper and wrote, addressing it to Inspector McNeil:

I hereby promise you personally that I am prepared to give information to you that will enable you to clear up a number of unknown crimes which occurred in the County of Lanark in the past two years. This promise is given that I might release my father and my family from any obligation or loyalties they may feel on my behalf. I wish to see my parents and make a clean breast with them first. The crimes I refer to are crimes of homicide. I further wish to stress that I volunteer this statement of my own free will without duress or pressure of any description being brought to bear on me.

On reading over this statement he did not seem too happy about it so he wrote a second one couched in roughly the same terms but with the added sentence, "I will lead information about the following specific crimes: 1) Anne Knielands 2) the Watt murders 3) Isabelle Cooke 4) the Smart murders."

Inspector McNeil said he would have to consult with the Procurator Fiscal to see if he could be allowed to see his parents and at this Manuel blurted out, almost desperately, that he wanted to tell them about the Smart murders. He said he entered the house around 6 a.m., on New Year's Day. He said he shot the man and then the woman and then the boy, although he said he thought the boy was in fact a man. He then stole some money, took the car keys and drove the car eventually to Florence Street where he left it. He threw the gun in the Clyde and the car keys in the Calder.

His parents were brought to see him and tearfully he told them, "There's no future for me. I have done some terrible things. I killed the girl Knielands at East Kilbride and I shot the three women in the house at Burnside."

Later that evening he was taken to Barlinnie to comply with the commital warrant. Although it was nearly midnight another warrant was obtained almost immediately to take him out again to show the police where Isabelle Cooke was buried.

It was a pitch black, bitterly cold night. He directed a cavalcade of police and press cars to a lonely field near Baillieston Brickworks where arc lights were quickly set up and shovels unloaded from vans. Handcuffed to two detectives Manuel walked up and down the field trying to get his bearings in the dark. He remarked that the field had been ploughed since the last time he had been there. Suddenly he stopped, looked around him and said, "I think she is in there." And he tapped his shoe on the dirt, "I think I am standing on her."

Her shoes were found first then the police unearthed her rigid, decomposing, semi-naked body.

A few days later by an extraordinary coincidence Mr. James Platt, whose house in Douglas Drive had been broken into the night before the Watt murders, walked into his local police station with a bullet which had been fired into his mattress. His wife who had been thinking of getting a new bed and had been examining the old one had just found it. The bullet was rushed to the police ballistics department and it was found to have been fired by the Watt murder weapon. Detectives then went back to Manuel's house and found an electric shaver which had been stolen from the Platt house.

Manuel's trial began at Glasgow High Court on Monday 12th May 1958. The judge was Lord Cameron (who had defended Patrick Carraher on his first murder charge) and the jury was made up of nine men and six women. The trial lasted sixteen days. The prosecution was led by Mr. M. G. Gillies assisted by Mr. Ronald

Sutherland who had to take over after three days when Mr. Gillies was taken ill. The defence was conducted by Mr. H. Leslie Q.C.

The indictment charged Manuel with all eight murders. (The taxi driver's murder could not be tried in Scotland and was left in abeyance for the moment.) Manuel put forward special defences: to some a simple 'not guilty'. To the Smart murders he put forward alibi, to the murder of the Watts he put forward impeachment and to both break-ins in Fennsbank Avenue he put forward the same defence. His impeachment in the murder charge was of Mr. Watt based on the Ferryman's story and the fact that the police had charged him; on the break-ins he blamed Charles Tallis and Mrs. Mary Bowes, the people he had claimed were responsible during his unusual conversations with Mr. Watt.

As regards his confessions to the police made at Hamilton Police Headquarters he now claimed they had been extorted by threats involving his parents. The evidence against him was formidable but he put up a strong rearguard action. He was now in his beloved position — the centre of attraction. The media throughout the world were full of him. Queues waited for hours outside the court to get a seat. It was, as they say, the biggest show in town. His name was on everybody's lips. This was his hour.

But as the trial progressed even this was not enough for him. He seemed to be a passive observer in the drama and not an active participant so he decided to take the stage himself. On the ninth day he dismissed his counsel and, like all those years ago at Airdrie Sheriff Court, undertook his own defence.

This time he was not to be so successful but, nevertheless, Lord Cameron complimented him on his quick brain and eloquence.

When Mr. Watt came to give evidence he had to be carried in on a stretcher and it was a grim sight to see, surrounded by all the hushed panoply of the Law, the wrecked shell of a man being baited, taunted and accused of his family's murder by the man who had committed the deed. It appealed to Manuel's sadistic sense of humour. Mr. Watt struggled to bear up under the onslaught and stoutly, repeatedly, denied all the innuendos and falsifications which Manuel flung at him. It was an added essence of torture for this most unfortunate of men.

As the trial neared its inevitable conclusion Manuel's self confidence began to waver. His hands shook, his face took on a yellowish pallor and he sweated a great deal. Gone was the old swagger and braggadocio. It was replaced with a dark, sullen moody stare.

The jury had no doubt about their verdict — guilty on all charges except the Knielands murder where there was not enough evidence to convict. Lord Cameron duly put on the black cap and sentenced Manuel to "death by hanging."

He appealed, again on the grounds that the confessions had been due to police pressure via his father (against whom all charges had been dropped once Manuel had confessed) but it was a hopeless gesture. The appeal was turned down. Deciding now to clear the records once and for all, and in the process doing an about turn that was an insulting gesture to the Appeal Court judges, he confessed to three more murders — that of Helen Carlin, a prostitute who was known as 'Red Helen' who had been strangled in Pimlico in September 1954 (preceding the first Lanarkshire murder, perhaps it too was a rehearsal); that of Anne Steele, a 55-year-old spinster found battered to death in Glasgow on January 11th 1956 (nine days after the Knielands murder); and that of Ellen Petrie, known as 'English Nellie', who was stabbed in Glasgow in June 1956 (midway between the Knielands and Watt murders). In all then, Manuel's known murder victims totalled a round dozen but there could have been others which for his own unfathomable reasons he did not want to reveal.

There were three motives behind Manuel's killings. The first was revenge against the Lanarkshire Police force who he believed had ruined his life because of wrongful imprisonment for rape and he sought to humiliate and tantalise with a spate of unsolved, lurid murders in a small area of their patch.

The second motive was sexual. Manuel was impotent and could only get sexual gratification through masturbation, the humiliation of women or the sense of fulfilment pulling the trigger of a gun gave him. In the Airdrie case where Manuel had earlier on in his criminal career successfully defended himself on an indecent assault charge, the victim had testified that her attacker had dragged her into a field and threatened her with a knife saying he had been "watching television and had a sudden urge to cut somebody's head off". He forced her to remove her underwear. Revelling in her terror, his threats of violence had become more and more extreme as his excitement mounted. Then he had suddenly calmed down and allowed the woman to leave unmolested. Later when he was arrested, Manuel's trousers were found to be stained with semen. The terror of his victim, coupled with her humiliation and the baring of her private parts, had aroused him to such an extent that there was ejaculation and no further action was necessary.

Similarly, with the murders there was humiliation but no sexual molestation or rape. Anne Knielands had her knickers ripped off, a nylon was stolen and her dress was up round her waist when she was found. Isabelle Cooke was semi-naked when exhumed and her panties and underslip were never recovered. In the Watt killings Mrs. Brown's green pyjama trousers had been ripped from the waistband down the right leg. Vivienne's pyjama trousers had been removed altogether, the buttons of her yellow and black pyjama top were strewn about the room, her pink brassiere which she had been wearing was torn off and there were semen stains on the cover of her bed. In the Smart killings, Mrs. Doris Smart's nightdress was ripped and she was found nakedly exposed. For Manuel the degradation of his victims was enough. Any kind of necrophiliac rape was unnecessary and it is doubtful if he was physically capable of such an act.

Manuel also seems to have taken a strange delight in making free with the houses of the dead. After the Smart killings, he returned to their home several times, helped himself to meals and fed their cat while the corpses lay in their bedrooms. He had a penchant for raiding the pantries of houses he broke into. This seems to have satisfied some weird childish desire to violate the domestic surroundings of his victims.

The third motive for the murders was simply that Manuel wanted to be famous. His egomania was a burning lust inside him which would not rest until he saw himself emblazoned across the front pages. This phenomena was fairly new and incomprehensible in Manuel's day but from Lee Harvey Oswald onward there have been plenty of small men wanting to go down in history for a seemingly senseless criminal act.

Allied to his egomania went Manuel's arrogance, his contempt for the law and belief that he was too clever to be caught, his certainty in his own ability to get away with it. This led him to take hair raising or, to him, thrilling risks. When he took the Smarts' car after their murder he gave a lift to a policeman who happened to be going on duty to help look for Isabelle Cooke's body. Manuel laughed and chatted with the policeman and dropped him off with the parting comment, "I think they're looking in the wrong place!"

Every killing took place during a public holiday. With Anne Knielands and the Smarts it was New Year. Isabelle Cooke was killed at Christmas and the Watt shootings took place during the September week-end holiday. This was Manuel's festive fare, his way of enjoying himself and at the same time shocking complacently celebrating society.

During his time in the death cell Manuel clammed up and never spoke to any of the prison officers. He put on two stones in weight and never showed any sign of remorse. His one comment on his terrible crimes showed how callous his feelings were, even on the threshold of eternity. As he was given exercise in the prison yard between two burly prison officers he said to a prisoner he knew, the only other one taking exercise at the time, "What do you think of that bastard McKay?" referring to 'Dandy' breaking the underworld code and giving information to Manuel's arch enemies — the police. He was more concerned and annoyed at this than he was about the blood on his hands.

He spent a quiet night before his death and on the morning of Friday July 11th 1958 he literally ran onto the scaffold inside the walls of Barlinnie Prison where the trap door dropped at one minute past eight. He could not get it over quickly enough.

The reign of terror was over. The mad wolf was dead.

1. Authors Paddy Meehan (left), safecracker and recipient of a Royal Pardon, and journalist George Forbes.

2. William 'Tank' McGuiness: responsible for the murder for which Paddy Meehan served seven years.

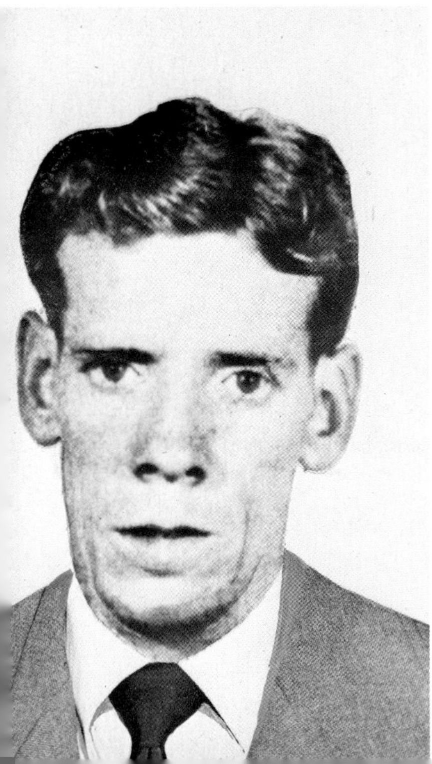

3. Ian Waddell: partner in crime of McGuiness.

4. A contemporary drawing of Madeleine Smith in court by William Brodie, R.S.A. acquitted by a 'not proven' verdict, nobody knows to this day who poisoned her lover, L'Angelier.

5. Glasgow High Court.

6. Outside Glasgow High Court as reporters fight over Walter Scott Ellis the arch-criminal acquitted this time on a 'not proven' verdict.

7. Sister Jessie McTavish: acquitted on appeal.

8. Gunman James Griffiths: turned Glasgow into a caricature of Chicago, shooting 14 people in just over an hour.

9. Oscar Slater: wrongly imprisoned.

10. Lorrydriver Thomas Young: preyed on prostitutes and girl hitch-hikers and jailed for 30 years.

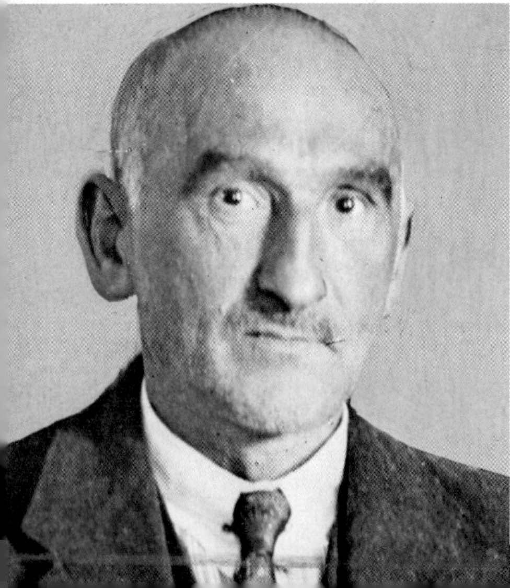

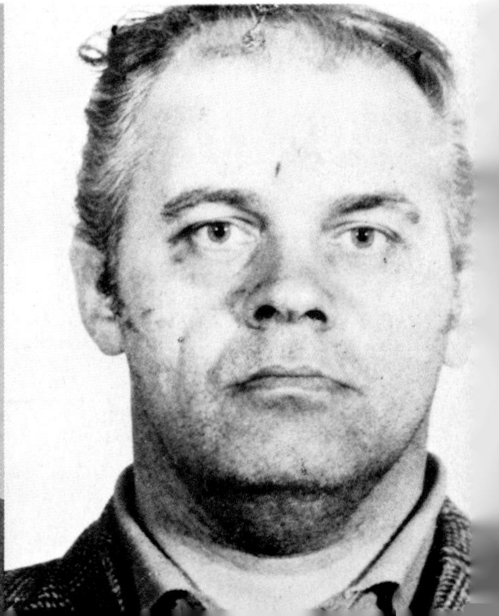

11. Street-killer Patrick Carraher.

12. Self-styled leader of the workers party for Scotland and bank robber Matthew Lygate.

13. Jimmy 'Babyface' Boyle.

14. Policeman turned police-killer Howard Wilson.

15. Peterhead Prison, Aberdeenshire, stands on a windswept promontory overlooking the grey north sea.

16. The grim forbidding sight of Barlinnie Prison, Glasgow. It was here the now famous 'Special Unit' was set up, Jimmy Boyle being its most notorious inmate.

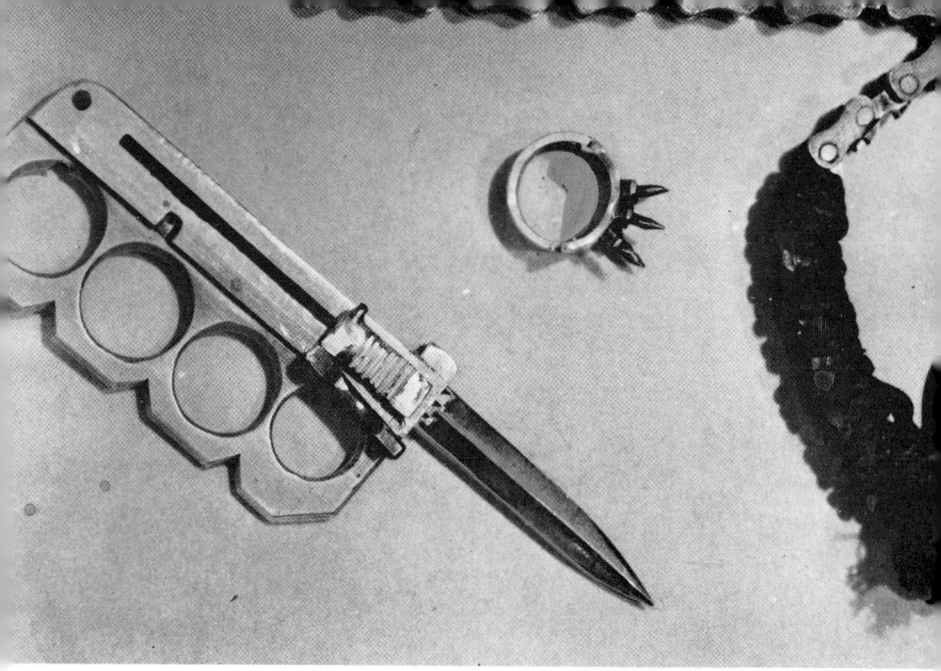

17. and 18.
Some of
the ingenious
and lethal
weaponry
collected by
City of Glasgow
Police and
exhibited at their
headquarters.

19. Moors murderer Ian Brady driven away after sentence.

20. Crime syndicate boss Walter Norval. His accomplices tried to burn down Glasgow High Court to abort his trial.

21. Peter Manuel was found guilty of the brutal murder of pretty young Isabelle Cooke. A sheet covers the spot where her body was found at Mount Vernon.

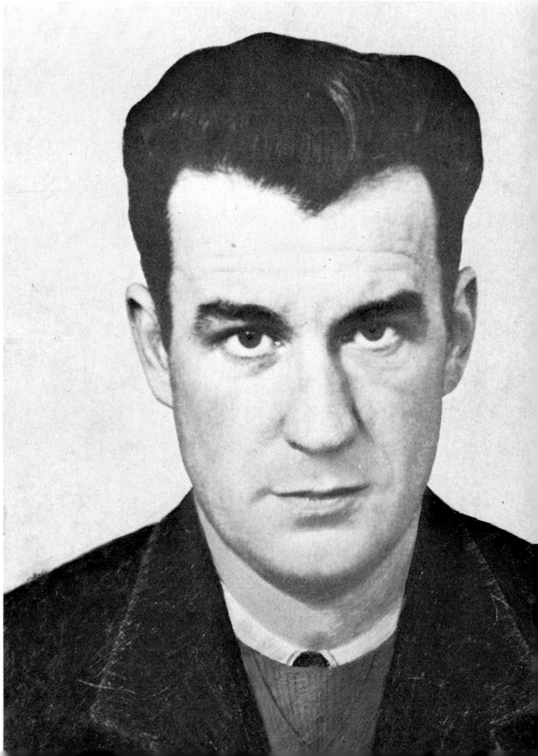

22. Multiple murderer Peter Manuel.

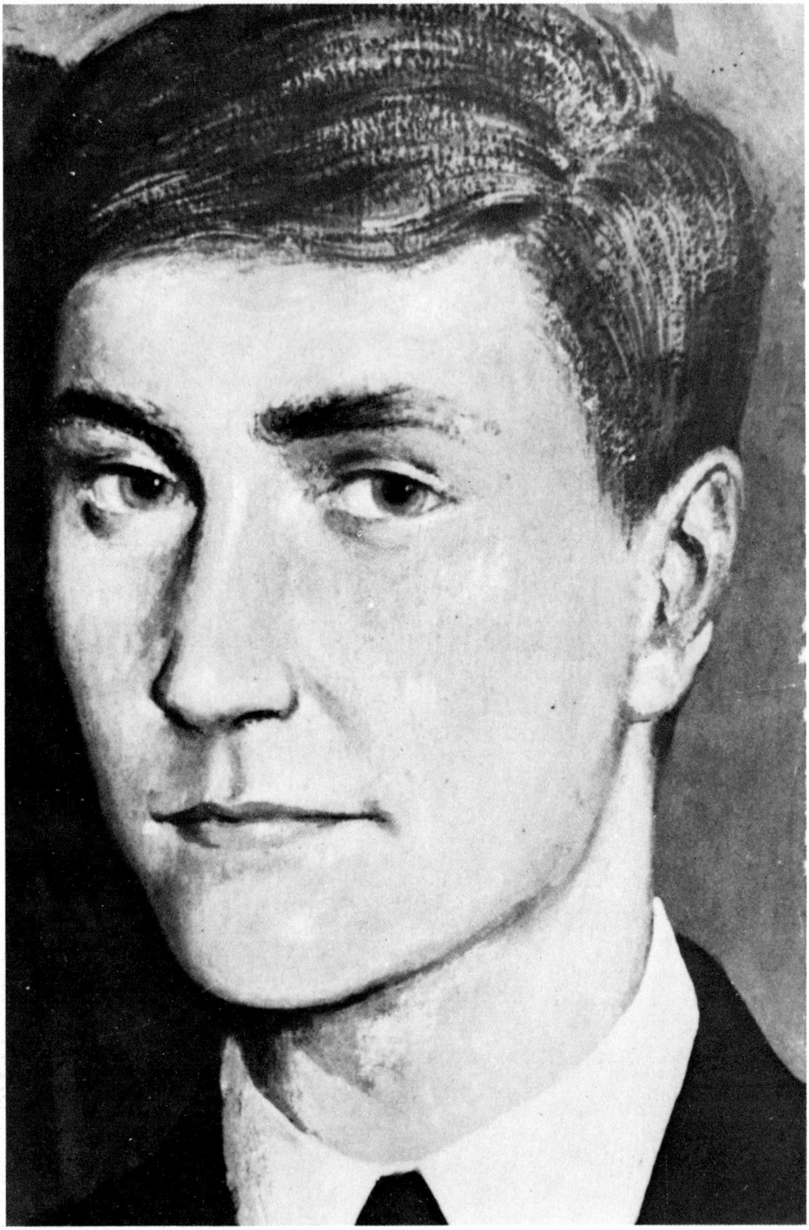

23. An artist's impression of Bible John.

24. and 25. Typical police searches following the discovery of a body in Glasgow. *Above,* Police frogmen search the River Cart for Patricia Docker's clothing in the Bible John investigations. *Below,* Police search Glasgow back courts.

26. A dramatic picture of a razor attack in Glasgow's St. Vincent Street. A plainclothes police officer draws his baton as a youth attacks with open cut-throat razor. *Photograph by Alan Milligan of The Scotsman.*

CHAPTER 10

Big Houses

Glasgow criminals took their dark codes, their folklore, their violence and their humour with them when they went into prison. The structured society of big villains, middle men and petty crooks which had existed in the slums was imitated within the prison walls with the heirarchy ruling the roost and trying to live up to their reputations. Prison officers had a hard time containing many Glasgow villains and much of what went on behind the high walls was kept very hushed up indeed.

Peterhead Prison was and is Scotland's toughest penal colony where all the worst Glasgow criminals go and it is also one of the toughest in Britain. This has been the case since it was built. Up until the Second World War its officers used to be armed with sabres which they carried on a heavy belt worn around the waist. In those days a prisoner was not allowed to approach within five paces of an officer. At any such approach the officer would place his hand at the ready on the hilt of the sabre and command the prisoner to "stand off!" The prisoner would then request permission to speak (the rule of silence meant prisoners were normally not allowed to speak at all) and only when permission was granted was he allowed to say what he wanted.

The chaining of prisoners was also common practice in those days, as was the use of the cat-o-nine-tails. The last man to suffer the cat in Scotland was Robert Meechan. While serving a sentence at Peterhead in the thirties, he floored the officer in charge of the punishment block then climbed on to the roof of A-Wing where he proceeded to pelt warders below with slates. By the time he was finished there were no slates left on the roof and A-Wing was closed for several months, much to the delight of the other prisoners.

While in the punishment block awaiting trial for the assault on the officer, as well as the demolition job on the roof, Meechan found himself without cigarettes (although smoking was forbidden, prisoners had devious ways of smuggling in tobacco). On the Sunday, Meechan decided to attend the prison Bible class where some of his friends would be able to slip him some tobacco. But when he got into the Bible class Meechan was required to sit well away from the other convicts, the officers being determined to see that he did not succeed in getting any tobacco or bits of paper with which to make cigarettes. As the Bible class proceeded with the singing of hymns, Meechan noticed the stem of a pipe sticking out of the pocket of the pious civilian gentleman who came every week to play the organ. He guessed, and guessed rightly, that in the same pocket there would be a tobacco pouch. As the congregation sang 'The Lord's My Shepherd, I'll not want", Meechan got to his feet and walked calmly across to the organist. Leaning over, he inserted both hands into the two pockets of the startled organist and whispered in his ear, "You don't mind if I borrow some tobacco, brother?" The terrified organist continued to play, pretending that he did not know Meechan was searching his pockets. The prison officers, sitting in their high seats in the balcony, were so taken aback by what was going on that it took them a few moments to react. Then they clattered downstairs and pounced on Meechan but he had a firm grip of the organist's tobacco pouch and would not let go. The officers dragged him off to the punishment block but they could not prise the tobacco pouch out of his grasp. In the end there was a compromise and they settled for the pouch minus the tobacco which Meechan was grudgingly allowed to keep to avoid further violence. The Prison Governor replaced the tobacco to pacify the organist who never returned again to soothe any savage breast with his music.

The cat-o-nine-tails did not hold any terror for Meechan. The officer who inflicted the punishment later told how when he was taken off the wooden triangle of planks to which he had been tied and then lashed twenty times, Meechan did a back sommersault, laughed like Douglas Fairbanks and said to the Governor who had to witness the punishment, "Give me a couple of cigarettes and I'll take the same again!" Some years later Meechan was serving a sentence at Parkhurst Prison on the Isle of Wight. One day a prison officer caught him smoking and tried to take away the cigarette. Meechan floored the officer and another who came to his assistance. For this he was again to suffer the cat-o-nine-tails which he took with his usual aplomb.

The officers at Peterhead also used to be armed with .303 rifles when on duty at the quarry which was some two miles from the main building. In the 1930s a prisoner serving ten years for a bank hold-up near Glasgow was shot dead trying to escape up the side of the quarry. The official account of this was that the officer who fired the shot aimed to wound but the bullet glanced off a rock and penetrated the prisoner's body, killing him.

In the late fifties, with the completion of the breakwater at Peterhead Bay (it was to build this massive breakwater that the prison was sited at Peterhead) the quarry was closed down.

In the mid fifties two prisoners working in the Admiralty Yard alongside the south wall of the prison tried to escape by commandeering a heavy lorry and speeding for the back gate. They had to run the gauntlet of the three armed officers stationed at intervals between them and the gate. The officers opened fire but the lorry swept through the back gate and onto the main road where, however, it crashed into a dyke and came to a halt, riddled with bullet holes. The prisoners, two Glasgow villains, were miraculously unhurt although one of the bullets had passed between the legs of the prisoner in the driving seat.

In 1959 a prisoner named Grockett making a run for it from a working party was shot and wounded by a prison officer. The bullet passed through the prisoner's arm and struck a granite rock which fragmented on impact. A piece of the granite then struck a prison officer in the eye, causing him to bleed freely. At first it was thought that the officer had been shot and this caused immediate panic. The prisoner's injuries were not really serious nor was the injury to the officer. But the fact that the officer had been injured caused the prison authorities to withdraw the rifles from service and, besides, with the closure of the quarry they were no longer felt to be necessary.

In every Scottish prison there used to exist groups of officers who indulged in beating up prisoners to enforce their own ideas of discipline. The system was once very much involved in the use of legalised violence: the cat-o-nine-tails, the sabre, the gun, the chains, the punishment blocks, the gallows. The 'batter squads' were as much part of the system as the cat. The object was quite simple. Just as Sillitoe's teams of policemen had physically hammered into the Glasgow gangs and tamed them so, inside prison, there were officers ready to do the same to recalcitrant prisoners. Unfortunately, unlike the cat the 'batter squads' never officially existed and therefore could not be legislated out of existence and they have continued even up to recent years.

During the seventies a 'batter squad' was very active in Peterhead Prison. Prisoners who fell victim to the squad very often found themselves charged with assault. Only in this way could the injuries sustained by such prisoners be accounted for. It was the practice then to prevent such prisoners, once they had been charged with assault, getting in touch with a solicitor before any court appearance. Since the prisoner, once he had been charged, was not likely to appear in court for as long as six weeks then any injuries he had received would have had time to clear up. Aberdeen solicitors, representing prisoners charged with assault on staff at Peterhead, had numerous complaints from clients that they were not allowed to contact lawyers for weeks after they had been charged.

In the summer of 1972 there was a great deal of unrest in prisons throughout Britain. This manifested itself in various ways: sit-down-in-the-prison-yard strikes, sit-up-on-the-prison-roof strikes, hunger strikes and work strikes. All this was in protest against the conditions. Supporting the prisoners was an organisation known as P.R.O.P. (Preservation of the Rights of Prisoners) that had been set up by a group of ex-prisoners in England.

In Peterhead where conditions were amongst the worst in Britain the prisoners were slow in responding to P.R.O.P.'s call. Prisoners in Scotland are notorious for their lack of solidarity in the face of authority, although they are never slow when it comes to fighting among themselves. But when they did decide to get their protest off the ground, 168 of them clambered on to the roof of the prison hospital and refused to budge.

The rooftop demonstration at Peterhead was to be a peaceful affair. All the prisoners involved had agreed on this. While on the roof some prisoners did call out insults to members of the staff but at no time was any violence done to the prison roof or to members of the staff. After twenty four hours on the roof the prisoners agreed to come down and return to their cells. But before doing so they extracted a promise from Chief Officer Boris Campbell that there would be no brutality against them from the prison 'batter squad'.

Chief Officer Campbell was not exactly popular with the majority of the prisoners. But the older type of prisoner, those who knew him from the days before he was made up to chief, had a great deal of respect for him. In the early fifties Campbell was in charge of the punishment block when the 'batter squad' entered, intent on beating up 'Dandy' McKay (the criminal Manuel tried to blame for the Smart killings). 'Dandy' had just arrived in the punishment block after flooring a couple of officers in the quarry. In due course he would be charged but first he had to be taught a lesson in keeping with the age old prison tradition. If you hit a prison officer you can only expect the worst.

'Dandy' McKay, as was mentioned in the previous chapter, was no ordinary crook. He was gregarious, a bit of a Beau Brummell (hence his nickname) and popular in the criminal fraternity. He was normally non-violent but when it came to a scrap was as tough as they come. As the 'batter squad' prepared to set about 'Dandy', Officer Campbell intervened in a way that earned him a lot of respect from other prisoners. When 'Dandy's' cell door clanged open and he saw the 'batter squad' encroaching he knew what was going to happen and shouted, "Why don't you come in here one at a time? You cowards?" And at this, Campbell, who was not in the 'batter squad' but had just arrived to find out what was going on, decided to accept the challenge. 'Dandy' was then led out to the small exercise yard at the back of the punishment block and he and Campbell squared up for action. The fight lasted several minutes and looked like lasting a lot longer when a prison officer named Shepherd arrived on the scene and intervened. At this point the 'batter squad' were about to attack 'Dandy' when Campbell told them that if they were to lay a hand on him, they would have to fight him too. After this incident the 'batter squad' took care that Campbell had gone off duty before they entered the punishment block.

When the 168 prisoners eventually came off the hospital roof after their protest, they had Campbell's word that none of them would be attacked by the 'batter squad' in reprisal. But once the prisoners were off the roof and locked away, Campbell, who had been on duty non-stop during the demonstration, went home. And while he was out of the prison the 'batter squad' went to work. They selected six of the men who had been on the roof. These men were led one at a time from the main cell block and in the corridor leading to the punishment block the 'batter squad' went to work. Four of the men involved were beaten unconcious before they reached the punishment block. This turn of events created a great deal of bitterness among the prisoners who felt that Chief Campbell had broken his word. And the situation was aggravated further when the prisoners who had fallen victim to the 'batter squad' went on trial before the visiting committee for the prison and were given loss of remission and spells in solitary. In due course, two of the prisoners who had been beaten up were transferred from the punishment block at Peterhead to the Special Unit at Porterfield Prison, Inverness. (An account of what happened then is given in Chapter 13.)

But life inside is not all violence. Even the occult gets a look in.

Every prison has its ghost story. In the early sixties the press gave a great deal of coverage to the ghost of Glasgow's Barlinnie. Staff on night patrol reported that cell lights were being mysteriously switched on long after they had been switched off. Since the switches were located outside the cells, out of reach of the prisoners, and since the staff denied all responsibility for this strange phenomena, the prison authorities began to take notice. A number of officers on night patrol also reported that they had observed a ghostly figure flitting along a corridor between C and D-Block (D-Block is where the scaffold used to be located). At one stage the prison chaplain decided to have the area exorcised. But this does not seem to have worked as even in the seventies there were reports that the Barlinnie ghost was still active.

The ghost of Peterhead Prison, although it has never received the publicity of its Barlinnie counterpart, seems to go back much further in time, to the thirties. For some reason the ghost never leaves the punishment block.

No-one has ever seen the phenomena. It was first taken note of in the thirties when an officer on night patrol entered the punishment block in the wee sma' hours. Then, as now, the night patrol was required to operate time clocks at different parts of the prison. In this way it could be established that he was carrying out his duties and not sleeping it out in the prison cookhouse.

On entering the punishment block the patrol officer approached the clock when suddenly he felt a violent push from behind. He turned but there was no-one there. For a moment the officer thought he had had a sudden dizzy spell but on operating the time clock and retracing his steps, he again felt himself being pushed from behind. This time he was in no doubt that he had been pushed by something he could not see so he ran out of the punishment block. The officer decided to submit a written report on the incident (he would do this to explain why he had failed to 'clock in' at the punishment block for the rest of that night) and when the story came out a number of others, staff and prisoners, let it be known that they had also suffered the same experience.

Today the ghost of Peterhead is known as Charlie. And the fact that Charlie never leaves the punishment block has given rise to the theory that he is the ghost of a prisoner who died there, either by taking his own life or by being beaten to death by officers.

There are numerous stories about Charlie. He has a habit of picking a cell for the night and between midnight and dawn is given to pacing up and down the centre of the floor. At that time the prisoner, if there happens to be one in the cell, would be fast asleep, leaving Charlie to walk around to his heart's content. But, since the Mountbatten Report laid down that the cell lights of A-Category prisoners be kept burning all night, things have changed. With the light on all night, the A-Category prisoner is liable to be pacing the floor himself at all times of the night.

In the early seventies, when the punishment block at Peterhead was nearly always full, a number of prisoners were left in no doubt about Charlie's existence. One prisoner, known as Big Davy, had never heard the story of Charlie and after being pushed several times he called out to the prisoner in the next cell, "Hey Tommy, I think this cell's haunted!"

Tommy, who had already experienced the presence of Charlie, called back, "Were you walking up and down and felt something push you from behind?"

"That's right," answered Davy.

"Well, that's Charlie," said Tommy. "He likes to walk up and down at this time so if you walk up and down and stay close to the wall you won't get in his way and he won't push you."

Normally a fearless Glasgow thug, Big Davy felt the hairs of his head prickling with terror. He hammered on his cell door until the night patrol officer arrived.

"Get me to f★★★ out of this cell!" Big Davy roared through the door.

"Can't you wait till morning," said the officer.

"Like hell I will," growled Big Davy. "This cell is haunted. And I'm A-Category and must have a cell to myself!"

Many prisoners who know about Charlie are not prepared to talk about him. They do not want to run the risk of ridicule.

But if Charlie is unwilling to leave prison, even in the afterlife, there are those only too willing to make a break for freedom. They are the escape artists, those for whom iron bars do not a prison make.

The record for the longest prisoner to remain on the run from Peterhead Prison is held by Teddy Martin who escaped from an outside working party in March, 1955. Martin remained at large for 31 days.

His escape was quite ingenious. A prison uniform was smuggled out of Peterhead and sent to Martin's accomplices in Glasgow where the convict's prison number was marked inside the collar. Then at the appointed time of the escape Martin, who was working in the Admiralty Yard, was given a quick leg-up by a fellow prisoner and was over the wall, into a waiting car and changing into civilian clothes within seconds. With sheer effrontery Martin and his accomplice went into the first hotel they came to, sauntered into the lounge and had a few malt whiskies as they watched the squad cars race by.

Meanwhile, back in Glasgow a diversion was being set up. Another accomplice, having allowed for the time it takes to get from Peterhead to Glasgow, made an anonymous phone call to the police saying that Martin was holed up in a derelict house in the Blackhill area of Glasgow. When police descended on the house they found the convict's shirt and were convinced Martin was in Glasgow. This meant the road blocks were lifted around Peterhead and there was no search up there. Martin and his pal were able to eat and drink and be merry at leisure while the police vainly turned Glasgow's underworld upside down. The pair eventually travelled at a leisurely pace to southern Ireland. They were caught a month later when they had to return to their old Glasgow haunts for funds and a 'snout' tipped off the police. (Seven years later Martin was shot and seriously wounded after a thieves' falling out by the accomplice who had put the convict shirt in Blackhill.)

The man who holds the record for escapes from working parties outside Peterhead prison was a convict nicknamed 'The Runner'.

'The Runner' arrived at Peterhead in the early fifties. He was serving six years for serious assault. Perhaps it was because he came of Romany stock but from the day he arrived in the prison he talked of nothing else but escape. Talking about one's intentions, especially in Peterhead Prison, is not a wise thing to do and it was not long before the Prison Governor got to know about the Runner's intentions.

"How are your escape plans coming along?" the Governor asked him when he was making his daily rounds of the work parties.

But the Runner did escape — eight times. Yet he never succeeded in staying on the run for long. All he succeeded in doing was to increase his six year sentence to thirteen years. But he did have a few amusing experiences during his brief spells of freedom.

On December 7th, 1954, the Runner took off from an outside working party yet again. He succeeded in getting clear of the immediate area of the prison but in the chase he lost his boots. Now December 1954 was a bad month for escaping. The weather was bad with heavy snow and temperatures below freezing. To protect his feet against frostbite the Runner crept into a farmyard barn and got hold of an old potato sack. This he cut into strips and wrapped them round his feet.

After travelling for a couple of miles the Runner realised that he was not going to get far without a pair of boots. In the distance he saw the light of a cottage and made for it.

When he arrived the Runner looked through the cottage window. Inside, sitting before a blazing fire, his stockinged feet resting on the hob, was an elderly, bewhiskered farmer. And beside the fender lay his drying pair of boots.

The temptation was too much for the Runner. He tried the door and opened the latch. Silently the Runner tip-toed into the room and, in full view of the old man by the hearth, stooped and picked up the boots before tip-toeing as silently out again. For a moment the farmer just sat staring at the departing apparition.

Then, as the Runner put on the boots and sped through the fields, the farmer regained his voice and the fugitive heard a plaintive shout behind him, "Maggie — someone's just stolen my best boots!"

After several escape attempts the Runner decided that the secret of a successful escape was getting under cover and lying low till the police gave up the search. After that, getting clear of the area would be easier. On his next escape, again from a working party, he covered as much ground as possible and then looked around for a place to lie low. He had figured that the best place to hide would be somewhere the police were unlikely to look, like the loft of a house that was quite near the prison. He chose a council house, waited until dark, climbed onto the roof and dropped into an attic through a skylight.

He could hear the occupiers of the house moving about below. Wrapping himself up in some old garments that were lying around, he settled down for the night. But as the hours passed it became increasingly cold and around 2 a.m. the Runner decided to drop down into the house where the occupants were asleep and get himself some food and some warmth. He silently made his way to the kitchenette and helped himself to some biscuits and slices of bread washed down with water. Then he spotted a small press under the stairs and deciding it would be warmer than the attic he quietly hid himself in its darkness behind some junk. However, after a while he felt an urgent call of nature and went to the toilet which was just beside his hidey-hole. It had been sometime since the Runner had exercised his bowels and the stool which his body now ejected was exceptionally large. The thought now occurred to him, after the deed, that he could not pull the chain without the risk of wakening the occupants of the house. As he was trying to figure out a solution to this problem he heard sounds coming from the upstairs bedroom and quickly crept back to the press under the stairs. He heard a man and woman talking and it was obvious they were up and getting ready for work.

The man went into the toilet and there was a long silence.

Then the man called out to his wife, "Bloody hell! Is there something wrong with your guts, Jean?"

"What do you mean?" replied the woman's voice as she went into the toilet.

There was a pause and then her voice declared angrily, "That wasn't me!"

"Well, it wasn't me," was the reply.

"It must have been you," said the wife. "You don't always pull the chain after you."

"I'm telling you I didn't do THAT!" said the man. "And if it wasn't me, it must have been you!"

At that the chain was pulled and the woman stomped out of the toilet.

"You'll be telling me next that someone comes in to use our toilet," she said.

When the couple had left for work the Runner came out and prowled around the house. The experience of the toilet had panicked him and he decided to find himself another place to hide. Once again he helped himself to some food and wearing a pair of trousers and jacket he took from a wardrobe, he left the house.

Within the hour he had found himself another attic to hide in. This was in the nurses quarters of a small hospital. All that day he spent in the attic. But at night he made his way down into the house in search of food.

This time he was lucky. The house being occupied by several nurses he could help himself without it being missed and he also found a warm cupboard to hole up in. He also used a milk bottle instead of the toilet.

He spent two days and two nights like this then became restless He crept out of his cupboard before the nurses had gone to bed and one of them disturbed him as he was helping himself to some bread and jam. He ran out of the front door and set off along the road in search of another hide-out. He was still running when a police car pulled up beside him and he was recaptured.

Over the years, Scotland's prisons have had characters like the Runner under their roofs but not all the odd people were prisoners. In the late forties there was a chaplain at Peterhead who was homosexual by nature and he was very popular with certain prisoners. Some prison officers suspected that in his repeated visits to these certain prisoners in their cells he administered to more than their spiritual needs. But no officer ever attempted to do anything about it. It was due to the treachery of a prisoner that he ended up in disgrace and the case ended up in the *News of the World.* But the chaplain was never prosecuted. One of the prisoners with whom he had sexual relations had decided to blackmail him after his release and it was due to a letter written by the blackmailer being found and opened by mistake among prisoners mail that the matter came to light.

The chaplain was dismissed in disgrace and was never the same again. The blackmailer was given four years.

Religion sometimes has strange side effects in the strained atmosphere of prison. In the early 1950s evangelism of the Billy Graham variety was all the rage in religious circles and one convert to this feverish style of preaching was a lay preacher who took weekly Bible classes at Peterhead and who was known simply as 'Brother'.

Every week for thirty years Brother had come into the prison to preach the Word to the convicts. His Bible class was always well attended, not because Brother was a star attraction as a preacher but because attending the Bible class gave the convicts the opportunity to swap magazines or circulate prison gossip. Brother was well aware of this but like a true Christian he practised tolerance.

Then one Sunday morning Brother arrived at the prison full of renewed zeal. He had attended a Billy Graham rally and been won over to evangelism. When the convicts had finished their usual transactions, Brother on this occasion rose slowly to his feet and asked them, "Has God spoken to you yet?" Then he really started. With a rising tempo, with sweat pouring from his brow, arms and hands gesticulating wildly, eyes glaring and voice at full pitch, Brother harangued them for an hour about the message of Jesus. The convicts sat mesmerised by this one man piece of theatre, wondering if Brother had finally gone round the twist.

Then he came to the climax of his performance. Pointing an accusing finger at them, he shouted, "Who among you has the guts to accept Jesus? I must ask you all to bow your heads and think for a moment on the terrible ordeal which Jesus suffered so that you might be saved. Is there one among you — just one — who has the guts to accept Jesus? If there is then let him raise his hand. Who has the guts to raise his hand for Jesus? Who?"

There was silence as Brother stared at them.

The prisoners dutifully bowed their heads to please him and glanced from side to side just to see in case anything was happening. Then slowly but surely a hand rose from the middle of the congregation. It belonged to Battling Peter, a Glasgow robber who no-one had ever said lacked guts since he was one of the toughest and most short tempered men in the prison as well as being built like a dam.

Excited, Brother almost jumped up and down, declaring, "There — I see a man who has guts. Raise your hand a little higher, brother."

Battling Peter did so amidst stifled sniggers but then someone from behind patted him maternally on his bald patch and all hell broke loose. Peter whirled round and started laying into those behind him with fists like bunches of bananas and blood and bodies went flying everywhere. As prison officers waded in a free-for-all started which did not finish until several heads had been broken and Peter was dragged off to the punishment block. Brother had collapsed with exhaustion and dismay, tears welling in his eyes. He was later warned by the prison authorities not to get his congregation as excited with his preaching ever again and thereafter Brother's sermons returned to their more subdued style.

All kinds find themselves in prison and in the fifties a regular resident of Barlinnie was a con man known as 'the Bishop'. On one occasion while he was awaiting trial he came into possession of a cell key which another prisoner had made. He decided to utilise his nefarious talents to get some enjoyment. The Bishop's speciality on the outside was to pose as a minister or priest and swindle the gullible out of their savings. Since he was a homosexual he had a soft, winning way, especially with old ladies.

Being an untried prisoner he was allowed to wear his own clothes and he was in a gallery with first time offenders who did not know him. Using the cell key and turning his collar, he made frequent visits to these first timers posing as an effeminate padre. After talking to the prisoner for a while he would let it be known that he could do the prisoner a lot of good in certain quarters in return for certain favours. Once these favours were given the Bishop was in the habit of leaving the conned convict with an address to go to on the outside, saying it was a male brothel. It was the address of a police inspector. The Bishop would then quietly return to his own cell, a smile on his face, knowing that being untried he would exercise separately from the first timers who had been sworn to keep their mouths shut about what was going on.

This went on for several weeks and the Bishop had enjoyed himself with quite a few lads when the trick went badly wrong. He entered the cell of one prisoner as usual, gave his spiel then started stroking the convict's leg. But this one was a former patient of a mental hospital who had a particular hatred for that sort of thing and he went berserk, almost killing the Bishop before astonished prison officers were alerted and pulled them apart. Another charge was added to the Bishop's list.

On another occasion a Glasgow thug called Benny was given six years and after he had arrived in the prison his hair began to fall out. He applied to the Governor for hair restorer to be sent in and after the prison doctor had confirmed that his hair was indeed falling out permission was granted. It was not long before a bottle a week was being sent to him. Then one Saturday night Benny's cell which he shared with two other men began to sound like a miniature music hall with Harry Lauder medleys echoing round the walls. On investigation the officers found the three men legless drunk. They had drunk three bottles of the hair restorer which they had discovered to their delight on reading the labels had a high alcoholic content. After that, Benny was allowed to go bald.

During the last war a prisoner at Perth Prison, one David McLeod, a Glasgow burglar, seduced a prison officer to the extent that whenever the officer was on night patrol and after they finished sexual intercourse McLeod was allowed to slip out of the prison, commit burglaries and be back in prison before the morning shift came on duty. McLeod was a former Inverness policeman who had turned to crime when he moved to Glasgow.

On one of his housebreaking expeditions McLeod left a fingerprint. When the police discovered it, they were baffled when a check showed it belonged to a man already serving a sentence. The Prison Governor, Mr. Mayo (who later became Governor of Barlinnie), was contacted and it was agreed that a close watch be kept on McLeod. A few weeks later the officer who was bent in more ways than one was again on night patrol and McLeod slipped once more out of the prison.

In the early hours of the morning McLeod returned to find a reception party waiting for him in the shape of the Governor and Chief Officer. McLeod was never prosecuted for the offences he committed while absent from the prison. Perhaps the authorities did not wish it to be known that a convict was able to leave the prison so scandalously easily in return for a few sexual favours. But McLeod was put in the punishment block for a long time while the officer was fined internally and dismissed the service in disgrace.

By prison rules prisoners are permitted to make complaints to the Secretary of State by petition. The prisoner making such a complaint is permitted to seal the envelope supplied with the official paper provided for the purpose. The authorities promote the belief that such petitions are sent out of the prison without being opened. The truth is that all such petitions are opened and read before leaving the prison, and where necessary the Prison Governor will add his comments for the guidance of the prison department to whom all such petitions are sent.

Where such a petition contains a complaint the reply is invariably: "The Secretary of State having considered the complaint has found no cause for complaint." It matters not how justified the complaint, or how strong the evidence in support of it, the answer is usually the same.

There is a widespread belief among prisoners that the petitions do not even leave the prison but are answered by the Prison Governor. There is another theory that the petitions are not even read. One prisoner in Barlinnie who believed the first theory to be correct decided to put it to the test. He applied for a petition to the Secretary of State and filled it up with meaningless words which he copied from a science fiction comic. It contained gibberish like Aaaaaagh Ugh Woweee Ka-thump.

About a week later Governor Mayo called the prisoner to the orderly room.

"I have here an answer to the petition you sent," said Mayo, handing the prisoner a sheet of paper. The prisoner was then ushered out of the orderly room. When he arrived back at the mailbag shop the prisoner unfolded the paper to read, "In reply to your petition the Secretary of State says Aaaaaaaagh Ugh Woweee Ka-thump . . ."

When he showed this around to the other prisoners who were all quick to offer advice the prisoner decided to take the matter further. Later that day, when Governor Mayo was making his rounds, the prisoner approached him and held out the answer to the petition.

"What does that mean?" he asked.

Mayo studied it for a moment and said, "It says, 'you have no grounds for complaint'."

Mayo grinned impishly, winked and handed it back.

Barlinnie Prison, the 'Bar-L', the grim, forbidding 100-year-old fortress on the nor' nor' east corner of Glasgow, has had its famous guests. When Buffalo Bill brought his famous Wild West show to Glasgow one of the Indian Chiefs got drunk on the local firewater and ended up in Barlinnie charged with being drunk and disorderly. Bill had to make a personal visit to the prison to "get the Chief the hell outa here".

John McLean, the rabble rousing socialist, was held at Barlinnie before being sent to Peterhead. (See Chapter 17).

In the old days the main industry at Barlinnie was stone breaking, oakum picking and mailbag sewing. Over the years the stone breaking was phased out and the stone yard used for further buildings.

Whatever purpose Barlinnie has served over the years, rehabilitation is certainly not one of them. The buildings, like the whole prison system itself, are outdated and the conditions primitive in the extreme.

Over the years there have been a number of riots at Barlinnie though none has been terribly serious. In the thirties there was the tobacco riot when prisoners rushed the exercise yard and broke into the cupboard where tobacco belonging to the untried prisoners was kept. In the late forties the prisoners in E-Wing rioted in protest against the quality of fish that was served at lunchtime, the fish being putrid. During this riot the staff vacated the wing and left the prisoners to it. In the fifties there was the 'batter squad' riot when a number of prisoners attacked a number of staff in retaliation for the beating up of a prisoner by a group of officers.

Barlinnie has had it's characters on both sides. There was the Governor named Walkinshaw who committed suicide by jumping out of a train. He was having an affair with an ex-borstal boy who was blackmailing him. After Walkinshaw came Governor Mayo in the early forties. The first hanging he witnessed was in 1946 when a 21-year-old soldier was executed for a gang murder in the Anderston district of Glasgow. After this, Mayo had to witness a lot of hangings. They had an adverse effect on his health and drove him to drink.

Executioner Albert Pierrepoint was not too happy either with the death apparatus he found north of the border, once describing it to a Commission on Capital Punishment as "antediluvian", by which he was referring to a fixed ring in the roof to which the rope had to be attached. Every condemned man has "a different drop" depending on his height, weight and muscular build, the more powerful the man the longer the drop. The ring allowed for no adjustment whereas in England the rope was attached to adjustable chains which made the length of the drop more flexible. Pierrepoint also resented the number of reprieves there used to be in Scotland, more than there were in England, although he was still paid half his fee and travelling expenses even if his services were not required.

The gallows at Barlinnie was certainly a primitive contraption. As happened when Patrick Carraher was hanged (Chapter 8) the trap door when it was opened caused a fearful bang and eventually had to be padded. When an execution was about to take place the prisoners, instead of being locked up, were taken away to worksheds where there was no chance of them hearing the ghastly noise of the gallows at work.

Horror stories of hanging men being strangled slowly instead of having their necks broken quickly, of prison officers hanging onto legs to break necks, used to abound in prison. It is curious to note that at the end of his career, after four hundred executions,

Pierrepoint changed his mind about hanging as a deterrent and concluded it was merely an instrument of revenge wielded by society and had no effect on the murder rate whatsoever.

In the fifties Governor Mayo appeared in a Glasgow court charged with a driving offence for which the Sheriff imposed a fine with the alternative of a spell in prison.

"I hope you can pay the fine," the Sheriff remarked, "otherwise you will end up in your own prison as Governor and prisoner."

The fine was promptly paid.

Mayo, who later died in a car accident, always made his views against hanging as widely known as he could without risking his job. This made him unpopular with virtually the hundred per cent hardline officers under him. Nevertheless, he stoically witnessed more executions than anyone else in the Scottish prison system.

Mayo may have tried to escape from Barlinnie through bottles of whisky but many of his inmates had more spectacular methods.

In the early thirties a youth awaiting transfer to borstal died when he dived into the nearby Monkland Canal, was trapped in the reeds and drowned.

In the early forties a prisoner got over the walls by using a sweeping brush tied to a length of rope. He then calmly broke into Governor Mayo's house and stole a suit of clothes before catching a bus.

In 1955 a youth, again waiting transfer to a borstal, climbed onto the roof of B-Wing and looping his belt round the telephone wires slid down and across the prison wall into a nearby drying green. Luckily for him the wires sustained his light weight. After that the telephone wires were put underground.

A similar escape to this took place in 1979. Three men went unnoticed into the shower room during a changeover in shifts early on a Sunday morning after slopping out. They chiselled their way into a small attic above and, taking a coil of rope with them which they had previously hidden, they clambered onto the high, slippery roof. An accomplice was waiting for them in a garden over the wall and the rope was flung to him and he tied it round a clothes pole while the prisoners secured their end to a drainage pipe. They then lowered themselves, hanging precariously in mid-air, down along the rope to freedom. The garden where they landed was at the back of a row of prison officers' houses and it was one of these off-duty officers who, glancing out his window, rubbed his bleary eyes in disbelief and raised the alarm by phone. By the time the siren sounded and other officers arrived on the scene the escapees had fled in a waiting car. They were caught in Glasgow a few days later having done nothing more dangerous than go on a pub crawl with cronies. A later inquiry into the escape found that the prison authorities had been tipped off by the police that an informant had warned an escape was in the offing. The officers on Saturday night duty had been told this and ordered to be on special alert. The shift they handed over to (at the time when the escape took place) had been given no warning instructions. Some of the prison officers were reprimanded. The incident became known as the 'Washing Line Escape',

Another prisoner escaping from Barlinnie hid himself in the Corporation refuse lorry that called to collect the prison rubbish. He was on the run for weeks.

Another great escaper was John 'Gipsy' Winning from Glasgow's East End, a middle-aged, six foot tall, heavily built, curly haired villain of tinker stock (like the Runner). In all he made eight escapes from prison (again like the Runner) but only managed four years of freedom since his early twenties. Despite this he married and contrived to have three daughters and a son. In 1954 he escaped from a bus taking prisoners from Barlinnie to Saughton Prison in Edinburgh when it slowed behind a tram and guards were overpowered. He was caught naked eleven days later when a showering constable recognised him at Shettleston Turkish Baths.

In 1960 while awaiting trial in 'C' Block in Barlinnie he filed through his cell bars, made a rope of bedclothes and lowered himself to the yard where a real rope was waiting for him to get over the outside wall where a car was also waiting.

On another occasion he escaped from a van nearing Peterhead when he freed himself from his handcuffs, smashed a window and dived out. When police visited a house in the Maryhill district of Glasgow on a tip-off looking for him they thought the place was empty until they noticed a television looked in a peculiar position and a carpet appeared to have been moved. On investigation they found 'Gipsy' under the floorboards.

On another occasion he scaled a security fence at Peterhead and stole a police van.

Charges of murdering William 'Tank' McGuinness, his partner in crime, by kicking him to death in an East End street were dropped and it was McGuinness's death which cleared up the Rachel Ross murder (see Chapter 16). Gipsy himself was eventually murdered in a drunken brawl in his caravan.

Over the years a number of Barlinnie officers have been themselves jailed (but not in the same prison), usually for trafficking offences like smuggling in luxury goods and being paid by the prisoner's pals on the outside. Despite their complaints about having a hard life, no prison officer has ever lost his life in Scotland in the pursuit of his duties and it is rarely they are involved in physically dangerous situations — even when this happens the odds are heavily in their favour. But patrolling a prison can be a depressing experience. Like crime, it takes a certain mentality.

However, in comparison to all the grimness surrounding the men's prisons, the opening of Scotland's womens' prison at Cornton Vale near Stirling in 1976 came like a splash of light and a breath of fresh air.

Spread out more like a university campus than a prison it can house around 300 inmates in comfortable small units where the cells are more like small bedrooms and even the bars have fancy, white painted designs so that from a distance they look like curtains. With gardening, cookery, garment making and various leisure activities, the prisoners time is kept occupied and a sympathetic staff working under an enlightened regime make sure that problems are brought out in the open and discussed rather than kept smouldering. An alcoholic unit deals with the problem which has caused virtually half of the sentences, whether because the prisoners themselves had a drink problem or because their nearest and dearest did. The recidivism rate is very low and it would be tempting to say that these women are lucky. A few minutes in the starkly horrific atmosphere of the bare, windowless, lightless stone punishment cell, where unruly offenders are kept for up to three days, would quickly dispel that notion.

Although Scotland has the highest number of prisoners per head of the population in Europe, this has brought no end to crime and violence. Prisons may be necessary but they are no solution. In the sixties and seventies 94% of male prisoners who were released after their first term of detention were back inside within a year. Barlinnie and Peterhead will never be short of business for the next hundred years.

CHAPTER 11

The Poisoned Dwarf

At what stage in their formative years do murderers go wrong is a question which has always fascinated sociologists, psychologists, dramatists, novelists and criminologists but in the case of Ian Brady there could be an excuse for believing the traditional Scots mother's pragmatic statement that there are simply people born bad with a taint of evil about them which can make one have second thoughts about the non-existence of the Devil. Brady and his mistress Myra Hindley cold-bloodedly tortured and killed their young victims and buried the bodies. This gave them their grim title in the annals of crime — the Moors Murderers.

Brady was born in a slum area in Glasgow rife with crime and during the first seventeen years of his life showed the first traces of the appalling abnormality which ended with one of Britain's most dramatic court cases.

Psychologists would say he suffered a disability even before his birth because he was born illegitimate. His father was a robust, hard drinking, newspaper reporter working in Glasgow and the mother Miss Mary Stewart, aged twenty eight, was a rather naive tea-room waitress whom he had, in the old fashioned phrase, "taken advantage of." The safe delivery was in Rotten Row Hospital, an unfortunate name for a maternity unit but in this case wholly applicable. The mother lied that she was married and said the husband was deceased.

The birth occurred on Sunday January 2nd, 1938 at mid-day, a time when the hungover city was just getting over the New Year revels.

Whether the father was alive or not, there was no move to help Mary financially and she had to leave her pal's house and find a single room in a tenement slum in Caledonia Road, Gorbals, at the time when the teeming area was notorious as a hotbed of crime and gang fighting. She took a string of part-time jobs and paid girls to babysit but after a few months she became exhausted and put an advert, not with much hope, in a shop window saying a working widow wanted a child adopted. But although she knew most families were overcrowded enough already she was in luck and a middle-aged woman who wanted simply to be known as Ma Sloan took the "wean" to nearby Camden Street. She had four children of her own, and her husband was hard put to even support them, but Mary helped out with expenses and also managed to visit every Sunday when she would wheel "wee Ian" to the nearby Southern Necropolis Cemetery for a walk and some fresh air.

The seeds of discontent were therefore planted from birth: a reckless father who was either dead or did not care and certainly no longer existed so far as the child was concerned, a feckless mother who could not afford to raise the child under the warmth of her love, the jibes of "bastard" which singled him out and the upbringing in a family where he was an outsider, the youngest and the weakest and one left to play his games and weave his dreams on his own. The surroundings were rough and adeptness at scrabbling out some sort of living using basic survival instincts were characteristics of both young and old. His exterior reactions were toughened whereas inside, in his own warm, private self his delicate self-esteem was nurtured and guarded carefully. He was always number one in his own eyes, but never in anyone else's and as his ego reached out for support and found none it turned back in on itself and glowered, waiting. But there again any Gorbals housewife would still have told you he was simply "a bad 'un."

Ian was a good reader. His mother said that came from his dad's side, but the cinema was really the entertainment that enthralled. In those pre-television days Glasgow had at least two cinemas in every district and with twice weekly changes of programmes the opportunities were limitless for Ian to indulge his fantasies in the darkened halls where the larger than life characters strode across the screen. Even when young he had a penchant for crime thrillers and his favourite was *The Third Man,* that atmospheric, brooding film with its darkened, ruined streets so reminiscent of the slum world and the enigmatic arch gangster lurking in the shadows.

In 1947 as part of the massive rehousing schemes the Sloans moved south west to Pollok. Ian was becoming more withdrawn, his film-going, always alone, more frequent. He was unpopular because of his aloofness, his self-imposed I-am-better-than-you attitude which had been with him from an early age. He could hardly avoid completely taking part in street and playground games and once when he was ten became over excited, unusual for him, during a game of cops and robbers, tied a boy to a post and vainly attempted to set fire to him with a burning rag. Playmates came to the captive's assistance and the matter blew over without anyone being injured.

On another occasion, on his first trip outside Glasgow, the Sloans took him to wild and picturesque Loch Lomondside and the mountainous scenery seemed to have a hypnotic effect on him. He disappeared from the party and was later found standing like Rob Roy on the rim of a hill staring into the distance, a position he had evidently been in for some time. Thereafter he always had a penchant for desolate countryside whose barren magnificence and isolation seemed to blend in with his personal delusions. This was to have fatal results later in his life.

When he was ten and a half and roaming through a bombsite in nearby Rutherglen, a wierd but favourite haunt of his next to a cemetery, he came across an emaciated black cat which tried to escape his leering, hunter's grin by scrabbling up a ruined chimney but it fell back into his eagerly waiting hands. The cat scratched him and he dropped it into an old string shopping bag and watched the trapped, terrified creature writhing in fear. He must have enjoyed the feeling of power, the superiority of one sinister, independent animal over another. He waited for the cloak of darkness to descend then went with the cat to the graveyard where he knew some kids had been digging mud pies next to a cracked marble angel. He heaved a slab of gravestone from over a foot deep oblong hole, released the cat down into it then swiftly slid the stone back across burying the cat which set up a pathetic wailing. He sat there in the moonlight, listening to it, then went home to slumber peacefully. The next day he could not resist boasting to his 'inferior' classmates in great detail of what he had done. They did not believe him but later in the day, without his knowing, they were passing the graveyard and decided to have a look. The stone was just as he had said, they prised it open and out slunk the black cat and away. Wee Ian was half pleased that he had been proved right but annoyed that they had let the creature go. The behaviour of a bad 'un, alright.

But at school there was nothing to complain about. He was neat, tidy and industrious and qualified to Shawlands Academy, even if teachers found him strangely reserved. He was poor at football and this did not help his introspection. Where the other lads started collecting cigarette cards and stamps he began to collect Nazi memorabilia, newspaper and magazine articles, relics the older men had brought back from the war but were fed up with, photographs, even swastika adorned daggers, anything he could lay his hands on. Hitler became a hero and although the intricacies of National Socialism philosophy were beyond him all he needed to look up to was that lone figure up there above the chanting masses.

The fact that the Germans had lost the war seemed a minor setback. His attitude was that the master race, the aristocratic blood brothers, know that they are superior and can and will strike at the inferior whenever it is necessary. Religions or morality he dismissed out of hand as a con trick. It was around this time he sat spellbound through *The Third Man,* the first of many viewings. And school colleagues recalled that even in Primary when the kids played

Yanks and Gerries nobody wanted to be the enemy except wee Ian who always volunteered, whether he 'died' a hero's death or not.

By now, aged thirteen, the formulative influences had crystalised: he was the outsider, an aggressor with a superiority fetish. All that was needed was action. He had to prove he could outwit the society around him which, to his twisted way of thinking, had forced him out into the cold. There was only one way: whistling the 'Harry Lime' theme from his favourite film he sauntered into a milk bar frequented by delinquents. He had a plan. He took out his neat school copy book and showed off addresses complete with house plans. One of them had a jemmy for gas meters, it was the Easter week-end, who could ask for anything more. They were impressed by his cool jauntiness, his new air of command as opposed to sulleness. He had been out on planning forays the nights before and had everything worked out.

A house was picked and Ian kept watch on the pavement because it was his first job. He had to dive into the bushes when a constable strolled past but did not have time or nerve or both to warn his accomplices which did not please them. Words were exchanged and Ian decided to take his eight shillings and scamper. But the superman's first venture into crime was not a success because the two amateur cracksmen went on to another house where they proceeded to get caught and spill the beans. It was a shock for the Sloans when the policeman appeared at the front door but Ian took it all poker faced, even the leathering from his foster father.

He was bound over for two years by the Juvenile Court but it made no difference because soon he was at the same thieving, seventeen shillings more was taken this time, and he was admonished and bound over again.

He was now fourteen and a half and risen to a healthy height. He eventually stopped growing at just under six feet. Big-boned and slim, he had large hands with which he used to tidy his brown hair, disdaining combs or brushes. He was always pale but with strange sunken grey eyes that were nevertheless large and penetrating and cultivated to be sinister. His lips were normally pulled down at the edges or pursed as if he were sizing something up. He was always tense and hardly ever let himself go in laughter. His sparse sense of humour was odd and cruel and when he did allow himself a grin it was usually at some mishap which had happened to someone. He was always clean and well dressed with quite finicky habits, like patting his lips with a breast pocket hankerchief for no apparent reason except perhaps to act the dandy. His clothes were conservative, nothing too modern or flashy, and he even sported a waistcoat where other teenagers would not be seen dead in one. According to his classmates during one of those secretive fag sharing and penis showing capers that lads get up to in school toilets Ian was surprisingly not averse to having his organ seen and apparently it won first prize, a fact which no doubt satisfied his secretly flourishing ego immensely. But despite this there were no steady girlfriends, or any boyfriends for that matter, because Ian was only in love with number one, himself.

Despite being above average intelligence he seems to have been keen to get out of school and conquer the world. His interest in literature had fallen away and his passions were still the cinema and his Nazi collection.

None of the professions or trades lured him because they all seemed so dull and mediocre and he left school to become an apprentice plater at Harland and Woolf's shipyard in Govan. But this was too menial, he was a teaboy most of the time, so he left after nine months and got his first protracted feel of blood in a Paisley Road butchers. He is remembered there, as everywhere, as a surly, morosely tempered fellow but the slaughterhouse conditions had no apparent effect except boredom. He returned to crime at night.

He had been given a taste of working life and he did not like it one little bit. They had tried to make him feel inferior, just another member of the drab proletariat and he was not having it. The time had come to hit back once more.

He went back to the milk bar, the cafes, the delinquents, the empty houses and the meter robbing. There was a romance of sorts with an ex-schoolgirl acquaintance but she soon severed all connections when she came out of a dance with another boy and there was Ian waiting, in one of his stormtrooper moods, brandishing a knife angrily. They had to shelter in a friend's house. She should have known better than to turn down Ian Brady but then he must have shrugged her off, to mend his bruised conceit, as just an inferior bit of slag who did not know she was on a good thing. Nothing more was heard of this matter. The girl, Evelyn Grant, did not realise until years later how lucky she was.

In Brady's career of crime the inevitable happened and he was once more nabbed by the constabulary. This time he avoided detention once more — but at a price. He appeared at the Sheriff Summary Court on several charges of housebreaking and theft. The benevolent welfare officer decided after deliberation with the Sloans, who were fed up with their sullenly rebellious and stubborn adoption, that Ian should go to his real mother. It was an unwilling decision giving the tall, pale-faced, sunken but darkly piercing-eyed lad the benefit of the doubt and one which the officer will no doubt always regret.

Mary Stewart had left her native land where life had been so rough for her and like so many others had been seeking her fortune down south. After six years in the Manchester area she had finally managed to get herself a husband, an Irish labourer called Brady. She had been out of touch with the Sloans for four years when the Welfare Officer wrote to her. Ian, who had always known he was a 'bastard', now had to be told that Mary who had visited all those years ago was not just a friend, and he was getting a new surname.

He packed his bag, including his Hitlerian collection and crime novels, told his criminal colleagues that they hadn't heard the last of him as he would be "in an' out o' the sewers down south", said good-bye to Ma Sloan and in December, 1954, shortly before his seventeenth birthday, entrained for Manchester.

His Scottish upbringing never left him and he cultivated it to suit his own image. He was known as 'Jock' Brady, the wild man from the notorious Gorbals. He had never cared a tuppence for his native country or its traditions but now he was the exiled Celt from his misty homeland among "a crowd o' bliddy foreigners." He acted the hard man, swaggering into the bar for the straight whiskies, perfecting a broader than broad Glasgow accent which he never lost, playing rough with the girls, picking arguments and exaggerating the grimness of the Gorbals. And his newfound low-life cronies, who seem to have been a tame lot, fell for it. He sank into petty crime with them and ended up in borstal.

With his arrival from Glasgow, Ian Stewart Brady had moulded himself into the perfect monster ready for the atrocities he later committed. At his eventual trial everyone was horrified as the cold facts were recited with no apparent explanation and no remorse on the part of the pale, staring prisoner in the dock.

But it was all there in his Glasgow past. The parentless boy dropped into a makeshift home in a criminal area who survived by creating his own fantasy world where he was King, a world which sympathised with cruelty, that identified with Nazism and which ended in a one man revolt in the sewers of the subconscious against the decency and morality of society.

It was not such a large step from burying a cat to burying a child. The principle is the same: possessing the power of life or death over another living creature, the only power with the electricity to move this monster devoid of conscience or normal moral restraints or emotions.

It is not the intention of this book to go into Brady's murders in detail but a study of his early life would not be complete without a brief summary of where it led.

He continued along his narrow path alone, enlarging his Nazi collection with books and photographs on concentration camps, buying records of Hitler and marching songs, learning German, obsessed by murder and horror films, spy thriller novels, keeping to himself, coming under the spell of the Marquis De Sade's life and writings whose cruelty was in accord with his own with the added piquancy of sex, becoming interested in photography and acquiring a tape recorder which was to have horrific repercussions.

In January, 1961 he met 18-year-old Myra Hindley, a slim good looking blonde who became a typist at the Chemical Merchants where he was then working. He ensnared her when she was in a vulnerable state of mind, trying to recover from the accidental drowning of a boy with whom she had been deeply in love. Brady with his outwardly strong personality took her over completely. She became his slave mentally and physically, accepting all his ideas and allowing herself to be whipped by him and photographed in obscene poses. She was the perfect partner for Brady: submissive, bitter and callous. He would probably have eventually committed murder without her anyway but her admiring presence added that extra thrill.

He loved the barren moorland country of north west England, reminiscent of the joy he had felt on Loch Lomondside, and the barren heathland where he could imagine he was master of all he surveyed. They would drive up there by moonlight, drinking wine and hatching plots.

In De Sade's teachings there is no room for love, only physical pleasure of whatever kind. In his philosophy there is no limit to pleasure, especially when it means inflicting pain and the ultimate in cruelty is death. They spoke of murder and the logical victims who would submit without too much trouble were children.

They set about their tasks coolly, sometimes photographing the victims before they were killed then burying them on the moors with snaps of Myra smiling over their graves.

Schoolboy John Kilbride was taken for a joy ride to the moors and his death on the week-end of the Kennedy assassination in 1963.

Lesley Ann Downey, aged ten, was forced to pose naked for pornographic photographs in the murderers house and her last hour was faithfully tape recorded before she was killed and buried on Boxing Day 1964. This harrowing tape was played to a hushed court at the subsequent trial.

In October, 1965 a young 'friend' Edward Evans was axed and strangled and put in a sack.

In addition, in the summer of 1963 Pauline Reade, aged sixteen, went missing for no apparent reason in the same area and her whereabouts has never been ascertained.

Also in the same area schoolboy Keith Bennet vanished in June 1964 under equally baffling circumstances and has never turned up.

The Evans murder was uncovered before they could get rid of the body and a search of the moors uncovered Downey and Kilbride.

The two were tried amidst hysterical scenes of wailing women and milling world pressmen at Chester Assizes in the spring of 1966. They pleaded not guilty to the three murders with which they were charged but Brady was found guilty of all three — Kilbride,

Downey and Evans — and Hindley guilty of the murders of Evans and Downey and guilty of being an accessory to the killing of Kilbride. They were given life imprisonment although there was the predictable outcry throughout the country that they should hang. Mary Stewart fled the furore to weep on the shoulder of Ma Sloan, back in Glasgow where they kept asking themselves what had gone wrong.

Throughout the trial the murderers showed no remorse, Hindley even sticking her tongue out at a staring reporter. She has made news even during her imprisonment after a lesbian affair with a warder. Brady's kingdom is like his wee room was back in the Gorbals, a solitary cell where all he has is his fantasies. (He did try to commit suicide by starvation but after being force fed decided to live on.)

Now he makes braille books for the blind, a drastic turnabout for someone who once believed in the survival of the fittest. He has also switched from reading Nazi memorabilia to gloomy Russian classics — Dostoyevsky's *Crime and Punishment* is one of his favourites. He has also expressed the wish that he and Myra should die in prison because of the enormity of their crimes and has claimed he will never apply for parole.

Prison visitor and professional do-gooder Lord Longford has professed the belief that Brady can be saved through Christian salvation and eventually allowed out. Relatives of the dead say they will kill the monster if by any wild chance this should ever come about.

CHAPTER 12

The Man In The Wood

Around 1.45 a.m., in the early morning darkness of Sunday 23rd July, 1961 in the middle of Glasgow's annual Fair holiday a taxi pulled up outside a house in the Castlemilk housing estate on the city's southern outskirts. The voices of two men were heard talking by people in the nearest houses. The motor was still running and the taxi radio's crackling could be faintly heard. Then there were two loud bangs. The curious who went to their windows saw under the streetlights a man running towards the darkness of a nearby wood. Doors opened, people became curious and glanced into the cab. The driver lay slouched over his wheel, dripping with blood and the windscreen was shattered. One of the shocked residents used the car radio to summon help while others dialled 999. Within minutes the street was packed with other taxis and police cars. But it was too late. The driver was dying from two gunshot wounds and his murderer had got clean away. The crime was apparently motiveless and for many the ghastly fear arose that a second Manuel had arisen to emulate the horrors of the first.

Three months later the man accused of this capital crime stood in the dock, a slightly built, medium sized, thirty-year-old criminal with a particularly pallid skin which served to accentuate his dark, slicked back hair and coal black eyes. Immaculately dressed with strong regular features, he appeared to many to be a cocky young prince of evil faintly reminiscent of Manuel. There was certainly something chilling and throughout the years he became known as one of Glasgow's most dangerous criminals. His name was Walter Scott Ellis.

The man he was accused of murdering was a mild mannered, hard working husband and father who had spent years building up his taxi fleet of five cabs. His name was John Walkinshaw.

Within seconds of the trial being over, it was obvious who was to be the feted hero of the hour splashed before the public's gaze in an unseemly scramble by newspapers to glorify the undeserving.

But at first things looked black for Ellis, not least because no lawyer wanted anything to do with his case. Partly this was because the Ellis family had little money (this was in the days before legal aid), but there was also strong public feeling against anyone trying to protect the accused in such a heinous crime.

However, at the end of the day this worked out to Ellis's advantage because he ended up with a young, up and coming lawyer who was ready to work 25 hours a day to make a name for himself. His name was Joseph Beltrami and he was the same age as Ellis. This trial was to make both their reputations although their paths were to go in diametrically opposite directions.

Before the trial began at Glasgow High Court, Beltrami had interviewed each of the 125 witnesses on the prosecution list at least twice. In addition he had visited the places involved dozens of times as well as studying forensic aspects involved in the case.

He chose to help a young advocate also keen to make a name for himself, Nicholas Fairbairn, who was later to become a Tory M.P. in Sir Alec Douglas Home's old seat, as well as Solicitor General for Scotland. This was the first big case that Beltrami and Fairbairn had worked on and they were to be a formidable team for several years, the first hardworking, rather dour but sharp as a scalpel, the second flamboyant with a touch of the actor about him. They both had that flair for publicity which is vital for all successful criminal lawyers — Beltrami even organised his own press conferences after trials and became as big a personality as anybody else involved in a case in the true Clarence Darrow tradition. He also had a penchant for getting himself photographed as much as possible, often clutching solidly onto the arm of a bemused accused he had 'got off' as they walked down the court steps. Disliked by the police and civil servants working in the Procurator Fiscal's department and not much loved by his fellow — rival — lawyers, Beltrami nevertheless contrived to be at the centre of many big cases in the sixties and seventies and built himself up into a considerable public figure.

But the fame was all still to come when he took up the Ellis cause and for him, as much as for his client, it was a game which had to be won. He also instructed a senior counsel, Ronald Bennet Q.C., to help Fairbairn because the defence was complex and the Judge, seventy-two-year-old Lord Patrick, approved the unique motion before the trial began that the defence would be split with Fairbairn cross-examining on technical aspects of the evidence and Bennet covering the straightforward factual questions as well as summing up.

Advocate Depute Norman Wylie was the formidable head of the prosecution team. He too was later to become a Tory M.P. as well as a Lord Advocate and Senator of the College of Justice.

The murder had taken place in Tormusk Road next to Glen Wood. There had been no eye witnesses to tie the accused in with the pulling of the trigger. For both sides the case was to revolve round purely circumstantial evidence as well as timing and distances which was to be expected with a taxi driver as the victim.

The trial began inauspiciously for Ellis. Beltrami and his two helpers decided to withdraw a Special Defence of Alibi. This was because they felt their client would not cut a very credible figure under cross-examination. He could be argumentative and aggressive and it was felt the jury should not see this side of his character but merely the neat, mute young man sitting unmoved before them. Besides Mr. Wylie was good at getting even the most credible defence witnesses tongue-tied. All that the defence could now do was discredit the prosecution evidence and rely on that alone.

After the black dressed widow had given evidence about having to identify her husband's body in hospital in the early hours of the morning (evidence unlikely to help the accused in the subjective minds of the jury), a map was produced in court and various taxi routes discussed.

The two most important streets involved were Mill Street, Bridgeton, on the south side of the city, where Ellis had been in a taxi shortly before the murder and Ardencraig Road on the other side of Glen Wood from the scene of the murder. Mill Street was almost four miles away from the scene of the murder and Ardencraig Road about a quarter of a mile.

Next witnesses were people at a party near the murder scene who told of phoning for a taxi, seeing Walkinshaw's and hearing the shots. Two witnesses told of seeing a man wearing a light suit running towards the wood carrying something white in his right hand which could have been a handkerchief. The defence made something of the light coloured suit since Ellis had been wearing a dark coloured one on the night of the murder but what the prosecution had failed to discover (possibly by not visiting the scene of the crime at night as Beltrami had done numerous times) was that the street lighting was of the orange sodium variety and liable to play tricks with light and shade.

What was agreed was that whoever ran for the wood knew the area because he made straight for a hidden stone bridge over a burn. It was also generally agreed that this man who vanished into the pitch darkness of the trees must have been the gunman.

It was also established that 10/4d was on Walkinshaw's meter when his body was found and that he radioed in and said he was dropping a fare at Tormusk Road shortly before he died there and that he was travelling from the south, the direction of Mill Street.

The most damning prosecution evidence came from another taxi driver who pointed to Ellis in the dock and said he was the man he had picked up in Ardencraig Road beside Glen Wood around 15 minutes after the murder, in other words the same time it would have taken the killer to run through the wood after the murder and turn up on the other side in time to hail another cab and get out of the area. Ellis had also been carrying a handkerchief in his right hand according to this taxi driver. The trip was only three quarters of a mile to where Elis's parents stayed and the fare was only two shillings, despite which the passenger gave the driver five.

The defence could do little with this witness. He had picked out Ellis at an identification parade and was unshakeable in his conviction that he had been the passenger. He even mentioned the dark suit. All the defence could establish was that the passenger seemed composed and reasonably talkative with nothing at all to indicate he had just ran through a lengthy wood in pitch darkness after a murder. In private the defence could not resolve this impasse with their client. He simply denied knowing anything about it and said the driver must be mistaken.

Things were not looking too good for Ellis at this stage but at least the next witness, a fingerprint expert, said he had found no prints of any value in Walkinshaw's taxi.

Police witnesses next told how they had saturated the area and among the people interviewed was Ellis who lied that he had spent Saturday night and Sunday morning at his parents house. In fact, he had been at a party in Mill Street until around 1.15 a.m., when he left in a taxi. There were plenty of witnesses who came forward to verify this, except one — the taxi driver who had picked him up. Despite newspaper appeals and personal written appeals to Glasgow's 1,280 registered taxi drivers not one came forward to say he had picked up Ellis outside the party in Mill Street. The inference was obvious.

When Ellis was arrested he insisted he had been indoors with his parents at all the relevant times. Next, detectives told of a visit they made to a flat Ellis recently bought on the south side. In a matchbox there they found eleven live cartridges but no gun.

However, returns in taxis from Mill Street to the scene of the crime threw up discrepancies. If Ellis had got into Walkinshaw's taxi at 1.15 a.m., from the party it would only have taken him ten minutes to get to the scene of the murder which took place around 1.45 a.m., and the fare would only have been 8/- and not 10/4d. But only the dead man could tell the times and places he had travelled through before his death.

What the police did discover by jogging through Glen Wood was that the man picked up in Ardencraig Road could have been the killer. What they failed to do was make plaster casts of prints in the wood immediately after the shooting and possibly crucial evidence was washed away with overnight rain.

Other witnesses told how when he got the taxi from the party in Mill Street Ellis had said he was going to his parents house in Castlemilk. The prosecution case was that after committing the murder Ellis had ran through the wood, picked up another taxi and made the short trip to his parents, and yes, neighbours of the Ellises had heard someone enter the close at the time in question but, no, they had no idea who it was.

Witnesses at the party said Ellis had been drinking heavily and when he left he had been carrying a small brown parcel and seemed very solicitous over it.

Police forensic evidence showed that green and clear glass fragments found in one of Ellis's shoes could have come from the scene of the crime where glass from the shattered windscreen and a broken beer bottle lay on the pavement.

Lengthy, often boring and technical questioning from Fairbairn on this point managed to take much of the sting out of this part of the prosecution's case. He established that the glass involved, both at the murder scene and on Ellis's shoe, was so common as to make a similarity almost meaningless. There was nothing definite to clinch the fact that the glass came from the two same sources, the windscreen and the bottle. Equally, the prosecution argued, there was nothing to say they did NOT come from the same two sources.

Another plus of sorts for the defence was the establishment that the bullets in Ellis's possession were not of the same kind which killed Walkinshaw. What could not be denied was that Ellis should never have had the bullets in the first place and the reason for their possession was never touched upon. Extensive searches by the police had also failed to uncover the whereabouts of the pocket pistol in the case which could have fired either type of bullet.

The Prosecution closed their case after three days of circumstantial but nevertheless powerful evidence.

The Defence began by calling a man who had been wrongly picked out at an identification parade, in which Ellis took part, by two witnesses who saw the runner to the wood. But they had only said the man was of the general build and appearance and anyway the man had been racing off with his back to them.

The Defence also established that the windscreen glass on the pavement could have fallen there after the killer had run off. A witness said he had also been drinking in a pub with Ellis shortly before his arrest and that the floor had showed remnants of recently dropped beer glasses.

When it came time for his summing up, Mr. Wylie put the Prosecutions's case forcibly. He pointed out to the jury, "My case consists of circumstantial evidence but such evidence is a perfectly valid way of establishing a criminal offence". The Prosecution maintained Ellis had got into Walkinshaw's taxi in Mill Street with the object of going to the Ellis household in Castlemilk, that Ellis had shot the driver then sprinted through Glen Wood to Ardencraig Road where the other driver drove him to his parents home. Mr. Wylie stressed the unshakeable identification made by the second driver and went on, "Is it not strange that Ellis should have required two taxis to take him home? My submission is that the reason he changed taxis is perfectly obvious — because he shot the driver who took him in the first place to Tormusk Road. We have a murderer running into a wood — and a quarter of an hour later you find the accused Ellis, standing at the opposite end of the wood looking for a taxi."

Mr. Wylie sat down after an hour and it was then the turn of the Defence. Beltrami, Fairbairn and Bennet had gone over this speech for hour upon hour as if they were preparing an oscar winning scenario and when Mr. Bennet stood up to deliver it the result was quite masterly. It had to be.

The first point made was that a guilty verdict would mean the accused swinging at the end of a rope. The onus of proof was on the Crown and they had to prove guilt "beyond reasonable doubt".

Mr Bennet stressed the lack of fingerprints, the lack of a weapon and the fact that the bullets in Ellis's possession did not match those which had killed Walkinshaw. He pointed out Ellis had not been picked out at an identity parade by the people who saw the man running into the wood, that Ellis had been drinking heavily that night and was in no state to run anywhere.

When it came to the evidence of the second taxi driver who had picked up the man in Ardencraig Road, Mr. Bennet said that if it had been Ellis he was wearing a dark coloured suit whereas one witness had said the man who had run into the wood was wearing a light coloured suit (ignoring the effect of the street lights which the Defence knew all about) and that the man, whoever he was, showed no indication whatsoever of having run through a thick wood in pitch darkness. And Mr. Bennet posed the question, "Would a killer attract attention to himself by hailing another taxi for a distance of only a few hundred yards and in the near vicinity of his crime?"

With regards to the glass particles, Mr. Bennet dismissed them thus, "There has been evidence, which is not in dispute that most clear glass is made by one firm — Pilkington's. That being so, little can be drawn from the fact that the clear glass found in the heel was of a similar density to the same type of glass found at the scene of the crime. Equally, the green beer-bottle glass was manufactured by the Scottish Central Glassworks of Alloa, who are the main suppliers to a number of breweries. These bottles are very common indeed, and the density of them cannot really vary to any marked extent."

The discrepancies in distances and fares between Mill Street and Castlemilk, between the reality of such a journey and the thesis as put forward by the Prosecution, were pointed out.

Mr. Bennet ended, "It is not sufficient for you to say that he might have done it. Before convicting you would require to be satisfied beyond reasonable doubt that he had done it."

Lord Patrick who now began his summing up was renowned for his impartiality and his address to the jury lived up to this reputation to an almost punctilious degree.

He told them, "The proof in the case, if there was proof, would depend wholly on circumstantial evidence. People sneer at that but these are uninformed people who do not understand that it is every bit as reliable as other evidence. Very often there are no eye-witnesses to a crime, and everything depends on circumstantial evidence."

Referring to the seriousness of the crime involved, he went on, "If the accused is found guilty he will be hanged by the neck. But that is not a concern of yours or mine." Some of the jury winced slightly at this. "You are here to hear the evidence and make up your minds on that."

Then he brought up one of the main arguments for the Defence, "It is important that you, the jury, should pay attention to the question of the burden of proof. You must be satisfied beyond reasonable doubt of the accused's guilt before you would be justified in bringing in a guilty verdict. It is not necessary to prove motivation. It is quite true, as both Crown and Defence have indicated, that the time factor is important. The theory of the Crown is that Ellis got in Walkinshaw's taxi in Mill Street and travelled to the scene of the crime where he shot Walkinshaw and then, in another street nearby, hired another taxi."

Referring to the fact that Ellis had lied to the police that he had been with his parents when he had been out at a party, Lord Patrick said, "Even if you hold that Ellis told lies to the police, that does not prove that he was there at the scene of the crime and committed it. There could be a number of reasons for Ellis's lying to the police unconnected with involvement in this crime.

"In this country suspicion will not do, proof on a balance of probabilities will not do — the Crown must prove matters beyond all reasonable doubt."

Remarking on the evidence of the glass found on Ellis's shoes, he pointed out that the Crown's point was the remarkable coincidence of the two types of glass being there — both clear and green — as there was alleged to have been beside Walkinshaw's taxi.

Finally Lord Patrick instructed the jury on the three verdicts they could return — guilty, not guilty and not proven. Those who had been actively campaigning for the abolition of capital punishment and who had shown an interest in this case wondered later if, at this stage, the punishment in prospect had been life imprisonment instead of hanging there might not have been a completely different attitude on the part of the jury.

When the jury retired it was generally thought that following a four day, complicated trial they would be out for some time. To everyone's surprise the jury bell rang after only half an hour. Ellis rose and in the total silence the foreman of the jury gave their verdict "Not proven — unanimously!"

Ellis, grinning with relief, shook the hands of his counsel as well he might while taxi drivers in the public gallery, who had organised an appeal fund for their dead colleague's widow, muttered about the deficiencies in the jury system.

The crowd of around three hundred gathered around the court steps were then treated to the unappetising spectacle of the city's press literally fighting to get their hands on Ellis for his exclusive story. A mass of tumbling fighting bodies fell down the court steps as blows were freely exchanged. One large photographer, before charging into the mêlée, took out his false teeth and placed them in his hip pocket for safety. He was promptly kicked in the behind and they were broken, much to his pain and anger. Ellis was eventually bundled by one daily newspaperman into what he thought was his paper's car. It in fact belonged to the opposition and sped off with Ellis in the back seat, leaving the reporter stranded and panic stricken. Beltrami was there on the court steps to start a lifelong love affair with the press and a less amicable one with the police who converged on the scene to restore order. Editors were later summoned before the Chief Constable to give a guarantee that such unseemly behaviour would not be repeated.

Ellis, smoking a cigar and jubilantly celebrating, was pictured on the front page of one newspaper. He had sold his story for a hundred pounds and was quoted as saying, "I think John Walkinshaw was shot by a roving madman lurking in the Castlemilk woods — by a man who may strike again. I had nothing at all to do with this ghastly, pointless murder."

It was to be the high point of Ellis's criminal career. Always keen on armed robbery, boastful that he had cheated the gallows and could flaunt the law, he eventually was too casual and was cornered trying to hold up a bank in Pollokshaws in 1966.

Sentencing him to a punitive 21 years for attempted murder and armed robbery, the judge said that while he was at large the lives of innocent members of the public were at risk.

At first, Ellis served his time quietly, saying to his cellmates that he wanted full remission so that when he got out he could shoot as many policemen as soon as possible. Then he started smuggling out letters to the press complaining that he, a model prisoner, was being treated harshly while others who had caused trouble inside had been moved to a life of comparative luxury in Barlinnie's Special Unit. He also complained to everybody who would listen that he had not been given any form of training or help to face the outside world on his release and that he feared drifting back to his old criminal ways and ending up back in prison.

His fears proved prophetic because a few months after his release (after serving 14 years) he made a bungled attempt at holding up a licensed grocer's shop, using a toy replica gun. Unfortunately for him the two shopkeepers behind the counter, 21-year-old Jack Mohammed and his 19-year-old brother Teddy, were karate enthusiasts willing to "have a go". Ellis, who was masked, shouted, "Okay sambo — hold them up!"

At first, the surprised brothers thought it was a sick joke then Ellis fired a blank and pistol whipped Jack. Teddy promptly grabbed a cheese knife, closed his eyes and ran at the robber. After a struggle and a 100-yard sprint along the street, Ellis was ignominiously disarmed and incapacitated by a few well chosen blows. The fact that he was drunk helped the brothers.

His appearance in court was pathetic and his snivelling, grovelling plea in mitigation, which he performed himself this time, was quite a come-down for the once arrogant gangster. In tears he said he had been "tossed out" of prison with no attempt having been made to rehabilitate him. He had no job, had been staying at a hostel and he told the Sherrif, "I was besotted by drink and, as often happens on these occasions, I had every intention of going straight but was tempted by the devil." He was sentenced to three years imprisonment. It was a long way from champagne and cigars.

CHAPTER 13

The Phoenix

In the sixties the Press correctly labelled James 'Babyface' Boyle as Scotland's most dangerous criminal and Glasgow's worst gangster following the eclipse of Walter Scott Ellis. But there was more to Boyle than that grim accolade. Not only was he unique in being acquitted on two separate murder charges before being 'sent down' on a third, but from sculpting human flesh with his bayonet he took to sculpting clay, having his exhibits displayed at the Edinburgh Festival, and from being the ringleader of one of the country's worst prison riots he ended up being at the centre of a controversy over a Special Unit which it is now recognised leads the field in prison reform.

His remarkable career in crime began in the Gorbals where he was born in a tenement slum in the spring of 1944, the third of a family of four. His father was a streetfighter and member of the notorious Bee Hive Gang (see Chapter 6) and although he died, partly because of wounds sustained over the years, when Boyle was young he was still talked about admiringly by local hoodlums long after his untimely demise and there was thus a violent reputation for young Boyle to live up to.

In the slum district's sub-culture men who were handy with their fists, as well as being rebels and outlaws generally, were admired. Many of the poverty stricken families who had to share in many cases single-ends (one roomed flats) or rooms and kitchens with their usually numerous children owed little or no allegiance to the Establishment or its representatives whether it be the rent collector, the clerk who handed out the dole money, the gaffer if you were employed, the education authorities or the police. And men who made their drab lives more adventurous or gave the 'V' sign to the authorities were often openly talked of as if they were local heroes. Brawlers and villains like Boyle's father or the venerated Dan Cronin, whose funeral was attended by more mourners than any Lord Provost's, were princes in their own society, people apart to be copied and Boyle, who felt himself to be a cut above the rest of his pals because of his bloodstock, saw nothing to stop him emulating his father's deeds and there were many who actively encouraged him.

Allied to their fighting abilities (and who is to say there is that much difference between a legal boxing match and an illegal bout in a back green), these toughs often had sidelines in crime and frequently had goods which had "fallen off a lorry". Again many people, including respectable money conscious mothers, saw nothing wrong in paying cheaper rates for stolen property which they could not afford on the open market. They asked no questions and answered none. Even Boyle's mother (although "straight" she had a weak, susceptible character) indulged in this practice and thought nothing of it. So for the youngster the twin threads of violence and crime took on a veneer of glamour and even necessity and certainly he saw nothing intrinsically wrong in taking the low road.

Street gangs were an intrinsic part of slumland sub-culture and it was inevitable that Boyle would drift into one, in his case the 'Wild Young Cumbie' from Cumberland Street of which he became natural leader, and he excelled in pitched battles, at this stage mostly with fists, with neighbouring gangs. The admiration more timid urchins had for him increased with this and he had not even reached puberty.

His first defiant criminal acts were nothing more than surreptitiously stealing sweets and cakes from shop counters but from there he graduated to breaking into empty shops at night. Again his schoolmates thought these were great acts of derring-do.

When he was 13 he had his first confrontation with the law. He had gone on a spree of breaking into chewing gum machines with three of his mates but one of them was caught, broke down and told all. To Boyle's mother's naïve amazement the family received a midnight visit from the constabulary and he was taken off, bubbling vociferously, to spend the night in a Young Offenders Institution. Here for the first time he was made to strip and put on uniform garb, had his fingerprints and photograph taken and his name was entered on police files, a document which was to grow to the size of a book over the years.

At the Central Police Court he appeared in the dock for the first time and was given two years probation after he swore that there would be no more trouble, sir.

Shortly after this he made a half hearted attempt to escape the Gorbals but only got as far as Edinburgh where he was found by a night secruity guard sleeping in a goods wagon. He then concentrated on shoplifting and stealing crates from brewers' lorries and he found no difficulty in getting rid of the goods. Quite the opposite. The demand was greater than the supply. But the police met up with him again when he was caught breaking into a hut to steal show pigeons and he was given two weeks detention.

On his release the routine began again: gang fights, breaking into shops and warehouses, caught, twenty eight days.

The violence always inherent in Boyle's nature now took a more serious turn and for the first time he started carrying a bayonet. In numerous gang fights on waste ground in the area he wielded this weapon indiscriminately, inflicting horrific injuries on his opponents while being spry enough to avoid serious injury himself. Most of his pals, and enemies, were likewise violent but even then he stood out for his reckless abandon in battle, what a Lord Advocate would later describe as "almost unimaginable ferocity", which was to mark him out as the most vicious of his violent fellows. The fact that his reputation among older criminals grew with every victory increased his bravado. In his own terms he was fast becoming the Young Pretender to the underworld's throne.

His thieving continued apace and it was while fleeing from the Kelvin Hall Carnival with a cash box that he was once more arrested. After serving a few months in an approved school he was allowed home. These periods of incarceration, after the initial shock had receded, did nothing to cure his criminality. Again the opposite happened: in these closed societies with the common enemy he was looked up to as a bit of a king-pin by those who felt rejected, downtrodden and forgotten. With his jaunty air it was easy for him to be superior even in these nether depths.

Once more he ran off, this time to the beckoning glories of London, was caught in a smash and grab raid and returned to approved school. After being released on probation he returned south once more and ran around with a mob of exiled Scottish hoodlums round the Kings Cross area, excelling himself to impress them in daring acts of robbery. He took to drinking heavily to emphasise his manhood, indulged in lengthy bouts of sex with prostitutes and dabbled in drugs. The streak of nihilism which scarred his life came to the fore at this time. His days were aimless, tomorrow held no meaning, relationships were empty unless based on bloody boasts and he did not give a damn about anything, especially life.

On his returns to the Gorbals he would bask in the reflected glories of his caperings in the Smoke and it was during one of these visits home that he was arrested for shopbreaking. This time it was Borstal for fourteen months. He was coming up in the world.

He found himself quite at home in this spartan world with its atmosphere of repressed violence — for many of his old chums were there. His sojourn did nothing to change his outlook on life except make him more depressive. It did help his criminal career, however, because on his and others' release he used the network of contacts he had built up to set himself up as a resetter of stolen goods. He also started a modest protection racket among pubs on the south side and took to carrying a Walther pistol in his waistband as well as his favourite bayonet rolled up in a copy of the *Glasgow Herald.* Borstal had taught him quite a lot.

However, his was not the only racket on the go and one night in Crown Street there was a full scale pitched battle with a rival gang in which he took his customary, expected leading part and the Royal Infirmary was kept busy treating the wounded casualties.

The Glasgow scene was now getting a bit too hot for Boyle so he retreated once more to London where he soon ended up in Wormwood Scrubs serving a six week sentence for police assault. Detectives met him at the gates on his release and he was taken to Glasgow High Court and found guilty of two charges of serious assault. This time it was Barlinnie Prison for two years. Even if he was only eighteen, he had come of age.

While inside he punched a prison officer who had insulted him and was put in solitary confinement for a fortnight which raised him in the esteem of many of the older lags. Barlinnie being the clearing ground for Glasgow's toughest criminals (see Chapter 10), whether they be *en route* to or from Peterhead or down for family visits, Boyle loved mixing and talking with these hard men and hearing tales of their prowess and vowed that when he got out he would make it big in crime. Reform never entered his head and as for the 'screws' they were merely objects of his hatred. He was one of the 94% of inmates who would never make it in the 'straight' world.

Physically at this time, Boyle was a stocky, well-built, cocky young man. He was good-looking with thick, black curly hair, a strong nose and jaw and features which could change instantly from jaunty, charming friendliness to cold ferocity.

He still had a reputation to live up to, so when the time came to step outside the prison gates some of his criminal cronies were there to greet him and let him know what was going on. Boyle was a willing listener and only too eager to join the newest criminal outfit — the Tallymen, whose leader was a Gorbals villain named Frank 'Tarzan' Wilson — as their chief heavy.

Their racket was simple. They loaned money, no questions asked or collateral needed, to whoever wanted it, repayable within an agreed time — at twenty five per cent interest. If the repayment was not forthcoming in time the interest went up ten per cent. If the borrower did not respond, Boyle was sent in and made sure, if the money could not be paid, that others were shown an example of what would happen if they did not play the game. Sometimes it was alcohol that customers needed, especially on Sundays when the pubs were shut, and the Tallymen kept their own stock. They were given their nickname because they went about with books in which the name and customer's tally was kept. Their favourite hunting grounds were the pubs and the thickset, smiling moneylenders with their wads of notes found the impoverished inebriated easy meat.

Boyle was the perfect strongarm man for the gang, even if he went about his task too enthusiastically at times. Only he knows how many customers he beat up, brutalised and terrorised at this time and, naturally enough, he is not saying. The majority of his victims were too scared to implicate him and many never even went to a doctor for fear of getting further involved. It has been estimated that Boyle's own league table of assaults was between eighty and a hundred, which gives an idea of the scale of the enterprise, and there was a rumour at one time, never properly substantiated, that he had crucified a customer to the floor of his home. Be that as it may, for every victim there were a dozen more ready to repay their debts even if it took months of handing over money to achieve this. Although the police knew what was going on they were frustrated at the impossibility of mustering enough jittery witnesses to make a case stand up in court.

In his spare time Boyle was also involved as a bouncer at shebeens and brothels throughout the south side where he freely partook of the available products. He was now approaching that peak of popularity he had always dreamt of in his murky imagination.

In December 1964 all that was threatened when he was arrested for the murder of a man named Lynch who had been a customer of the Tallymen. He was also charged with robbing Lynch and slashing a second man. But the usual frustrating problems of finding witnesses and corroborative evidence faced the police and at the High Court trial in March 1965 the charges were withdrawn and Boyle, beaming all over, marched down the court steps where he was mobbed by his cronies and the Press. He accepted an invitation into the *Daily Express* car but when the photographer later went into a phone box to phone his office Boyle followed him and presented a knife, slipped to him by a crony, at the photographer's throat threatening that if he was not promised "a lot of dough" for his story the photographer would be cut there and then. When told nothing would be forthcoming Boyle grudgingly let him go.

His reputation as the man who could freely commit murder, his place of honour in the underworld, had now been achieved. He was feted in Gorbals pubs by all the villains of the day, held in awe by the weak, spoken respectfully to by the cautious, the darling of the girls, the king of the hoodlums. For a while life was one big party, it was drinks on the house all the time and the police were furious at his effrontery.

But he still could not keep out of trouble and only ten days after his release he was involved in a fight with two other hoodlums who had mistakenly decided to take this big-head on and at the same time make a name for themselves. Defending himself with a broken bottle, Boyle gouged one of their eyes out and almost severed the hand of the other.

While on the run from this he attended a party in a city centre tenement which ended in a free-for-all with knives, bottles and glasses being used as weapons, the end result being two brothers stabbed, one fatally, and a series of multiple injuries. Boyle was arrested when he carelessly and drunkenly returned to his mother's house and he was charged with murder and three serious assaults.

But again witnesses were not forthcoming. The lights had gone out. Everyone was fighting each other. No-one could be certain about anything. The Procurator Fiscal announced that the murder charge against Boyle would be held "in abeyance" for the moment, the first time this had ever happened in a murder trial.

Just in case any of the witnesses had ideas about getting their memories back, one of their houses was blown up by a gelignite bomb while she was out shopping.

At the trial in October 1965 the murder charge was withdrawn but Boyle pled guilty to a reduced charge of pushing and jostling and was given a mere three months. This was tantamount to a second escape from life imprisonment and the villains talked admiringly about the lad's lucky star even more.

On his release he returned to the Tallymen and found business was booming as ever. Not all the profits were squandered, much of it being used to subsidise ancillary crime projects. The gang were now so confident of immunity that they took to carrying around guns and there were several shooting incidents with rivals who wanted to chisel in on the bonanza.

The Kray Twins were busy building up their crime empire in Soho and Ronnie, through a contact named Big Pat Connolly, made several visits to Glasgow to hire hit men to do flying jobs for them. His favourite was Boyle although sometimes even Ronnie, always wanting a front of respectability and sophistication, became a trifle alarmed at some of the wild Scotsman's methods.

When the Kray's rival gang leaders in Soho, the Richardson brothers, were shot in the kneecaps, Scotland Yard were tipped off that it was two top Scots boys who had flown down on contract to do the job, returning home the same day. But no names were forthcoming. The 'Scots boys' also developed a penchant for crossbows which they would use on whoever opened the door of the intended victim, whether it was the right man or not. And they were linked with the disappearance of Mad Axeman Frank Mitchell whom the Krays 'sprung' from Dartmoor as a vainglorious prank before getting rid of him when he became an embarrassment.

Boyle did not just visit the Krays on business. He often went south on holiday or when he felt the Glasgow C.I.D. were annoying him too much and getting on his nerves.

He was now confident of his abilities, sure that he had the scene under control by use of his bayonet, with the top mob in command and the customers keeping the cash flowing. But his life was one of danger and mayhem and although he was riding high he must have known deep in his pessimistic soul that it could not last. Nothing ever had lasted.

His downfall came in the spring of 1967. He and another villain called William Wilson, 'Tarzan's' brother, on a wet, blustery night visited the Kinning Park flat of a pimp known as 'Babs' Rooney who owed the Tallymen money. A drunken argument arose over nonpayment and Rooney was fatally stabbed in the chest. The pair ran off but when word spread that the police had found his fingerprints on a beer can in the kitchen of Rooney's house Boyle fled south to the Smoke where his old pals the Krays hid him in a 'safe' house. But after a couple of months he made the arrogant mistake of summoning three of his Gorbals henchmen for a conference in a London pub. They were followed by C.I.D. men determined he would not get away this time. A large furniture van drew up outside the pub and suddenly the place was swarming with armed police and, manacled and furious, Boyle was escorted back to Glasgow.

However, he was not too despondent, confident that his pals on the outside would help rig the evidence, get at witnesses and get him off the hook as they had in the past. He was further heartened when he was told, as had happened before, that a gelignite bomb had exploded outside the house of a witness who had seen him in the vicinity of 'Babs' Rooney's flat at the time of the murder.

He went for trial at Glasgow High Court before Lord Cameron and security was strict with armed police in the building and others with walkie-talkie sets on surrounding rooftops.

Gradually, the evidence mounted — the bloodstained murder weapon found under the linoleum of his house, brave witnesses who testified that they had seen him flee the scene. But key witness Mrs. Sadie Cairney, who was 'Babs' Rooney's blonde girlfriend, and had been in his house at the time of his murder, swore on oath that it had been a stranger and not the accused who had killed her lover. Boyle smiled but at this crucial stage there was an adjournment during which, under police pressure, Sadie broke down in the cells under the court and admitted she had been intimidated and had lied.

After the recess, the Crown Prosecutor asked for Sadie, who had technically finished her evidence, to be allowed to go back into the box: but Lord Cameron turned this down, However, the jury could see Sadie sitting crying between two policewomen in the public benches and it was obvious to all and sundry what was afoot.

The Prosecutor made an eloquent speech and the jury retired for two hours. Boyle was finally doomed — Guilty, unanimously. Lord Cameron then described him as a menace to society and sentenced him to life imprisonment with a recommendation that he serve not less than fifteen years. All the top brass of Glasgow police were there in the public benches and shook hands with each other.

The intimidation machine which Boyle's gang had successfully used for years had finally failed. At its most sophisticated it had worked through the gang's own crooked lawyer, James Maxwell Latta, a respectable but ambitious middle-aged father of three whose twin hobbies were collecting antique pistols and mixing with unsavoury underworld types. It was this slumming which was his undoing because he found it easier to bribe and threaten witnesses than live up to his professional code of conduct and he loved the kudos attached to getting guilty men off, being prepared to stake his livelihood and freedom for the glories of appearing to be Glasgow's Clarence Darrow. His 'interview room' was often a bar in the Gorbals, the 'Hi-Hi', where, along with sundry colourful characters like Boyle, 'Tarzan' Wilson and 'Bandit' Rooney, evidence was concocted and he was also handed *ex gratia* payments to be the crooks' lawyer in court.

Following Boyle's murder of 'Babs' Rooney and subsequent conviction, Latta was jailed for eight years for trying to induce Sadie to say it had been one of two unknown men in light raincoats who had come to her home in Kinning Park and killed Rooney and not Boyle.

Lord Grant, passing sentence, told Latta, "There is no doubt that the administration of justice in Glasgow has been suffering over recent years because witnesses — whether persuaded or intimidated — have failed to give truthful evidence. It has been a crying scandal.

"Furthermore, the tracking down and conviction of the perpetrators, the instigators, is a difficult and, in many cases, impossible task."

Lord Grant then told the city's senior magistrate who was in court to hear sentence being passed, "I believe we have been bedevilled in Glasgow in past years, time and again, by acquittals which have resulted in guilty men going free because witnesses have been tampered with, intimidated, and false evidence given.

"That, I believe, is the experience of every judge who has sat here in recent years and, probably, though I cannot speak with first hand knowledge, of most counsel."

It was a frank admission of the power of the Tallymen but now their reign of terror was over. With the threat of Boyle lifted, other ringleaders and their cohorts were rounded up and jailed on various charges ranging from intimidation and extortion to serious assault and attempting to pervert the course of justice. 'Tarzan', the brain behind the whole operation, was given twelve years.

Although now inside for life, Boyle's hatred had by no means run its course. He gave the Governor in Barlinnie an uppercut which sent him flying off his seat and broke his cheekbone, an offence for which he was given a severe beating and a further eighteen months. His preliminary hearing in front of a Sheriff on this charge was unique in that it took place in cells under the court and he was surrounded by armed police. (It was also like a military operation when he was allowed to attend his mother's funeral in the Gorbals several months later with van loads of armed police surrounding the cemetery.)

On arriving at Peterhead Prison he assaulted two prison officers, biting one of them and punching the other, for which he received four years. At Porterfield Prison in Inverness (nicknamed Siberia among prisoners) he and others were involved in a scrap with prison officers during which there was much punching and kicking for which he received a month in solitary confinement.

This violent catalogue of numerous assaults on prison officers, and occasionally prisoners, continued for five bloodstained years and for most of that time Boyle was confined to solitary and received a dozen hammerings from the 'batter squads' in Peterhead, Barlinnie and Porterfield. None of them wanted him, none of them could contain or repress him, he was labelled as uncontrollable and the lengthier his barbaric record became the less he seemed to care. He only wanted to inflict pain and suffering, to hit back, to take as many 'screws' with him as possible.

The first solution the prison authorities came up with only made the situation worse and led to tragedy. They reasoned, in a narrow, blinkered way, that if Boyle insisted on acting like an animal then they would treat him like one. They penned him in a specially constructed block at Porterfield Prison which became notorious as 'The Cages'. These were six cells and within each was a small cage.

Boyle, stark naked, was kept in one of these cages which was hardly big enough for a large dog to turn around in. There was a two inch gap which opened at feeding time and food was shoved through as if to a creature in a zoo. There were no toilet facilities whatsoever, no furniture, nothing. Opaque glass and heavy wire mesh deliberately made it impossible to tell if it was day or night. A dim light burned all the time. 'The Cages' were designed to degrade and dehumanise and they succeeded.

For two hours a week the prisoners were allowed into a small recreation room. The place was a time bomb and for someone like Boyle a spark was all that was needed.

There are two versions of the riot which took place on the evening of December 28th 1972 in the recreation room. The prison officers' official version claimed that it was a pure and simple attempt to escape and that they were attacked by the prisoners without warning and had to fight for their lives.

The prisoners version is that they had sat down and linked arms in a peaceful protest against 'The Cages' when they were suddenly set upon by the prison officers and had to defend themselves.

Either way the room erupted into a mini battlefield with batons splintering, knives flashing and blood gushing as four prisoners and six prison officers desperately fought each other. It was claimed the prisoners had in their possession a rope of sheets, three knives, a weighted sock and a radio which it was presumed would be used to monitor news of their escape once they got over the wall. How they were supposed to have acquired these implements was a mystery which neither side could or would clear up.

Boyle, of course, was named as the self-appointed ringleader and the others were Howard Wilson, serving life (see next Chapter), Larry Winters, serving life, and William McPherson, serving 25 years (see Chapter 18). Boyle, according to the staff, kept screaming, "Kill, kill, kill!" and stabbed one prison officer, who was a former professional boxer, fifteen times before he was overpowered and beaten unconscious. Another prison officer lost an eye in the mêlée and another one, who was stabbed three times, had to struggle through a rain of blows before he could press the alarm bell. He said later that he had been flattened by a chair then saw Winters advancing towards him "in slow motion with a smile on his face", before the door burst open and help arrived.

Boyle almost lost his life over this riot following the sustained and systematic beating he received once he had been hauled back to his cage. A doctor who later examined him said he was surprised he had lasted the night. He was like a carcass of raw meat.

At the trial held at Inverness High Court, again with massive security precautions, the four prisoners were found not guilty of attempting to murder the six prison officers but all were found guilty of assaulting five officers and attempting to escape. They were all sentenced to an additional six years.

Before the sentence was passed Boyle asked if he could address the judge, Lord Wheatley, on his own behalf. This was refused but through his counsel he was allowed to say that he considered he had been brutally treated and severely injured but that he felt it had all been worthwhile as it had brought their grievances to light.

Twelve of the 55 prison officers at Porterfield resigned after the riot, including some of those involved.

The prison authorities now decided to try a new tack with Boyle. Word filtered through that he was to be transferred to a new Special Unit that was to be opened up at Barlinnie. At this stage only the Home and Health Department knew what this Unit was to do and Boyle was very alarmed since there were rumours that it was to be a cross between a prison and a psychiatric ward and he feared he was going to be drugged or lobotomised into subjection. It had been nicknamed the 'Nutcracker Suite'.

But after he had got over the first shock of not being assaulted, of being able to walk around and do the toilet without being supervised, of being able to wear his own clothes, of being addressed as 'Jimmy' by the friendly prison officers, he became the Unit's star inmate. He was now being treated as a human being and from being a cornered animal he was transformed into a creative personality.

The Unit is based on the principle of self reliance, of giving the prisoners what Boyle describes as "a sense of freedom" within the confines of four walls. Weekly meetings are held at which the inmates put forward suggestions to improve conditions. They are allowed to criticise the staff and if any of the inmates step out of line he is put in the 'hot seat' and asked to justify his actions or apologise. The inmates do their own cooking and eat round a table. They are allowed to study educational courses, have a television and transistors and are allowed regular visits from their friends and relatives. Books and writing material are freely available.

Prison officers throughout Scotland heaved a sigh of relief that at long last Boyle was out of the system and since his move to the Unit there has not been any serious trouble in Scottish prisons. At the same time the Unit can be said to have proved itself an outstanding success since Boyle has not been in any trouble since his removal there. The Prison Officers' Association have gone on record as giving the Unit their hearty approval.

Thanks to the visit of an art teacher Boyle, who had also been taking a correspondence course in psychology, found he had a talent for sculpting clay and some of his work, with clenched fists and chains a recurrent theme, went on display in an Edinburgh gallery. Boyle was allowed out for the day under supervision to attend this exhibition, an occasion which almost reduced him to tears.

In addition, he collaborated with playwright Tom McGrath in writing a drama about his experiences in prison, particularly in 'The Cages', which was titled *The Hard Man* and which was performed throughout Britain.

Boyle also wrote his memoirs, aptly titled *A Sense of Freedom,* which deal at great detailed length with prison brutality while being an apologia for his own atrocious crimes. So much of his long criminal career is glossed over or whitewashed that this part of the book is worse than worthless: it is downright misleading. Nevertheless, considering the nature of the author it is a remarkable achievement.

It was later made into an extremely violent film for television which seemed to give the impression that daily riots and beatings were on the prison rota just like slopping out and meal times. The character of Boyle was heavily romanticised and the scenario managed to keep his crimes at a distance or off-screen altogether while gloating on every injury inflicted on him by the Gestapo-like prison officers.

In September 1977 the future of the Unit was threatened with the death of inmate Larry Winters. He was found dead in his cell, his naked corpse sitting on a chamber pot, and a post mortem revealed he had died of an overdose of tranquillisers. His relatives later claimed it was easy to get drugs, drink and sex in the Unit and said women were free to visit the prisoners in their cells. No solid evidence was found to support these allegations but, nevertheless, as a result of Winters' death security was severely tightened up and there were changes in staff.

Amidst the hysteria it was forgotten that Winters' death was particularly poignant because he had shown the makings of being a writer and poet as well as being expert on the guitar. He died at the age of 34, having been in prison for 13 years, two of them in solitary confinement. A toughened character in the Boyle mould, he had been one of the first 'lifers' after the abolition of capital punishment. Since he had held up and shot a barman he would almost certainly have been 'topped' in the old days. After his death, scraps of manuscripts were collected from the Special Unit and published under the title *The Silent Scream.* One example will give a taste of his bitter, garish style.

ELECTRIC DREAMS

the dream goes on
through winding sandstone streets
where bewildered ancient gas-lamps & cracked paves
look on as the electric drunk & his favourite sword
baffle the Bluesteel guards & the red-eyed Boar
the dream goes on
in derelict tenements the Python coils
& wild wolves howl through the crystal film
& shadows mask the mouldering walls
the dream goes on
& the dream goes on . . .
tiers
of tears &
lobotomised heads
empty smiles
& bluefaced guards with tranquil guns
ah the dream goes on

with E.C.T. &
brainbursting drugs &
faceless men in soothing suits
sit silent sit silent silent
& the dream goes on
of plastic plates &
rubber knives & hollow heads hanging
ah weary the watchful walls
weary and wistful the wings void
of woe the warder whistles
& the dream goes on . . .

Prison officials from abroad have visited Barlinnie's Special Unit and have gone away impressed. It seems to have solved that nightmare for prison officers which arose with the abolition of capital punishment — the recalcitrant prisoner who knows he is as good as dead and does not give a damn what trouble he causes.

A lot of good may come at the end of the day from Boyle's irrepressible rebelliousness, against all the odds and expectations. The fact that the Scottish prison service has admitted that once money becomes available a lot more similar units will open in other prisons is testimony to the Unit's success.

Boyle, always one with a romantic bent and a flair for making headlines, was apparently determined that all should end happily ever after when he married a psychiatrist and prison visitor, Dr. Sarah Trevelyan, the attractive brunette daughter of the former broad-minded British Film Censor.

Despite pleas that he had undergone a spiritual change and was ready to be released, the authorities were determined he should serve his full sentence as Lord Cameron had ordered. Perhaps one day after he is released he will write another volume of his memoirs. But it is highly unlikely that he will ever allow the full story to be made public.

CHAPTER 14

On The Make

There is nothing more pathetic than the downfall of a bright and good young man whose ambition if properly tethered would have made him a success but who goes sadly awry and brings disaster — not only to himself but also to innocent people around him. This was the case with Howard Wilson, at one time a bright spark in the Glasgow Police whose desperate expectations ended in a bloodbath. Starting off as someone who always wanted to be different, above the rest, he ended up a total outcast, banished by his fellows on both sides of the law and left to revolve the rest of his days round the black void that used to be his life.

Impatience allied to ambition proved his fatal flaw. Many policemen become disillusioned with their job, the strict regimentation, the uniformity, the necessity of always having to obey, the long hours for indifferent pay, having to mingle with the garbage of society while having to suffer abuse and physical violence, while at home wives wait and worry. It is a vocation. It requires dedication. It needs restraint.

Of those who fall by the wayside some simply leave for employment elsewhere. But others become tainted with the corruption they daily deal with and the open sore of cynicism poisons their outlook on life. With Wilson, the bitterness was deeper than most and when he turned his back on the law he not only ended up hitting back at society which he thought had cornered him but he hit back with a vengeance at the symbols of that establishment which he felt had rejected him.

Wilson, the son of a newsagent, came of a respectable family with no criminal history. He was educated at Glasgow Academy and in December 1958 he joined Glasgow Police. He had always wanted to be in the force and nurtured dreams of being a top crimebuster like Sir Percy Sillitoe and with his keen intelligence, athletic body and driving enthusiasm, prospects seemed exceedingly good. But his was the sort of snap-to-attention, eager-to-please approach which can backfire if it comes up against a slow, orthodox method of career advancement. In other areas, kudos and promotion can be won quickly by spectacular successes but with the police, who naturally put great store by years of experience in their higher echelons, the process takes time and as Wilson saw some of his non-police chums driving about in sporty cars and natty suits he became gradually dissatisfied with the routine paperwork and petty offences that were his lot. It seemed that the day he would be cracking those big cases and getting in the headlines receded with every plodding step he took forward. He began to think his superiors were thick and narrow minded in not recognising his undoubted capabilities. Although only in his twenties, he became restless and realised that if he had to change course it would have to be soon or he would be stuck in the force, possibly doomed to be always in uniform for the rest of his working life. Gradually his talk in the locker room became more critical and he began to drift apart from his more patient colleagues.

Meanwhile during his fourth year in the force he married an attractive girl, Julia, and the couple soon had two baby boys. This intensified the wish to improve his lot, now not only for himself but also for his family.

After several years on the beat — during which time he had to wait in ambush for killer James Boyle in the latter's house while he was on the run — Wilson thought things were at last looking up when he was given a job with promotion potential as a turnkey at the Central Police Office.

In his spare time he retained his school interest in rugby and played in the police team as prop forward. A team photograph of him at this time shows a grinning, broadfaced, seemingly happy man with a high intelligent forehead and receding thinning hair. There is nothing to suggest anything sinister. He looks just one of the boys.

He was also gregarious on social occasions and known as an ebullient cracker of jokes and a telling impersonator. He became a member of Bearsden Shooting Club and shared his interest in guns with fellow policeman John Sim (who also shared the same shifts at the Central) and prison officer Ian Donaldson. It was to prove a doomed friendship for the trio.

The Glasgow which Wilson patrolled in the sixties was a restless, changing environment which seemed full of new opportunities. The old tenements were being cleared away and new high-rise flats were taking their place. The city's population was declining. It had lost its right to be called the second city of the Empire, Birmingham's population of 1,112,000 beating it by 22,000. But where there used to be 500 people to the acre in Glasgow there was now new space in which to breathe and feel free. In addition, there was a fresh spirit about, there was new affluence, there was upward social mobility in careers, old taboos were being demolished along with decrepit buildings and it was said the bad days were gone forever. Heavy industry was declining but there was still plenty of work around in other areas and there were plenty of ambitious people 'swinging' with the times as in the rest of Britain.

But for Howard Wilson 1967 brought the sour taste of defeat. He was put back on the beat for no apparent reason. For a man who, throughout his nine years of service, had three times been commended by his Chief Constable for zeal and initiative it was the last straw. After a discussion with his wife, he resigned. It came as no surprise to his colleagues.

Fancying himself now as a small-time business entrepreneur who would build up a thriving chain of shops, he opened a greengrocers business near his home in Allison Street. Although now out of the force, Wilson frequently met his ex-colleagues because his ground floor flat in a gray tenement block was opposite Glasgow's Southern Police Station.

His former colleague John Sim had also become disillusioned with police work, for similar reasons to Wilson's, and had opened a garage service and Ian Donaldson, their friend in the shooting club, had left the prison service to become a motor mechanic.

But things began to go badly wrong for Wilson's presumed business acumen and he found trade was not as he had expected while his debts mounted rapidly. In conversation with Sim and Donaldson during their shooting practice he joked about the perfect crime, the one-off job, that could solve all his problems and after a while in the course of these gradually more serious talks he discovered the three of them had a factor in common — insurmountable debts and the prospect of ruin.

Each of them knew all about crime, how it was committed, how foolish mistakes led to capture, how with a bit of planning a job could be carried out with successful expertise. Wilson was now no longer the super detective; he was to be the arch criminal. Society had dealt him a lousy hand and he felt no regrets about hitting back to get himself out of the mess.

The robbery joke had now become a haunting reality and plans were laid for a big bank job. At his later trial Wilson's Q.C., Mr. Nicholas Fairbairn, eloquently stated that debt was a cruel and relentless master, creating in its victims the fantasy that one visit to Aladdin's cave would result in the terrible burden being gone forever "and so they took the fateful decision".

The target was the British Linen Bank in Eastwood — Mains Road, Giffnock, Renfrewshire. Wilson decided to bring in a fourth man on the job, his business partner in the greengrocer's shop twenty-one-year-old Archibald McGeachie who acted as driver in the raid, he being as desperate for money as Wilson. The raid took place on July 16th, 1969. Their faces covered by masks and wielding guns as well as bottles of ammonia they charged into the bank, threatened, tied up and blindfolded the staff before wrenching out phones, opening the safe and escaping clear in the revved up getaway car round the corner with £20,876 — all in a matter of minutes.

Cock-a-hoop with their perfect crime, the raiders calmly strode into Wilson's house opposite the police station and split up the loot.

But the euphoria did not last for long. True, Wilson and McGeachie paid off their debts on the grocery business and Sim and Donaldson settled their motoring commitments amicably: but after this had been done there was nothing left and the foursome's legitimate business expertise proved no more profitable than before and once again the spectre of mounting debts returned to haunt them.

Emboldened by the success of the bank raid, Wilson decided that just one more time would prove the clincher that would make them all a success and the dream of the good life — fat cigars, champagne, good food, a villa — kept him awake at night in his cramped flat. So he suggested to his accomplices another job but this time he came up against opposition from two of them.

Donaldson was not a man of violence and the prospect of another ordeal in a bank robbery frightened him: but, after persuasion and the promise that there would be no rough stuff, as well as the financial and emotional pressures imposed on him by his thalidomide daughter, he eventually nodded agreement.

The other dissenter was McGeachie and for Wilson he was a much harder obstacle to overcome. He was adamant that he wanted no part of any further job or indeed of Wilson. In addition McGeachie had not got rid of his spoils to the same extent as Wilson but yet at the same time he refused to help bail out his floundering business partner. Relations between the two men deepened into distrust, enmity and bitterness.

All that can be said about the hapless McGeachie is that he was never seen alive again after December 23rd, 1969. But his disappearance took a bizarre turn three years later when his parents claimed he had been murdered. They applied to the Court of Session in Edinburgh and as a result he was officially pronounced dead and it was announced he had left £9,432 according to a confirmation of his estate lodged with the Sheriff Clerk. Mr. McGeachie senior said he believed his son's murdered body had been buried by a labourer paid to carry out the grisly task in the concrete foundations of the multi-million-pound Kingston Bridge which was completed seven months after his disappearance. It proved scientifically impossible to confirm this, short of knocking down the bridge, but by that time more drastic events had superseded the disappearance of the amateur bank robber.

It was two days before the New Year that the fateful second job which was to cure all the robber's ills took place, twelve days after the abolition of hanging had gone through the House of Lords and seven days after McGeachie, who had known so much, had vanished. It was December 30th, 1969 cold and bleak with a widow's wind blowing icily, when Scotland was looking forward to the Hogmanay festivities and a feeling of light-heartedness was traditionally in the air.

The three well dressed men who quietly entered the Clydesdale Bank at Bridge Street, Linwood, Renfrewshire in the afternoon looked like ordinary customers there to pick up some cash before the bank closed for the holidays. The fact that they were carrying suitcases only reinforced the impression that they were no doubt going away over the holiday period and would need some money. When one of them, Sim, politely asked if he could open an account for a plant hire business he was ushered into the office of the assistant manager. But no sooner had the door closed than the assistant was flung to the floor and Sim pressed a pistol against his temple and hissed, "Listen, you will hear me release the safety catch!" Wilson held a knife at his throat and muttered, "If we have full co-operation no member of your staff will come to any harm!"

A pillow case was taken from a suitcase, put over the assistant manager's head and his hands were tied behind his back. The keys to the front door were located and the three men came out of the office, rounded up the other clerks and a customer and placed them, bound and hooded, beside the assistant before locking the front door. But one woman customer with her two-year-old son came to the door knocking urgently to get in as it was not yet closing time. Realising she could attract attention, the raiders let her in then glared at the startled woman and said that she had better behave or her baby would be shot. They then manhandled the youngest clerk and made him show them were the money was kept. The raiders began to fill suitcases and a box with money from the safe and counter drawers. Their greed to take silver coins as well as notes later proved to be their undoing. Again all the phones were ripped out before the three locked the manager's office then calmly walked to their car outside. None of the shoppers round about noticed anything unusual.

They returned as before to Wilson's house to split up the proceeds. They took the notes into the tenement without any bother. There was a discussion as to whether they should just leave the loose change in the car and sort it out later or risk being seen bringing it in. But they decided that the chance of being thought suspicious was remote and, besides, nothing had happened before because they reasoned their open brazenness allayed suspicions which shiftiness would arouse, and what was more to the point — the more money the better. However, they, with their thieves' instinct, did not trust just one to go out and get the rest of the loot so all three strolled out to the car.

Inspector Andrew Hyslop was driving towards the Southern Police Station at this precise moment. His colleague, Constable John Sellars, was in the squad car with him and they were returning from a routine patrol. The two policemen noticed the three men carrying suitcases into the close. Inspector Hyslop, knowing of Wilson's flagging greengrocery business, suspected he could be resetting stolen whisky. The police in Allison Street involved in the events to follow did not know of any bank robbery.

Inspector Hyslop went to the police station for assistance while Constable Sellars stopped Wilson at the close mouth. The bank robber said he was merely going to a shop nearby and that he himself was a former policeman. Constable Sellars returned to the squad car and was joined by Inspector Hyslop who had brought along Detective Constable Angus McKenzie, aged 30, and Constable Edward Barnett, aged 24, and a Constable Campbell. When Wilson returned with a bottle of lemonade he was asked about what he had been unloading into his house. Wilson was polite and co-operative and they all entered his house where he offered them a drink which was turned down. Inspector Hyslop opened a case and found it contained bags of cash stamped 'Linwood'. The officers now dispersed throughout the kitchen, bedroom and bathroom to see what else they could find. At the first arrival of the police Donaldson had escaped through a window while Sim had dumped a pistol in Wilson's bedroom wardrobe.

While the police were searching the house, Wilson slipped into the bedroom and, having found out from a terrified Sim where the gun was, he grabbed it and reappeared in the hallway to come face to face with Inspector Hyslop who had just emerged from searching the bathroom.

Wilson raised his right extended arm and aimed at the frozen policeman's head. He was later to tell fellow prisoners that he would never forget those seconds and the astonished look in the eyes of Inspector Hyslop as he stared at death.

Wilson tried to fire but there was a click indicating that the pistol had jammed. He pulled back the sliding jacket to clear the obstruction and aimed again but by this time the Inspector had gained his senses and was rushing at him. But it was too late and a bullet struck him on the left side of the face, spinning him round. He fell to the floor, paralysed but still fully conscious.

It was later said in Wilson's defence that he had no sensible recollection of using the gun, that he was numb with fear, irrational, shouting and yelling without meaning, the whites of his eyes blazing and that he was in an uncontrollable state. That was not so He had a clear idea of what he was going to do (he had probably formulated it while going for the lemonade). He was going to kill all the officers and dump their bodies and car in a loch or shoot himself in the process since life would hardly be worth living anyway.

While Inspector Hyslop lay helpless staring at the horror unfolding a few feet away from him, Detective Constable MacKenzie rushed into the hall from the living room and Constable Barnett appeared at the kitchen door. Wilson aimed with his marksman's precision and accurately shot MacKenzie in the head before swinging round on Barnett and shooting the startled constable again on target in the head. Wilson felt his hobby of shooting had come in handy at last and at this point the insane notion flew through his head as to what he would tell his wife Julia when she came in from work.

Barnett was obviously dead but MacKenzie seemed only stunned so Wilson calmly and cold bloodedly, with the helpless Inspector Hyslop staring on aghast, stepped forward, took deliberate aim at MacKenzie's head and fired, killing him instantly. A post mortem later revealed that MacKenzie would have lived had it not been for this second shot.

While this was going on Constable Sellars had managed to spring into the bathroom over the prostrate Hyslop and lock himself in. He had something Wilson had not bargained for — a pocket radio. Sellars started shouting frantically but vainly for help into the radio while Wilson fired at the bathroom lock and yelled, "We'll need to get this bastard — he's got a radio!"

Wilson then shouted to Sim, who had a spare round of ammunition in his pocket, "You'll need to get me more rounds!"

But Sim only swore and said they should give themselves up.

Sellars now saw the bathroom door opening and, grabbing the handle, pitted his strength against Wilson's. The door opened an alarming inch but at this point Hyslop, lying at Wilson's feet, managed at last to make an agonised movement. The killer saw this and, relinquishing the bathroom door for the moment, decided to finish Hyslop off.

For the second time in minutes Hyslop gazed at the barrel of the pistol and thought this time he was finished: but now Constable Campbell appeared at the living room door and instinctively launched himself across the hall at Wilson. Both men fell struggling to the floor.

As they wrestled there, Wilson shouted for Sim to get more ammunition from the car but the accomplice, realising all was lost, made no move of any kind.

Campbell grabbed the barrel of the pistol, punched Wilson and pulled the gun free. He struggled to his feet and, covering the two men, edged backwards into the close where he shouted to a passer-by to get help.

The street was soon flooded with squad cars and ambulances and Wilson and Sim were marched in the midst of a swarm of policemen across the road to the cells.

It says much for the restraint of the police at this time that there was never any accusation of brutality alleged against them as regards Wilson. Probably they were too stunned and, in any case, every top officer from the Chief Constable down arrived on the scene.

The drama sent shock waves throughout the city and the Lord Provost, politicians, councillors and churchmen publicly expressed their utter horror at the deed. It was a black New Year for the Glasgow Police Force.

That evening Donaldson, when he heard the news in a bar, fled distraught to the Gleniffer Braes where he contemplated suicide but decided he did not have the courage. A haggard, hollow figure, he went back to his Paisley home to face the inevitable with resignation. The police were waiting for him and he gave himself up meekly. He simply had nowhere to go. It was the end of the road for the once respectable hard working father who had been in and out of a dozen uneconomic jobs since the birth of his tragically deformed first child, the object of his affection and despair who had been an innocent contributor to his downfall.

Constable Barnett left a 24-year-old wife and two sons. Detective Constable MacKenzie left a young widow. Both widows were understandably bitter about the repeal of the death penalty and asked for its reintroduction as, vociferously, did the Police Federation. The dead men were posthumously awarded the Queen's Medal for bravery. Inspector Hyslop, who recovered after a lengthy sojourn in hospital, and his rescuer, Constable Campbell, both also received bravery awards.

Detectives interviewed Wilson in prison about the missing McGeachie but he was telling nothing.

When the case came up at the High Court in Edinburgh two months later the three accused pleaded guilty to all the charges against them. Lord Grant sentenced Wilson to what was then Scotland's longest sentence, twenty five years minimum, and Sim, aged 22 and married with a two-year-old son, was sentenced to twelve years as was Donaldson, aged 31, and married with three young daughters. None of the accused standing erect in the dock showed any emotion as they were sentenced.

Lord Grant told Sim and Donaldson, "Those who indulge in armed robbery play for high stakes and must realise that the penalties are equally high."

Before the sentence was passed Wilson's counsel, Mr. Fairbairn, said that his client had specially asked that his profound apologies be extended to Glasgow Police for having by "his appalling actions" impugned their good name and that he also wished to express his profound apologies and deepest sympathy to the widows and their families and to Inspector Hyslop and his family.

The severity of the sentence, however, was not enough for most people. The then convener of Glasgow Corporation, Bailie James Anderson, said the punishment was "grossly inadequate and simply an invitation to murder because I honestly feel that, Heaven forbid, crimes of this nature will be repeated." He said Wilson should have been executed or at least have been given life, meaning the rest of his life, and that Sim should have been given 30 years minimum and Donaldson 25 years minimum. This was in line with popular opinion at the time.

There were petitions, questions in the House, the Police Federation had a meeting with the Secretary of State and predictably got nowhere, there were outraged letters in the Press, a flood of donations — tens of thousands of pounds — to a widows' fund, stormy scenes at Glasgow Corporation meetings over hanging and whether it should be brought back, and there were debates as to whether the police should be armed and, if so, where and when should authority be given for use of guns.

Meanwhile, Wilson was having a very rough time in prison. Normally, sentenced people who have been formerly respectable (what the villains call white collars) are sent to soft option jails but this was not on for a man who had killed two of his own. He was sent at once to Peterhead, where the 'cons' despised him as being an ex-policeman and the 'screws' loathed him for his crimes. The 'cons' sent him to Coventry, insulted him or threatened him with violence. He always had a shattered, hunted look about him. The 'screws' were arrogant and gave him more menial tasks. He was forever cleaning out cells, emptying slops, washing out toilets. He was classed as a top security prisoner with all the close restrictions and constant surveillance which that entails. As a result of the strain, Wilson took part in the prison rooftop protest in August 1972 and shortly afterwards, along with Jimmy Boyle, was transferred to 'the Cages' in Porterfield Prison. (His part in the riot there and consequent move to the Special Unit in Barlinnie has already been recounted in Chapter 13.)

A month after he was sentenced on the riot charge his wife Julia, then 33 and having been forced because of abusive letters to move to Easterhouse, divorced him on grounds of cruelty. The action was not contested and she was granted custody of the children. A visitor who was there when he had to sign the papers described him as looking like a living corpse. He was haggard and wan, had lost most of his hair and had grown a dark, straggly beard.

The bright young man who had dreams of being head of Glasgow C.I.D., then of being a big business tycoon had ended up spending the long hours in his cell working on Braille books for the blind, like Ian Brady.

The politicians, as is their wont, let the storm over the shootings calm down and disappear. If public feeling riding high could not get them to budge on the issue of capital punishment at that time then it is obvious that it will have to take a much greater and longer groundswell to get Parliament to change the law on hanging. But even if the Lords decision had somehow been delayed in the winter of 1969 it is highly debatable if the prospect of the gallows would have crossed Wilson's mind before he pulled the trigger on that fateful December afternoon.

CHAPTER 15

Dancing With Death

The most extensive and longest manhunt in Scottish criminal history took place in the late sixties and centred on a shadowy, elusive figure who haunted a brassy Glasgow ballroom. He was an immaculate, well groomed gent who was well spoken, polite and, possibly, even religious. He was light on his feet, a good dancer and his charm was literally fatal. It was a case in which the police received massive nationwide help, had all the advantages of modern forensic science at their fingertips, as much evidence as any detective could pray for and a murderer who picked the most public of places, a dance hall, where people went *deliberately* to eye up others — and yet that final clue proved as difficult to pinpoint as the man who terrorised the city.

At that time the Barrowland Ballroom just east of the city's High Street was a popular night spot where the dance floor was nightly packed, the music loud and lively, the atmosphere raucous and abandoned and, in the shadows round the walls, jabbed occasionally by neon lights, the eyes of the boys on the town hungrily eyed up the 'talent'. On Thursday, Friday and Saturday nights of the week it was well known that bored married women took off their rings, popped them in their handbags and loosened up for a spree and a bit of fun. On these occasions it was easy pickings for any presentable young man out for a night's sex.

It was on the night of Friday February 23rd 1968 that a vivacious 25-year-old brunette in a sexy black dress called Pat Docker was gyrating to the music and letting herself go after a busy week at the Victoria Infirmary where she worked as a nurse. She danced with several young men in the semi-darkness that night but no-one could later recall in whose arms she enjoyed the last waltz.

The following morning, a Saturday, some boys were playing in a lane beside Pat's home in Carmichael Place, Langside, when they saw what at first glance appeared to be a broken tailor's dummy lying on the ground. On investigation the grim truth was obvious. It was the stark naked, strangled body of a girl.

It did not take the police long to establish that the dead girl, who had been throttled with her own tights and raped, was Pat Docker. Her distraught father identified her.

Nor did it take them long to discover that a press photographer had been holding a large, noisy party, attended by nurses, in his nearby flat. Detectives took over editors' offices in newspapers throughout the city and interviewed everyone who had been at the party, much to the embarrassment of some of the reporters who were supposed to have been touring the police stations in radio cars on calls duty that night.

But no clues were forthcoming, no-one had seen or heard anything suspicious and, anyway, Pat almost certainly was not at the party but was down in the lane with someone. Her clothes and handbag were never found and, despite intensive investigations lasting months, neither was her murderer.

Business at the Barrowland continued as usual until the night of Saturday August 16th of the following year when slim, dark haired 32-year-old Jemima McDonald, an unmarried mother of three, decided to let herself loose at one of the dance hall's notorious swinging singles nights. She too wore a black dress and enjoyed herself, laughing and drinking and getting up with whoever asked.

She left the dance hall with a man and walked in the direction of her older sister's house in Mackeith Street, Bridgeton, where she had arranged to spend the night. But when she failed to arrive back the sister became alarmed in the early hours and decided to go out looking for her. It did not take her long to find Jemima's body which lay sprawled on derelict property a few yards away.

Death was due to strangulation by her own tights and she had also been raped. Her handbag was missing. Apart from the other coincidences with the Docker murder — the dance hall, each having dark hair and dresses, each young, attractive and available, each meeting their deaths in the same way and having their bags stolen — both women had been having their periods.

But this time the police seemed to be on better ground. They had a description. Several people had seen Jemima leave with her last partner and they had both been seen strolling through the midnight streets.

The police assembled an Identikit picture and issued it to the press, the first time this had been done in Scotland. It showed the pleasant, well balanced face of a clean shaven, fresh faced man in his late twenties with dark eyes and short, brushed back reddish fair hair. In addition, he was described as being six feet tall of slim build and immaculately dressed in a blue suit of good quality with hand stitched lapels and a white shirt. If this was indeed the man then one could well imagine women finding him attractive and allowing themselves to be escorted away by him.

As in the Docker case the police appealed to patrons of the dance hall to come forward but they had to deal with the frustrating problem that many of the dancers were wives who should not have been there in the first place and who had no intention of getting involved. Only a smattering of staff and dancers who had nothing to hide volunteered statements and they could add nothing to the description. Not quite certain yet if there was any connection with the Docker case the police nevertheless went over every possible angle — relatives, friends, possible motives of any boyfriends — with their usual painstaking thoroughness and the investigation was still continuing when the thunderbolt really struck.

Mother of two Mrs. Helen Puttock, a chubbily attractive 29-year-old brunette whose husband was serving in the Army, was not bothered by press theories that there might be a strangler on the loose at the Barrowland Ballroom, knowing as she did that it could never happen to her and, anyway, she was a good judge of character. Ten weeks after the McDonald murder, on Thursday 30th October, she too decided to go out for a night on the tiles and she too, apparently, could have danced all night in her sexy black dress at the ballroom.

She went with her sister, Mrs. Jean Langford, and in the dimness of the hall she tried to get some cigarettes from a machine which jammed. A well dressed young man stepped forward and offered to help get her money back and the two got into conversation. They then had a drink and a dance, he said he would see her home (you couldn't be too careful these days) and towards midnight they met in with Mrs. Langford who was leaving. The three got into a taxi to Scotstoun where the sisters lived and Mrs. Langford was dropped off at her home before the taxi went on to near Helen's house in Earl Street where she and her well-spoken, new found friend, who was called John, alighted. It was the last time anyone, except John, was to see her alive.

The next morning a woman emptying out rubbish found Helen's corpse in a back court a few closes from the dead woman's home. She had been strangled with her tights and raped, her bag was missing and she, too, was in her bad week. The hue and cry now really began in earnest.

Thanks to Mrs. Langford and the taxi driver the police now not only had a minutely detailed description of the murder suspect but also facts about John's background which he had revealed in the taxi.

First the physical description which was possibly the most accurate in Scottish criminal history. It was issued by Detective Chief Superintendent Elphinstone Dalglish, then head of Glasgow C.I.D.

John was clean shaven, in his late twenties, six feet tall of slim to medium build with light auburn reddish hair styled short and brushed to the right, all of which fitted with the last man seen with

Jemima McDonald. In addition, he had blue grey eyes, nice straight teeth with one tooth on the right upper jaw overlapping the next tooth, fine features and was of smart appearance. On the night he met Helen he was dressed in a brownish, flecked, single breasted suit, the jacket of which had three buttons and high lapels. There were no turn-ups on the trousers and the suit generally was in modern style. He also wore a knee length brown coat of tweed or gaberdine, a light blue shirt and a dark tie with red diagonal stripes. He had a wrist watch with a broad leather strap of military style and smoked Embassy tipped cigarettes. He frequented the Barrowland Ballroom on his own. He could have had scratch marks on his face and hands as a result of his attack on Helen.

As to his background, he had a sister and had been brought up strictly by his puritanical parents who were very religious and teetotal and who had vainly tried to instill in him a dislike for alcohol. He could quote extracts from the Bible. He was well spoken despite a Glasgow accent and did not appear to be engaged in heavy manual work. He could play golf but was not very good at it although a cousin had recently scored a hole-in-one. He was a bachelor who lived with a relative, probably in the Castlemilk area of Glasgow. He was personable, handsome and probably occupied some place in society where he had some authority. It was this respectable, clean-cut image which helped protect him.

An evening newspaper news editor now dubbed the murderer 'Bible John' and the name caught the public imagination and stuck. The heat was now on the police to come up with results.

There had only been two recent manhunts in the city comparable to it. One was for the Box Man, a pederast who preyed on young boys in the Partick district by saying he had a present for them in a box thus enticing them into a backcourt where he would bugger them. And the other for a labourer in the St. George's Cross area who would take little girls into back closes and sexually assault them with a chisel. Both were pathological sexual perverts who otherwise led normal lives and despite large-scale police investigations and 'sex patrols' both had only been caught by luck, one running away from an assault and the other through a suspicious workmate. But both were dwarfed by the massive Bible John hunt.

The police now had a second picture of Bible John following Helen's murder but this time, instead of using the Identikit method, they took the unusual step of hiring an artist to paint a portrait of the wanted man. It was broadly similar to the Jemima McDonald murder picture and showed a very presentable young man who looked as though he could be trusted. Tens of thousands of these posters were distributed in public places throughout Scotland and to police forces throughout Britain as well as to military units abroad.

Detectives now definitely and openly linked all three murders and a Bible John H.Q., was set up in the Marine Police Station, Helen's murder having taken place in its area. More than a hundred detectives were assigned to the case and forces throughout the country were asked to co-operate. More than fifty thousand statements were taken in door-to-door inquiries or volunteered from members of the public, from taxi drivers, bus drivers, dancers and dance hall managers and staff, publicans, hoteliers, anyone involved with religious groups like the Mormons, ministers and priests, religious seminaries and colleges, nurses, newspapermen and much of the huge sprawling estate of Castlemilk was 'checked out'. Records were methodically examined, lunatic asylums visited, prisons and borstals visited, state hospitals visited. Barber shops were visited and asked about John's hairstyle and golf clubs held special meetings attended and addressed by senior detectives in an attempt to place John and his elusive cousin's hole-in-one. Dentists were asked to check their chart records and Helen's distraught husband, discharged from the Army to look after his two little sons, offered a personal reward of £200 for information at a specially organised police press conference. The Armed Forces were thoroughly checked and detectives travelled to N.A.T.O. countries to see if suitable leave passes coincided with the murders. The Special Investigation Branches of the Army, Navy and Air Force travelled throughout the world, even as far as Hong Kong, during the investigation and gradually, with masses of statements, documents and photographs piling up, the murder H.Q., where a special 24-hour switchboard was installed, began to take on the appearance of a mini British Museum.

The media were constantly badgered to appeal for information and there was a unique B.B.C. documentary compiled, with the Lord Advocate's blessing, which graphically reconstructed the night of Helen's murder. The part of John was portrayed by an upholsterer who had been interviewed but cleared by the police and the roles of the dead woman and her sister were taken by policewomen who looked similar. There was even a dramatic appeal over the air by commentator Hugh Cochrane which was couched in Biblical terms and asked John for his sins to give himself up. This programme alone brought a flood of a thousand calls to the murder H.Q.

Even the underworld offered its services. The stepping up of police checks, raids, patrols and general intensification of investigations into the criminal element was making life distinctly uncomfortable for several dubious characters and, anyway, villains generally have a deep-rooted antipathy for the lone wolf slayers of women or sexual perverts — not just because the underworld has its human side too but also because they give crime a bad name and can make routine 'jobs' more difficult (as was the case with the Manuel murders). But here the underworld came up against the same problem as the police — the killer apparently had no record and was not one of their number so how could they track him down? Solemn conversations in the back rooms of pubs, mini summit conferences in certain slumland houses and various messages tapped out on the underworld grapevine brought no results and villains had to stoically suffer the police harassment and sit out the manhunt in the hope that the killer could be caught by more conventional and official detection methods.

But the hunt had its humorous side too. One gentleman, a printer, was one of several young men who had the misfortune to be the double of one of the posters. He became sick fed up with conscientious passers-by making citizen's arrests and dragging him off to the nearest police station as he protested his innocence. On one occasion he was calmly walking along a city street when he suddenly found himself face down on the pavement with his legs trapped. A husky citizen had him pinned in a rugby tackle. This was the last straw and, knowing that the police had cleared him at the outset, he insisted that the Chief Constable give him a signed certificate saying he was not, definitely not, Bible John.

Many innocent men had the embarrassment and misfortune to be interviewed by the police and be told people had always had their suspicions about them and many a one became distinctly uneasy when being stared at while sitting in buses or trains and later being followed by alert citizens, not to mention downright cranks.

And a night out at the Barrowland Ballroom could be an amusing activity at this time. The murders had meant a decline in business but the floor was still packed, except many of the dancers were exceptionally well groomed and behaved. They were all P.C.s and W.P.C.s in plain if fashionable clothes and anyone who was not had the uncomfortable feeling of dozens of pairs of eyes sizing them up. The murder squad was christened the Marine Police Formation Team and one detective said on the T.V. documentary, "We must be the best dancers in the country by now. We are there at least twice a week and this has been going on for months. But people must think we are strange. We don't look at the women but the men."

And as the months went by without success at least one senior detective had to be given sick leave because he would leap from his car in the middle of traffic to grab and interview neat young men on the spot before summarily clearing them after a few minutes of questioning. And when asked what he wanted for Christmas he growled at his wife, "Bible John — in wrapping paper!"

The end result of all this frenetic activity, with all the modern aids to detection in full use, was — nothing. The file is still open.

Every time a sexual murder is committed the ghost rears up once more but so far as is known there were only three Bible John murders.

Or were there only two? One theory was that the first, the Pat Docker murder, was separate because she was naked and her clothes were never found, suggesting she had been murdered in a house and dumped in the lane. The murderer would hardly have taken the time and trouble and risk of discovery involved in stripping her in the lane and she would not have voluntarily been naked in the open air in mid-February. Yet all the other coincidences would suggest it was the same man, even if the murder did not actually take place in the lane.

Of course, there were plenty of theories. One was that he died after the last murder — but a healthy young man does not simply die because he has committed murder. Another solution put forward was suicide but no reports of this fitted. He emigrated, he was shut up in an asylum, he was imprisoned — take your pick.

The police were probably thrown off the scent by the two identity pictures. The only people who saw him for any length of time did so in places of semi-darkness, a dance hall, a street, a taxi — and, as was proved, the main features could fit an awful lot of men. And it is well known that witnesses under pressure from the police will agree that his eyes were like this or his nose was like that, just to get some peace.

As regards the statements he made about himself, if he was astute enough and deliberately planning a murder, he could invent a false background for himself to throw witnesses and the police completely off the scent. But it still seems more likely that the statements were true and that he had no preconceived aim of killing but did so in the frenzy of the moment.

Sexual murderers with no records are the most difficult to catch and luck is needed by the police. On this occasion the dice rolled for Bible John.

The favourite theory, based on the fact that these kind of killers never stop, is that he is still around. He has a strong sexual urge which when denied him through the menstrual cycle turns to murder and rape. He has probably been imprisoned for rape, not necessarily in Scotland, since the last murder. Or he could have been incarcerated in a mental institution. The police had one suspect who was later imprisoned for sexual assault but evidence was too tenuous to make a case stick. A relative almost certainly knew the truth but out of misplaced loyalty and a belief that it would not recur remained silent. If he is still alive he is only in his late thirties with time on his hands . . .

CHAPTER 16

The Spider's Web

A personal statement by Paddy Meehan

In the early hours of Sunday July 6th, 1969, a vicious crime was committed in the holiday town of Ayr. An elderly bingo hall owner, sixty-seven-year-old Abraham Ross and his seventy-two-year-old wife Rachel were asleep in their bungalow home at 2 Blackburn Place when two masked men broke in and attacked them. Despite his years, Mr. Ross put up a fierce struggle and at one stage it looked as if he would overcome his assailant.

"Get this c★★t off my back, Pat," the man called out in a panic.

At this stage the other intruder left off beating up Mrs. Ross to go to the assistance of his accomplice. Wielding an iron bar, he struck Mr. Ross several vicious blows on the head. When Mr. Ross ceased to struggle the two thugs then proceeded to bind the old couple with rope.

The intruders were two Glasgow villains, William 'Tank' McGuinness and Ian Waddell. Robbery was the motive for the crime. Acting on information received they had come to rob Mr. Ross of the large sum of money he was reputed to hold in his safe (some of it, it was alleged, from resetting stolen goods). Closing the bedroom curtains, they switched on the lights and proceeded to the next part of their plan — to force Mr. Ross to disclose the whereabouts of the safe and hand over its keys. To this end they beat the old man about the face and head without mercy until he told them what they wanted to know.

From the safe, which was concealed in a hall cupboard, they removed a small case containing more than £3,000. This, added to other money found around the house, brought the haul to almost £4,000. But time was on their hands. It was part of their plan to remain in the house until well after dawn, when the normal morning traffic got under way on the Glasgow road. So they spent the next couple of hours ransacking the house and drinking Mr. Ross's whisky.

After a while, McGuinness told Waddell, "You wait here. I'll go and fetch the car."

McGuinness came out of the house into early morning sunshine. To avoid suspicion the car had been parked well away from the house and McGuinness made his way towards it as if he were out for a nonchalant stroll.

But just a few minutes after leaving the house a police car drew up alongside him. The police had no real suspicions about McGuinness but wondered what he was doing in such a wealthy area so early in the morning. McGuinness, with some Ross jewellery weighing down his pockets, had a story ready for them. He told them he had been in the area on the Saturday night but had been legless drunk and, as a result, had missed the last bus back to Glasgow. Since it was the height of the holiday season when many Glaswegians made day trips to Ayr the story sounded authentic enough. The two constables in the car then obligingly gave McGuinness a lift to the bus station.

Shaking with fright, McGuinness waited until the squad car was out of sight and made once more for the direction of the parked car. Realising if he was caught the jewellery would be found, he dropped the stolen articles down a drain. Just as he straightened up he saw the same police car again in the distance. The constables also saw him but concluded that since the bus services had not started yet he must be looking for a cafe to get a cup of coffee. They left him alone and went on their way.

It was with some relief that McGuinness eventually slid into the seat of the getaway car and drove back to the Ross bungalow.

The two thugs took a roundabout way back to Glasgow just in case an alarm was raised and road blocks were set up. They split up the loot in a lay-by and went to separate houses, Waddell to a house in Parkhead where another villain called Donald Carmichael had promised to give him an alibi for the night and McGuinness back to his home in Milton. He told his wife about the police picking him up in Ayr and said he would have to flee south to England which he proceeded to do. In his haste he had, deliberately or otherwise, forgotten to telephone the operator, as he had told Waddell he would do, to give an anonymous tip-off about an old couple tied up in Blackburn Place. The Ross couple lay bound and injured all day Sunday and throughout that long night, their cries for help going unheard.

Meanwhile, Ian Waddell was less cautious than his accomplice. He was soon drinking with cronies in a lounge on the outskirts of Glasgow and between paying for all the rounds he told of the Ayr job and laughed about McGuinness being picked up by the police.

It was not until the Ross's cleaning lady arrived on the Monday morning that the old couple were found and rushed to hospital, seriously ill. Mrs. Ross, who suffered from a respiratory illness, later died. A full scale murder hunt was now launched and Mr. Ross, partially recovered, tried to help detectives as best he could.

In Glasgow the Serious Crime Squad got wind that Waddell had been flinging money about on the Sunday night and boasting of his part in the tie-up job. They tried seeking him out for questioning. Waddell in turn heard of this on the underworld grapevine and discussed his best course of action with an ex-criminal who was now the manager of a pub in the Gallowgate. He advised Waddell to call in at the office of a solicitor called Carlin and get his advice, which Waddell proceeded to do giving Mr. Carlin a wad of £200 for his trouble. He explained to the lawyer this was to be his fee in the event of he, Waddell, being charged with the Ayr murder. He wanted Carlin to organise his defence.

They both decided it would be better if they approached the police first rather than wait for the inevitable knock on the door so they made their way to a police station where Waddell was promptly interviewed by detectives as to his whereabouts at the time of the break-in. He gave his alibi and Donald Carmichael, who was also interviewed, duly supported it. Waddell was then allowed to go and he repaired to the Gallowgate pub to celebrate and, again in his cups, boast to his cronies about how he had pulled the wool over the eyes of the police.

Down in Ayr, Detective Chief Superintendent David Struthers, who was in charge of the investigation, was busy giving press conferences. He said he believed one of the men was called Pat, that they had broad Glasgow accents and that they had not left the Ross bungalow until around 6 a.m. For some reason he did not mention the two constables picking up McGuinness in the area at the relevant time although a report to this effect was in his hands.

Then the Ayrshire C.I.D. received a phone call from the Special Branch who had been tapping my phone for some months previously. As a result of this so-called tip-off, Struthers and a team of detectives arrived at my flat in the Gorbals to arrest me. I was then put on a rigged identity parade (we shall come to this in due course) and was charged with the Ross murder.

At about the same time as I was being kicked on the steps leading into Ayr Sheriff Court by an enraged lynch mob, an Englishman named James Griffiths was shot dead after a chase through the streets of Glasgow (see next chapter). He was my alibi and I knew just how serious the trouble I was in when the Crown Office issued a unique, astonishing and shameful statement: "The Crown Office can confirm that with the death of James Griffiths and the arrest of Patrick Connoly Meehan the police are no longer interested in anyone else in connection with the crime against Mr. and Mrs. Ross at Ayr". So much for being innocent until proved guilty!

On the 21st October 1969 I went on trial at Edinburgh High Court, Lord Grant presiding. Two special defences were lodged on my behalf. Firstly, alibi and, secondly, impeachment against Ian Waddell and another man.

The trial began with Mr. Ross in the witness box. He told how he had picked me out at an identity parade at Glasgow Central Police Office because of my voice. He insisted the two men had Glasgow accents. Griffiths my co-accused on the indictment had a broad Lancashire accent.

He said he believed the men called each other Pat and Jim. This was correct — it was the two names Waddell and McGuinness had decided to use when talking to each other in the bungalow. I have never been called Pat in my life, always Paddy.

Then Mr. Ross was questioned about scraps of paper in the drawers of his house safe. (The Ayrshire police were claiming that scraps of paper 'found' in the pocket of a car coat belonging to the dead Griffiths were identical to paper used by Mr. Ross to line the drawers of his safe.) Mr. Ross replied he knew nothing about any paper lining the drawers of his safe.

He was absolutely certain that when the two intruders had left it had been full daylight.

The police gave evidence that, contrary to what Mr. Ross had said, there had been paper in his safe which had also been found in Griffiths' car coat. Both safe and coat had lain side by side locked away in the C.I.D. department of the Ayrshire constabulary for months.

The Prosecution placed great emphasis on the fact that Griffiths and I had been travelling in Ayrshire on the night of the break-in, a fact I freely admitted. We had been casing a motor taxation office in Stranraer and it was from there that I had phoned my wife at home thus tipping off the eavesdropping Special Branch that we had been in the area at the time.

When it came to the turn of the defence, our journey was gone into in great detail. It was established that Griffiths and I had indeed motored down to Stranraer which is 52 miles south of Ayr and that we had not left there until 2 a.m. Several witnesses verified this. It was also established beyond doubt that around 3.30 a.m. at a spot seven miles north of Ayr we had gone to the assistance of two girls who had claimed they were being molested by kerb crawlers. We took the girls to their respective homes in Kilmarnock and continued on to Glasgow where I arrived home around 4.30 a.m. just as dawn was breaking.

When it came to the defence of impeachment against Ian Waddell, a number of witnesses from the underworld, horrified by the nature of the crime, testified to Waddell's confessions of involvement in the break-in.

When Waddell went into the witness box he denied everything, even giving the £200 to Mr. Carlin. Months later Waddell pleaded guilty in connection with a perjury charge resulting from this denial and was imprisoned for three years.

In his summing up to the jury, Lord Grant came away with the remarkable theory that Griffiths and I could have been in all these places and still have committed the crime. To drive up the twisting coast road from Stranraer to Ayr and later to have been able to have come across the two girls would have meant the break-in being like a five minute silent comedy instead of the long drawn out torture it in fact was. And, anyway, it was still pitch darkness during our travels in Ayrshire and Mr. Ross said it had been full daylight when the intruders left.

However, the jury in their wisdom, after being told by Lord Grant to disregard the impeachment defence entirely, felt there was enough evidence against me and I was found guilty and sentenced to life imprisonment.

Being completely innocent of the crime, there was no way that I would accept the life sentence without a fight. My family and a number of lawyers, all convinced of my innocence, pledged their full support in the struggle ahead.

Thanks to the untiring efforts of my eldest son Patrick, startling new evidence about the way the police had handled the conduct of the identity parade came to light. It had been rigged and in a way that proved beyond doubt that the police officers concerned were involved in a conspiracy.

In the conduct of an identity parade it is the practice of the police to go out into the nearby streets and invite members of the public to return to the police station to assist by acting as stand-ins. This is what the police did following my arrest on Monday 14th July. I make this point to bring home that the men who volunteered to act as stand-ins can be considered completely neutral witnesses in what took place when the identity parade got under way.

Six witnesses, including Mr. Ross, were brought to the police station to view the line up. In the course of an identity parade it is a firm rule that witnesses who have already viewed the line up should not come into contact with the witnesses yet to view it. To achieve this, three rooms — call them A, B and C — are needed. The witnesses are first assembled in room A, are called in to view the line up in B and are then conducted to room C. In this way, all the potential witnesses who were initially assembled in room A will end up together in room C.

When the identity parade held at the Central Police Office got under way the first witness called was Mr. Ross and the others assumed he had gone to view the line up. In fact, he had been taken to room C without seeing anyone. The other witnesses were then called and this time they did view the line up, ending up in room C where Mr. Ross was still waiting in an apprehensive state to take his turn. He started to ask the witnesses coming in who they had picked out and among them were the two Kilmarnock girls who had correctly picked me out and now proceeded to tell Mr. Ross where I was standing in the line up and what I looked like.

When it finally came his turn, Mr. Ross let it be known that he could not pick anyone out by sight but he might be able to recognise a voice. He went along the line up until he came to where I was standing at the end, as he knew I would be. He then asked me to say what one of the intruders had said, "Shut up, shut up, we'll send an ambulance." This I did in my normal Glasgow voice and Mr. Ross said, "That's him. I don't need to hear anyone else."

Having successfully rigged the identity parade, the police now set about covering up the conspiracy. First, they falsified the identity parade schedule to show that Mr. Ross had been first to view the parade when in fact he had been last. And second, two police officers committed perjury at my trial by saying Mr. Ross had been first in and that the schedule was a true account of what took place.

When, as a result of the inquiries made by my son, the parade rigging came to light, the witnesses who were in the line up all gave statements to my solicitors. In addition, two Glasgow solicitors who were present in room B while the parade was in progress signed statements that the police version was untrue. And Mr. Ross confirmed to newspaper reporters that he had indeed been last to view the parade but had not thought anything about it.

I tried to bring a private prosecution against the police officers involved in a conspiracy against me and I told the High Court of Justiciary in Edinburgh that I believed I had been framed by the police acting under instructions from the British Secret Service.

Their Lordships turned down my right to bring a private prosecution and in their judgement said that because the crime of perjury was a crime against the public interest, the decision whether or not to prosecute must be left to the independent and impartial decision of the Lord Advocate and he had decided, without needing to give any reasons, that I did not have the right to bring a private prosecution.

Their judgement went on, "It would require to be a very special case indeed to justify a departure from this general rule, and this broad consideration of public policy must normally outweigh the private interest which an individual may seek to qualify."

In other words, in Scotland the individual has no effective remedy against a political frame-up.

This carries certain logical implications: that those who were instrumental in the frame-up were aware they would not be prosecuted if any conspiracy came to light because they would be protected by the deliberate inactivity of the highest arbiter for deciding on prosecutions in the land, the Lord Advocate.

To follow through the implications of the term 'political frame-up' it must be remembered that the office of Lord Advocate is a political appointment. He is a member of the party in power and elected by the Prime Minister of the day and is also subject to the pressures and advice of the Establishment. Therefore the law and politics are not, as the general public are led to believe, things apart. It therefore follows that a Lord Advocate could, if he thought it in the public interest (as well as his own), protect policemen guilty of conspiracy to pervert the course of justice.

When it comes to the highest court in the land the judges have simply to rely on the integrity of the Lord Advocate and through him the people advising him (including the police) in turning down private prosecutions. If the same thing had been true in America during the Nixon era he might still be President!

In Scotland, to take on the police, the legal Establishment (even more conservative than it's English counterpart) and the Secret Service and win, especially if you are a convicted criminal serving a life sentence for murder, is mission impossible.

However, there was a victory of sorts. On the 19th of May 1976 — after seven long, harrowing years in self imposed solitary confinement — I was given a Royal Pardon and released (although how I can be pardoned for something I did not do is a mystery).

This only came about because 'Tank' McGuinness was found murdered in Springfield Road in Glasgow's East End. 'Gipsy' Winning, the great escaper, was charged with the murder then released for lack of evidence. This meant that McGuinness's lawyer, the ubiquitous Joe Beltrami, could drop the rules of confidentiality and tell the Lord Advocate that his client had confessed to him in private that he and Waddell had committed the Ayr murder and that I was not involved. Waddell's confession to this effect had previously been splashed across the front page of the now defunct workers co-operative newspaper, the *Scottish Daily News* with, of course, no subsequent action whatsoever being taken. If McGuinness had not been murdered I would still be rotting away alone in self imposed solitary (the only protest I could make). So whoever did the killing did me a favour.

A few months later the Secretary of State, under pressure from M.P.s, appointed a High Court Judge, Lord Hunter, to conduct a private inquiry into the case. Immediately following this announcement, the Lord Advocate made his own announcement — any person who chose to give evidence to Lord Hunter would not be prosecuted for any offence committed in the course of the investigation into the Ross murder or in the course of my trial in Edinburgh. The police officers who had committed perjury at my trial had been given immunity from prosecution as had anyone else involved in the conspiracy. As I have said, the term 'political frame-up' implies that those instrumental in organising it act in the knowledge that, in the event of their criminal conduct coming to light, they will be protected from the consequences. And there is absolutely nothing the ordinary citizen can do about it. So much for the veneer of democracy.

With regards to the involvement of the Secret Service, when I went behind the Iron Curtain while on the run in the mid sixties I was held by the K.G.B. for months and questioned about British criminal life and especially prisons and, especially, Wormwood Scrubs where the spy George Blake was imprisoned. The Russians eventually dumped me across Checkpoint Charlie and back into the lap of the British Secret Service who did not know what to make of the situation. I warned them repeatedly that Blake was going to be sprung, saying when and how I thought it was going to be done. I was ignored, either deliberately or otherwise, and Blake duly escaped.

When I was released from my prison sentence shortly before the Ayr murder I found my phone was tapped and I was being watched and followed. This was not paranoia but fact. It is my contention that the Secret Service tipped off the Ayr police that I was in the area on the night of the murder because there was absolutely nothing else to lead the plodding Ayrshire constabulary to my door.

I also contend that the Secret Service and the Ayrshire C.I.D. (who may have felt themselves pretty much out of their depth on this one) combined to frame me while deliberately ignoring or suppressing evidence pointing to the obvious real culprits. And when they could not get enough evidence against me they rigged an identity parade and planted bits of incriminating paper in Griffiths' car coat.

I was framed because I was an embarrassment, a liability and, in their eyes, potentially dangerous from a security point of view as well as a political one. I knew too much about the interlocking workings of the Secret Service and the K.G.B. and suspected that Blake had been deliberately allowed to escape. Allied to this the Secret Service had no way of knowing if during my sojourn in Moscow I had not been trained as a K.G.B. agent who would lie low for a considerable time before going into action. It was decided in certain elite quarters that I had to be put away for a long time and the only problem was the method. Then murderous events played right into their hands.

At a time when every year brings revelations of Soviet 'moles' in high places and of sophisticated wheeling and dealing and skulduggery in the secret services of all countries, the general public blandly accept fictionalised accounts in books, films and on television of elaborate espionage plots. In my case, truth really was stranger than fiction.

End of personal statement

CHAPTER 17

The Romantic Gunman

James Griffiths was born a romantic and died a romantic. In Glasgow folklore he will go down as the man who turned the city streets into a caricature of Chicago in the twenties.

He was born in Rochdale, Lancashire, in 1935, one of a family of seven. He started to get into trouble from the age of six when he stole articles from his own home and sold them, as well as pickpocketing his school mates.

From the beginning he always had a childish impetus to be the centre of attention and this acute feeling of vanity never left him. Although taken to a child guidance clinic and put under the supervision of a woman probation officer, the stealing continued and at the ripe old age of nine his mother took him before Rochdale Juvenile Court and said he was beyond her control. The court chairman was not pleased when he was told both Mr. and Mrs. Griffiths were out at work all day and told her, "It is felt you are losing more than you are gaining by not being at home looking after the children. It is absolutely essential that you should be there to give them a proper home where they would know they were being cared for."

Nevertheless, a year later Mrs. Griffiths had her troublesome son committed to an orphanage because she could not control him. This had a traumatic effect on James who felt totally unwanted by the harsh world and decided to wage a one man war against society.

At the age of thirteen he was back in front of the Juvenile Court for breaking and entering and theft. He was sent to an approved school where he became a sullen, morose individual, hardly exchanging any more words than were absolutely necessary with those around him.

After release he indulged in what was to become an obsession with him — stealing cars — and was sent to Borstal. This served to toughen him up and, on release, he joined the Army in the Ordnance Corps. He also got married and had two sons and for a time his life seemed to settle down.

But it could not last and in 1956 he broke into his brother's house, stealing goods and cash. When charged he also admitted stealing from an army camp. Sentence was suspended for twelve months and, before going on a tour of duty in Cyprus, he stole a car and changed the number plates and licence. On his return from abroad he was given six months.

At this time he had developed a muscular, good-looking, tousled hair physique. Snub nosed with wide, enticing eyes, he had a childlike charm which made women want to mother him and he had a rich line in patter. But his lies and bragging could become wearing. He claimed he was a top class paratrooper and had a string of qualifications from a public school. Already he had begun living in his own fantasy world.

When he came out of prison he found to his chagrin that his wife had been having affairs. His vanity badly bruised, he plunged headlong into a life of crime. He was given 18 months for fraud by forgery and a further 15 months for burglary.

After this he claims he managed to avoid arrest several times by making regular trips abroad, living in the best hotels and hitting the high spots, "After each job I got my money together and went abroad, living in the best hotels and I did what I wanted. When the money was getting a bit low I came back to this country, did some more and went back abroad. I've been caught two or three times, but there's more times I haven't been caught so I consider it was worth it.

"As regards violence, if there's one or two people come on the scene of the crime, and I've got no weapons at all, I'm captured unless I can do something about it. So I either carry a gun or a knife for self-preservation, and to cope with dogs or anything like that."

Griffiths kept himself fit with mountain climbing and potholing. He also loved romantic classical music and went regularly to concerts. He was especially fond of Russian music (Tchaikovsky and Rimsky-Korsakov) and had a large record collection with fixed views on certain conductors (Klemperer was tops but Toscanini was over-rated).

In 1963 he was back on one of his criminal money raising visits. Armed with a bayonet and along with an accomplice who had a gun he broke into a Blackpool boarding house. But the accomplice fell down in the dark and his gun went off, alerting the sleeping occupants. Griffiths, however, was not to be deterred. Two men appeared and he promptly stabbed one on the side of the head and in the thigh and almost sliced off the fingers of the other man. He then tried to comfort the injured men, getting a wet cloth compress. The two thieves made off with £700 but shortly after they were arrested and two guns were found in Griffiths' flat. An inspector at the time said that he was convinced if Griffiths had not been surprised by the swiftness of the police reaction he would have been ready to shoot it out.

He was sentenced to four years and ended up in Parkhurst on the Isle of Wight from where he staged a daring escape. He simply walked away from an outside working party when no-one was looking and got the local bus to Ryde where he paid for a day return on the ferry.

Although he was wearing prison overalls no-one paid any attention and he actually shared a railway compartment with a prison officer and his wife on the journey from Portsmouth to London. He was one of the few men in the prison's history to make a successful escape to the mainland.

He retreated up to Scunthorpe where he hid out in a caravan, protected by local villains. He returned to burglary and car theft but the law eventually caught up with him and he was given another four years and returned to Parkhurst.

There he met up with Paddy Meehan and Roy Fontaine, whose real name was Archibald Hall and who was nicknamed 'the Butler' in the criminal fraternity. A Glasgow-born psychopath, the Butler's racket was to enter the service of a wealthy family then rob them. He later became notorious as the Demon Butler, having murdered a string of victims and accomplices and buried their bodies throughout England and Scotland. This three made an odd trio but Griffiths admired Hall's high class ways and avidly read society magazines that the Butler ordered. Griffiths was always putting on airs and graces, talking with a posh accent and, when he was on the outside, dressing flashily with jewelled tie pins and cuff links. He was unpopular with most of the prisoners who found him a fake and a bore. Meehan found him faintly amusing.

Griffiths was eventually transferred to Gartree Prison where he was among a group of prisoners interviewed for a television documentary. He boasted about his climbing and potholing exploits, about being a loner, about his love of classical music, about being punctilious, well-dressed, polite and well spoken.

He also was certain he would not mend his criminal ways, "I'm not going straight when I've finished because I don't feel there's any future in going straight. I'm going to get some money when I get out of here. I shall either get the money and live very well in South America for the rest of my life, or get buried.

"Under the new penal laws a man like me with more than two indictable convictions could be sent down for a long stretch, even for a quite minor offence like stealing a bottle of milk. So when I get out of here, I know I'm going to face a big sentence if I'm caught — fifteen or twenty-five years.

"Under these circumstances, my course is clear. I don't go out with the intention of committing violence. But if in the course of my going on a job, it means either I get caught and put in prison, or I whack somebody over the head and they die, that's their hard luck. And there's no point on a job in turning back because you get as much for starting as you will for finishing, so if a policeman charges at me shouting, 'Stop, stop, stop', and he caught me a blow with that truncheon, if I had a gun in my possession, I would use it. In fact I WOULD use it!"

It was almost as if he was foretelling his own doom.

On his release, due to conversations he had had with Meehan and Hall, Griffiths decided to move to Glasgow and to make the city, where he was unknown, the base of his future criminal operations. Hall was still inside but supplied Meehan's address in the Gorbals and one evening the immaculate, polite Griffiths turned up on the doorstep. He had some stolen jewellery and an antique clock which had to be reset.

He was still the old suave Griffiths, boasting of his luxury flat, his position with a jewellery company, his new expertise at karate, showing off a tattoo on his arm consisting of a snake, dagger and skull and crossbones.

Within weeks he had broken into the home of former Secretary of State Michael Noble and stolen antiques worth tens of thousands of pounds. He compulsively stole flashy, expensive cars (in the boot of one he found a thousand pounds) and when he had seven or eight secreted in garages throughout the city he would drive some of them up to Loch Awe in Argyllshire and drive them off a cliff into a steep, deep stretch of water he had discovered. This stealing of cars for Griffiths was as much for pleasure as profit. He was always driving Meehan about, getting introduced to other crooks and pleading with the safeblower to "crack a bank" with him. From cars outside sporting hotels in the Highlands he stole a shotgun and two rifles.

It was one of their jaunts, this time to Stranraer, which had fateful consequences for both Meehan and Griffiths as has been recounted in the previous chapter. They had been casing a motor taxation office with the object of stealing documents for Griffiths' fleet of stolen cars while, unknown to them, the Ross break-in which was to lead to murder was taking place further north in Ayr.

Once Meehan was charged with murder, Griffiths was in a quandary. He wanted to clear his pal but he knew if he gave himself up he was going away for a long time. He tried phoning reporters he knew but could not get in touch with them. He phoned Tom Goodall, the head of Glasgow C.I.D., three times and told him Meehan had nothing to do with the murder. He told him about the Stranraer situation and Goodall said he should give himself up for Meehan's sake. Griffiths said he could not give himself up.

Then the inevitable happened. Meehan had to give the police Griffiths' address to clear his name. On the day that Meehan was appearing at Ayr Sheriff Court the police came for Griffiths.

What will always remain a mystery is why Griffiths had not moved out but was waiting for them at his attic flat in Holyrood Crescent, on Glasgow's north side. With his criminal expertise it must have been obvious to him that Meehan was bound to give him away to save his own skin. Yet Griffiths made no attempt to flee, almost as if he was willing to go out with a bang. The squad car pulled up outside his flat and five officers got out into the bright sunshine. They went up to the attic landing and knocked on his door loudly, saying who they were and demanding that he open up. A radio was playing and this was switched off. There was no answer. Again the knock and again the demand to open up. Then the detectives charged the door and burst it in, only to be greeted with the sight of Griffiths charging at them with a shotgun.

Since they were unarmed and taken by surprise, the officers promptly turned about and fled down the stairs as fast as they could go. Griffiths raced onto the landing, firing after them and wounding the last man in the back. They took cover behind their car which Griffiths sprayed with bullets from the attic window.

He had once boasted to one of his Scunthorpe cronies that when he went he was going to take as many with him as he could — he was not going on his own. Popping benzedrine tablets into his mouth, he started firing at startled passers-by, both men and women, wounding several. He brought a police van carrying reinforcements to a halt and, using a rifle with a telescopic sight, fired at figures in windows as the curious came to see what was happening. Soon the air was thick with flying and ricocheting bullets. Ambulancemen tended seven injured people, running under a hail of bullets. Police dogs barked and steam hissed from damaged car radiators. Armed marksmen took up positions in houses opposite while the Army despatched a Ferret Scout car. Every policeman on the city's north side was put on alert.

Then for a long spell there was silence in the street.

Unknown to the police, Griffiths, armed with his .12 bore shotgun, .22 rifle and two bandoliers, had crept downstairs, out a back window and into a lane. He ran for several streets until he saw a blue Ford Anglia outside a pub. He blasted the driver through the passenger window then dragged him out and drove off at high speed.

News of this was flashed over the airwaves and every police car converged on the surrounding area. Taxi radios were used to try and pinpoint the fugitive's whereabouts but for ten minutes it was not known where he was.

Then Griffiths crashed the Anglia at a crossroads known as the Round Toll and staggered into the Round Toll Bar. There were six men quietly sipping their pints out of the glare of the warm noonday sun when the dishevelled figure crashed through the door. He fired two shots into the ceiling, went to the bar and said to the landlord, "Don't mess me about! I've already shot some people this morning. Nobody moves or they've had it. Give me a bottle of brandy."

The terrified landlord did as he was told and Griffiths took a swig from the neck of the bottle. One of the customers, an elderly newsvendor called Willie Hughes, nervously reached for his glass of whisky. Griffiths saw the movement out of the corner of his eye, whirled in a panic and shot the old man dead.

Griffiths then ran out and leapt into a stationary lorry. He drove off as a beat police constable commandeered a passing taxi and gave chase in the best "follow that car" tradition. Radio messages now went out pinpointing Griffiths' position as he sped northwards through the Springburn district.

In a main road the lorry screeched to a halt at a traffic jam caused by faulty lights and did a right angle up a side street called Kay Street which turned out to be a short cul-de-sac.

Diving out, Griffiths ran up the stairs of the last tenement to the top floor and shot away the lock of a flat which had been vacated only minutes previously by its tenant. Taking up a position at the window he started firing, for no sane reason, at people in a playground opposite.

The police converged on the area in force, sealing off and evacuating Kay Street. He was not going to escape this time. It was to be his last stand.

While detectives fired at the window from the playground, two officers, Chief Superintendent Callum Finlayson and Sergeant Ian Smith, crept up the side of Kay Street, hugging the wall until they came to the last close. On tip-toe they then swiftly ascended the stairs.

Finlayson lifted the flap of a letter box in the door of the gunman's eyrie and looked through. Griffiths turned at the sound of the flap, saw the eyes and made for the door, guns in each hand.

Finlayson said later, "It was either Griffiths or myself. I took my revolver and aimed it, through the letter box, at his shoulder and fired. We then pushed open the door and sprang at him. He fired at us but missed, and slumped to his knees. We grappled with him and took the guns from him."

His feet hardly touching the stonework, the two men took the slack body down the stairs to the close mouth where it finally collapsed to the ground. He was dead which surprised Finlayson who had only managed to get off one stray shot. It turned out that the bullet had ricocheted down Griffiths' rib cage, tearing his insides apart.

That day in just over an hour he had killed one man and wounded thirteen others, taken on the whole of the Glasgow police force and had gone out Dillinger-style through a freak shot. He had been given the ending he desired.

CHAPTER 18

Come The Revolution

The 'Scottish Che Guevara' was the epithet given to an armed bank robber and would-be revolutionary in Glasgow who took his political ideals into the realms of crime and became one of his country's rare phenomena, the violent activist against the so-called corrupt system. Many communists believe that the only really worthwhile contribution made by Stalin to the cause was in his early days, just after the Russian Revolution, when he became a bank robber in Tiflis and gave the proceeds to the Party. Every revolutionary movement needs money — the centres of wealth are closed to them and budding revolutionaries, most of them dangerously naive with a simplistic outlook on problems and solutions, tend to believe that the cash in bank accounts of business enterprises is legitimate plunder for the enemies of capitalist society.

But when they robbed the rich to save the poor, these latter day Robin Hoods found that the Establishment could react with savagery and in Glasgow in 1972 they were effectively put out of circulation for good. The rebel in this case was 33-year-old Matthew Lygate, founder of the Workers' Party of Scotland. He was a highly intelligent political theorist who believed in the doctrines of Mao and Marx.

Lygate was born on the south side of Glasgow and became interested in politics soon after he left school at the age of 15. He took a job as a tailor's cutter and early in his working life became interested in communism and joined the Young Communist League. In his early twenties he went to New Zealand for six years and while there he again immersed himself in politics — what he described as "the struggle of the oppressed worker against capitalist doctrines". Once he had been converted to communism there was no going back for Lygate. It was his one true and trusted faith and one for which he was to become a martyr.

On returning to Glasgow one of Lygate's first steps was to create the Workers' Party of Scotland with himself as leader. In 1969 he stood as a candidate in a by-election in the Gorbals but polled the lowest number of votes, even fewer than the official communist candidate. Evidently the proletariat were not yet ready for the message. During the campaign he made it clear that if he were to win he would refuse to take his seat in the House of Commons but would set up the country's first soviet.

The Workers' Party were in favour of complete separation from England and making Scotland a republic. Their policies were in accordance with those of John MacLean, the charismatic Red Clydesider of the twenties who was made the first Soviet consul in Britain by Lenin himself.

MacLean stood for the Gorbals in 1923 and, in his election address, just ten days before his death, said, "My policy for a Workers Republic of Scotland debars me from going to John Bull's London Parliament. Last year I told you I would not go as I could get nothing there." Lygate was following this philosophy to the letter.

The tenements of Glasgow are a ripe breeding ground for ultra-left wing politics. The city is predominantly working class, the civic local authority has been mainly socialist, the M.P.s have been mainly Labour and, in the early seventies, there was a generation of young men brought up with illusions of personal and political freedom which were a legacy of the liberated sixties. The decline of the shipyards and heavy engineering, lengthening dole queues thanks to greater computerisation and another deepening recession all seemed ample proof to many young idealists that the decline and fall of the capitalist system was imminent. Strange cult figures like Trotsky, Mao and Guevara seemed to offer a ready made solution for many to this apparent decadence and at street corners and in bars cloth capped youths could be heard in lengthy debates about the overthrow of the Establishment just like their forefathers, who had seen tanks in George Square quelling workers' unrest.

In 1972 there was a spate of robberies in the city. Four banks were raided by hooded men carrying sawn-off shotguns and more than £20,000 was netted. Tellers were clubbed and warning shots were fired. In addition, a haulage firm was robbed of £3,500 and British Rail employees in a wages office were temporarily blinded with ammonia while a safe on the premises was emptied of £5,500.

Acting on a tip-off, armed Special Branch detectives burst into a small bookshop which Lygate ran and which sold nothing but communist and revolutionary literature. The Special Branch had been keeping an eye on him and his shop for some time, well aware that he was a potential troublemaker, a fact which Lygate never tried to disguise.

In the basement of his shop they found guns, hoods and stolen money. Similar tell-tale articles were found in his nearby flat, as well as a radio tuned into the police wavelength. The political theorist was arrested along with the caucus of his Party, 24-year-old Ian Doran, 35-year-old Colin Lawson and 31-year-old William McPherson.

Doran had met Lygate through a mutual sympathiser of the communist cause and had stayed in Lygate's flat for a while. He was a second hand car salesman. Lawson joined the Party after meeting Lygate, again through a mutual acquaintance. He camped down in Lygate's flat before taking up his stance in a sleeping bag in the bookshop where he assisted Lygate and received the princely sum of £5 per week. He had evinced no interest in politics until coming under Lygate's talkative, almost hypnotic influence. A single man, he had been a psychiatric nurse and had joined a religious order, working at Nunraw Abbey in East Lothian. With Lygate he had found a new messiah.

McPherson was a professional gambler, a drifter with no settled address. He lived in hotels in Glasgow, London and Manchester, paying his bills from winnings he garnered in private houses in the three cities. He too was persuaded to join the Party after meeting Lygate through a friend and he became a leading protagonist at many of the Party's committee meetings. A rootless person, he seems to have been given some purpose in life after being given a cursory lesson in Marxist economics.

This then was the motley crew of misfits who were going to release the chains of the Scottish working class and show them a new Jerusalem. When their trial started at the High Court in Glasgow all four were charged with armed robbery, assault and forming a criminal conspiracy. Lygate, who was the dominant personality of the four and was treated by the Prosecution as the ringleader, admitted that he knew there were large sums of money, various firearms, masks and clothing in the basement of his bookshop.

But he declared defiantly, "I have been associated in many parts of the world with guerilla tactics on behalf of the working classes. And last year I was approached by some of these people and asked if I was prepared to participate in bank robberies. I refused as I felt this would jeopardise my position as a political organiser and chairman of the Workers' Party of Scotland."

Lygate said he was approached again later and asked if he would at least keep various articles. And he said he would. He told Nicholas Fairbairn, his advocate, that he put "the tools of the trade" in the basement himself but that he had not taken them to his flat. The evidence found there was, he claimed, planted by the Special Branch.

He denied having taken part in the robberies, much though he appreciated and sympathised with the fact that people were prepared to take violent actions to liberate the downtrodden proletariat. He went on in the witness box, "If that means liberating money from banks to furnish materials for us to move forward in the struggle, I support this."

Midway through the trial Lygate became annoyed with Fairbairn's attempts to defend him and dismissed his counsel on an assurance from the Judge, Lord Dunpark, that he would be allowed to make his own closing speech as well as one in mitigation should the need arise.

The Prosecution summing up emphasised an element of identification (some of the accused, but not Lygate, had been hesitatingly picked out by bank staff as their attackers) and the overwhelming circumstantial evidence of the guns and the booty being found in the possession of the accused.

Lygate told the jury he had known what was going on, had helped store the weapons and other articles involved as well as the stolen money, had supported the raids in theory but not in practise.

The jury were out only a brief while before finding all four guilty on all charges.

Lygate, in his plea of mitigation to the Judge, said that what had brought him to court was violence against the working class, the same violence that had put 150,000 persons out of work in Scotland at that time (the figure was to rise throughout the decade), and the violence which had caused the withdrawal of free milk and led to children again suffering from rickets.

Lord Dunpark impatiently told Lygate that such matters were irrelevant in regard to the sentence which would be imposed. However, with this warning he allowed the prisoner to continue.

But Lygate was never one to take a warning and after several more minutes of political haranguing Lord Dunpark again interrupted, "I have given you a good deal of licence. You must not make a political speech."

Lygate then said that people could not get work so that their only alternative was to join the Army and fight in Ulster "and murder Irishmen and women."

Lord Dunpark said that violence in Ireland had nothing to do with the sentence to be passed. His Lordship became increasingly annoyed with Lygate's attempts to take over his court.

Lygate continued to declaim about the oppression of the working class and ended by warning that a day would come when those who judged him and his fellow accused would themselves be judged. It was not the sort of speech likely to endear him to any judge and was the complete opposite of mitigation as he sought to justify his crimes, almost glorying in them.

Lord Dunpark reacted strongly. Although he had no previous convictions, Lygate was sentenced to twenty four years' imprisonment. The Judge described him as a highly dangerous insurrectionist who had taken part in a deliberate criminal conspiracy over a lengthy period of time and had supported bank robberies "presumably because they were aimed against capitalist institutions."

McPherson, the one time gambler, was jailed for twenty six years, Doran, the ex-car salesman, was jailed for twenty five years and Lawson, the former monk, was given six years because he had only participated in one raid.

As the four ashen faced prisoners were taken to the cells, Lygate and McPherson suddenly raised their arms in a clenched fist salute and shouted, "Long live the workers of Scotland!" There was silence from the public benches and the revolutionaries were hustled down out of sight.

A news conference was held at the end of the trial by the Workers' Party of Scotland at which their new secretary Mr. Thomas Murray, aged 71, said that the time might come when his party would use bank raids to obtain funds to help the working classes to overthrow the capitalist system. But the time had not yet come. He said proposals at party meetings to use robbery as a way of funding the movement had always been turned down. But the Party was now demoralised and virtually out of action.

One of its last acts before retiring from the limelight was to issue an official statement a few days after Lygate had started his long sentence. It said that the Party deplored an association between members of the Party and non-members in activities alleged to have been carried out to benefit the working classes (ignoring the fact that all four accused were members). It said there had been "no consultation whatsoever" with the Party about the armed raids and said, "Those who committed them were wrong to carry out these deeds."

There were consequent attempts by Lygate's parents to get his sentence reduced and he considered appealing to the Court of

Human Rights in Strasbourg against the severity of the sentence after the parole board twice turned down his applications for freedom. He told them he would not step outside the law again to further his political aims — but he was not believed. His father, shortly before a premature death brought on by the ordeal, also hired a private detective to find evidence to get the sentence reduced but all to no avail.

The deep fascination with politics remained unabated throughout Lygate's long years in prison and psychiatrists described him as fanatical in his beliefs and unshakeable in his communist convictions, which he made no attempt to hide. He organised a food strike at Peterhead Prison and a campaign for political rights for prisoners, barricading himself in his cell and struggling in vain against a transfer to another prison.

As time went on he was allowed to work on V.A.T. and prisoners' wages in an office in Craiginches Prison at Aberdeen. He told his brother on one visit, "I suppose I could have made out that I had seen the light and become religious or something but even if it means I must stay here and serve my full sentence I still could not compromise my integrity, honesty and principles.

"Even when I get out I may have to emigrate, if I can find a country to accept me, because the police will be keeping a special watch on me.

"I'm not bitter. I live from day to day. It's the only way to survive reasonably intact. You couldn't serve a twenty four year sentence any other way.

"People say why shouldn't I be released when a man like Jimmy Boyle is being trained for freedom. Good luck to Boyle if he is a reformed character and no longer vicious. But I don't want to be compared with him or any other prisoner. I want to be judged as me."

One judgement must be that he paid an exceptionally harsh price for bucking the system.

CHAPTER 19

Sister of Mercy

Glasgow, with its great medical teaching hospitals and university faculties of medicine, has for almost a hundred years been a leading centre for the healing sciences. The city has produced a string of stern, high-minded doctors and researchers who have revolutionised medicine the world over and made the dour, abrupt physician with the bedside manner and the harsh Scots accent almost a national caricature. These men had religion deeply embedded in their characters and felt they were doing the Lord's work when they improved methods of healing.

But with the decline of religion and the rise of a more consumer orientated society, new (and some would say sinister) ideas began to be discussed, like abortion, euthanasia and artificial insemination.

The decline in religious values was symbolised in the city by the growing number of derelict kirks to be seen while those that remained open had increasingly smaller and older congregations. Glasgow at one time had the highest church going Presbyterian population in the world but by the late sixties and seventies this had declined drastically, thanks to more liberated younger generations either being cynical or turning away from the dank, restrictive dogmas to freer fields for spiritual nourishment. Redevelopment saw whole districts demolished, made parts of the inner city into deserts and scattered church flocks and in the process also accelerated the slackening of the hold of Bible teachings.

In particular, the practise of euthanasia was openly discussed at medical schools and its ethics debated, something which would have been unheard of but a few years previously. Questions like this were open and shut cases to the old medical pioneers. The taking of human life under any circumstances was against the law of God and that was that.

But with the growth of the hospice movement and the rise of voluntary societies like E.X.I.T., dedicated to the final alleviation of pain, with the lessening belief in the sanctity of human life and a more practical approach to creature comforts, young medical theorists began to wonder if it was not their duty to end a life if all hope was gone and it appeared merely to be a case of prolonging the agony.

Euthanasia of sorts occurs in a surreptitious way with a cloak of professional rectitude drawn over it. Often a switch has to be put off to end the life of a human vegetable or medical help is withdrawn to let nature quickly take its inevitable terminal course. These circumstances are accepted by a silent medical profession and often grateful members of the public.

But open euthanasia, the blatant taking of a patient's life, is another matter altogether. Ironically, the controversy was raised in all its complexity with a 1974 murder case in Glasgow, the ancient bastion of kirk-led ethics and morality in the medical field. The case excited public comment, private discussion, angry letters in the press and ended in an about turn on the part of the Law.

It centred on Ruchill Hospital on the north side of the city where relatives of patients in a geriatric ward became suspicious, on comparing notes, at the rapidity of patients' deaths. The C.I.D. were called in and found they had a major headache. Short of spending months digging up bodies it would be a problem to find out in entirety what, if anything, was going on. They solved this by concentrating on certain cases and leaving it up to the city's pathologist to analyse the evidence.

The result was that in October of that year Sister Jessie McTavish, a 34-year-old spinster, was charged in Edinburgh High Court with murdering an 80-year-old terminal patient, Mrs. Elizabeth Lyon, at Ruchill Hospital by repeatedly injecting her with insulin. She was alleged to have committed the offence after watching a detective programme on television which dealt with a method of killing involving the use of lethal drugs which left no trace in the body. It was maintained she thought the insulin would be burned up by the still functioning juices in the corpse so rendering discovery impossible. Death would be put down to heart failure, if in fact there would be any post mortem at all on such an ill and elderly patient.

She was further charged with four assaults by syringe on elderly patients in her geriatric ward number five at the old redbrick hospital, this time by using "substances unknown". After a fifteen day trial, during which most of the evidence was medical and technical, the jury found her guilty by a majority of the murder charge and three of the assault charges, with an acquittal on the fourth charge.

The neat brunette in her red leather coat, having been sentenced by Lord Robertson to life imprisonment, was led from the dock between two policewomen weeping hysterically, "I never did that! I never did anything like that!" There was silence in the crowded courtroom.

But only six months after starting her sentence at Gateside Women's Prison in Greenock she was freed. A hearing at the Court of Criminal Appeal in Edinburgh quashed her conviction because Lord Wheatley, the Lord Justice Clerk, held that Lord Robertson had misdirected the jury on an essential matter.

The rule he had failed to observe in his charge to the jury was that, having referred to police evidence of an alleged admission of guilt made by the accused after she was charged, he failed to present her side of the story — that she had, in fact, made no admission at all. The Judge's role was to guide the jury on points of law but proof of the facts was for the jury to decide. And it was essentially a matter of fact whether or not there had been an admission of guilt.

Lord Wheatley in quashing Jessie McTavish's conviction referred to the ruling by Lord Aitchison in a 1935 case and quoted from it, "I reach this conclusion with regret. It can never be a light thing to interfere with the verdict of a jury on a charge of murder. As I have already said, there is in my view ample evidence to support the verdict.

"But by the Law of Scotland an accused person is entitled to have his case tried with an adequate direction to the jury and if on any vital matter the direction is so inadequate as to amount to misdirection, it is our plain duty to set the verdict aside."

Cheers and applause from a packed public gallery greeted this decision. Sister McTavish's supporters, and there were many, overlooked the fact that the three assault convictions still stood. However, she was allowed to go and she sped off to freedom in the sports car of a private detective who had helped the defence — and a beaming crowd watched her go.

Miss McTavish later claimed she had been made a scapegoat and forced "to carry the can" for atrocious conditions at the hospital where she worked. She said she had never believed in euthanasia and never would and wanted no part of any public debate on the matter. She claimed she had only given the dead woman an injection of sterile water and not insulin although medical evidence at her trial had contradicted this.

After her release she declared she wanted to return to nursing — "my first love" — and she told reporters over a celebratory magnum of champagne. "When I was told I was free it was like being handed my life back. I really did not grasp it for the first few minutes."

She had received a thousand letters of support while in prison as well as 106 Christmas cards. She claimed she had had a dream a few days before the hearing that she would walk out of court free and that another female prisoner would have her sentenced halved. Both events had happened.

An inquiry into working conditions at Ruchill Hospital, built in 1895, was held after her trial and Miss McTavish claimed the report vindicated her while condemning the wholly incompetent way the establishment was run. The inquiry was ordered by the Greater Glasgow Health Board and, as she had suggested, found evidence of appalling conditions and serious neglect by junior doctors. Statements in the report about the problems caused by junior doctors who showed little interest in the geriatric patients were in agreement with her evidence at the trial. The committee of inquiry found that the hospital had no clear leadership and that junior doctors were doing locum work when they were supposed to be on duty at Ruchill, that they were reluctant to visit wards when asked, that they ordered injections and prescribed drugs by telephone and failed to verify deaths properly, that there was remote management, poor communications, serious under staffing, overcrowding and loss of job satisfaction for the staff. And in addition the geriatric wards were too widely scattered for satisfactory supervision.

Miss McTavish was a ward sister and the report said that on occasions one sister had been left in charge of twenty wards. Describing their task the committee said ruefully that they "had to consider whether the fact a nursing sister in Ruchill Hospital stands guilty of charges of assault in itself represents a circumstance which should reduce public confidence in the hospitals on which they depend."

The report went on to state that "an error of judgement" might have been made when the background of Miss McTavish was not examined at the time she resumed her nursing career after a stay in Canada.

She had become a ward sister in 1965, went to Canada two years later and eventually had been appointed as a sister at Ruchill in 1969. When she took up this appointment a medical certificate was provided saying she was fit for duties as a nursing sister. It made no reference to any psychiatric history.

Yet nurses gave evidence that she made no secret to her friends and associates that she had had emotional problems and psychiatric help prior to her appointment in 1969. Some witnesses said she was emotionally unstable. Staff records early in 1973 showed she was anxious to please and kind to patients but easily upset. Differing views were expressed on whether she had behaved abnormally but one point of agreement was that she appeared to be devoted to her patients. One sister said she ran one of the best wards in the hospital and favourable comments were made by patients' relatives. She had ordered flowers for all her patients at one stage and had arranged a bus run for them without getting proper authority.

But the insulin cupboard was not supervised and had been easily accessible to her or any unauthorised person.

Two weeks after the report, the General Nursing Council for Scotland struck Miss McTavish's name off their register for professional misconduct. She was surprised at the decision because she had not been given an opportunity to present her case properly. They demanded the return of all her nursing certificates and badges. When told the news she said she was desperate to return to nursing as it was the only life she loved. But this time her appeal fell on deaf ears.

Exactly a year to the day after she was freed on appeal she married a 39-year-old warehouseman who had been a friend since her primary schooldays. They were later divorced but she was granted custody of her baby daughter.

The question as to her guilt or innocence, morality or immorality remained open for individuals to decide. Cynics would argue that her only mistake was in being found out but, regardless, she was seen to contravene the basic tenets of her profession and there was no question of her being accepted back.

Her case also raised the legal question as to whether a convicted murderer should be allowed to go free on a legal technicality at the Appeal stage or whether it would not be better to have a retrial, regardless of the inconvenience to witnesses and the legal profession. To date the subject of retrials, although examined by committees at the highest levels, has not been acted upon and considering what Shakespeare dubbed 'the Law's delay' there seems little likelihood of any action. Killers may continue to walk free given a flaw in the Judge's summing up.

On the medical side of the McTavish case, one can only wonder what Lords Kelvin and Lister would have made of it all. They would probably have decided their advances had not really taken mankind as far forward as they had thought.

CHAPTER 20

Rogues Gallery

Every city has it's characters on the fringe of criminal activity and Glasgow has had more than its share. Generally harmless, they live by their wits, hard drinking, two fisted when it comes to a personal injustice, with a penchant for gambling in all its forms. They are non-conformist even in the criminal world and bring a touch of eccentricity to that strictly structured society.

In the twenties and early thirties one of Glasgow's best known characters was a man named Mickey Casey who lived in a model lodging house in Buchan Street in the Gorbals. But despite the meanness of his residence he dressed and spoke like a gentleman. Not that Mickey was a man of means. He just dressed and spoke like one. He was in fact a pauper and petty thief who stole good clothes to boast his vanity.

The fine clothes he wore (in those days the tailed coat and bowler hat were fashionable) made him stand out, at least in the Gorbals.

As Mickey walked along the street swinging the cane he always carried, the women of the area would gaze after his tall erect figure in admiration.

But Mickey had two weaknesses, drink and gambling. And with some alcohol in him, Mickey would do anything for a bet. He once walked along Glasgow's Argyle Street, under the influence of too much champagne, on a Saturday afternoon, dressed in spats and a bowler hat — and nothing else.

Another time he dressed up as a priest and went into the confession box at St. John's Chapel in Portugal Street. Sitting in the gloom of the confessional Mickey heard a few confessions and handed out absolutions. Then one of his friends from the lodging house entered the box, a man whom Mickey suspected of cheating him at cards. In the course of his confession the man admitted the sin of cheating. "Was it at cards?" Mickey asked. "Yes, Father," said the man. "Was it Mickey Casey you cheated?" "Yes, Father," said the man. "You must return all the money you cheated from Mickey Casey, then come back here for absolution", said Mickey.

But the man made no attempt to return the money and after a couple of weeks Mickey, who had a few too many at the time, let it be known to the man's gambling cronies in no uncertain terms that he was definitely not to be trusted, even with the threat of damnation hanging over him.

It was Mickey's love of fine clothing that was his undoing. One day he came out of the lodging house wearing a pair of brown boots he had acquired from a pal who had filched them from the house of a country gentleman. As he proceeded down the stairs to the street, the boots got their revenge, Mickey slipped and fell, the fall breaking his neck. There was not even time for the last rites.

But being a popular figure in the district, Mickey was spared the indignity of being buried in a pauper's grave. His body was taken to the home of a woman in the district and there the customary wake was held, with his pals from the lodging house in attendance. After a great deal of drink had been consumed, it was decided to give Mickey a proper send off by taking his body from the coffin, propping it up at the table, and dealing him a last game of cards. In the course of the game the lady of the house walked in and fainted at the sight of the corpse sitting at the table. It is said that Mickey did not win his last hand at cards — someone was cheating.

In the thirties and forties a similar figure around the Gorbals and the city centre was a man known only as Bee Baw Babbity. If he had another name then very few people knew what it was. Like Mickey Casey, Bee Baw Babbity was a beggar and thief. It is doubtful if he would have agreed with this description, preferring to describe himself as an entertainer.

Several times a week Bee Baw Babbity would do his rounds of the Gorbals. He would stand in the centre of the back-court and sing a song, and the song he sung was the one that earned him his name: Bee Baw Babbity. The song had these words and no more: "Bee Baw Babbity, babbity, babbity, Bee baw Babbity, Lassie or a wee laddie," and so on.

After a while the windows would go up. Sometimes a few half-pennies would come out, sometimes a cup of water, and sometimes a pot of urine, (one of the reasons why Bee Baw Babbity always stood in the centre of the backcourt) and sometimes the only thing that came out was abuse from some housewife because Bee Baw Babbity's singing had 'woken up the wean'.

The kids of the Gorbals used to have great fun with Bee Baw Babbity. Whenever they heard him in the backcourt they would scrounge a halfpenny 'to throw to the auld man in the back'. They would throw the halfpenny to the old man alright, but before doing so they would heat it up on the fire or the gas ring. At such times Bee Baw Babbity would not only sing but dance. It was a dance of pain as he picked up a halfpenny that was red hot.

Until recently a familiar sight, albeit a disturbing one, around Glasgow's city centre was the figure of a handless, blind beggar wearing a placard around his neck. This beggar's name was Tom Galloway. In the early fifties, Tommy was a criminal who sometimes indulged in a little safeblowing. His knowledge of explosives was somewhat hazy and that, plus the fact that Tommy was a heavy drinker, made him a danger to himself and those around him. In the late forties Tommy and another man blew the safe in a wholesale butchers in Errol Street, Gorbals. As a result of overloading the safe with gelignite a piece of metal flew off the safe door and entered

Tommy's neck. The injury was a serious one and resulted in Tommy losing a lot of blood. But his accomplice managed to carry him out of the premises and so got clean away.

It was in the fifties that Tommy lost his sight and both hands. This came about when, in a state of intoxication, he attempted to pay off a grudge against a shop owner in Glasgow's Castle Street. He made up a gelignite bomb and attempted to throw it into the back window of the shop. His aim was bad and the bomb bounced back on him. As it did so he caught it. At that moment it went off. For the rest of his life Tommy was a beggar who often haunted Glasgow's Argyle Street. In 1977 he was found dead in a city centre close. Death was due to malnutrition and pneumonia.

Another character was Big Mull, a beat policeman in the Gorbals during the 1940's. Being originally from the Western Isles, he liked a drink and found his police pay inadequate to meet his need.

If drink was Big Mull's vice, his pet hate was 'neds' — the young, shiftless, male hooligans. But Big Mull had a lot of respect for 'earners', men who were criminals but harmed no-one, apart from the safes they blew. No doubt Big Mull had his own personal reasons for distinguishing between the 'earners' and other members of the criminal fraternity. Earners usually had money. And money was something Big Mull was always in need of.

In the forties a number of safeblowers lived in the Gorbals, and it was common knowledge among them that they had nothing to fear from Big Mull, provided they did not practice their trade on his patch. And provided they paid their dues to Big Mull for the protection he extended to them. The safeblowers accepted Big Mull just as he accepted the backhanders they gave him when in the small hours of the morning they returned from a nights work to find him standing outside their home.

One night Big Mull was on duty in the Gorbals when he decided to collect some money from a local pub that happened to be closed. He called at the home of a safeblower and suggested that the safe in the pub was ripe for blowing. The safeblower agreed and off they went. While the safeblower was busy in the pub Big Mull stood guard outside. After a while the safeblower came out and borrowed Big Mull's police torch, the batteries in his own having become flat.

The job was successful and Big Mull and the safeblower went to a local house and cut up the money from the safe. After that they began to partake of some whisky taken from the pub.

They spent the night drinking and when it came the time for Big Mull to go off duty he discovered that his police torch was missing. The safeblower had inadvertently left it in the pub. There was no time to return to recover it, and anyway the safeblower was by this time too drunk to stand up.

When the owner of the pub opened up that morning and discovered that his pub had been burgled he came running out into the street in search of a policeman. By chance an off duty policeman in the shape of Bill Mull happened to be passing. Telling the publican to stay where he was, lest the villains might still be on the premises, Big Mull entered the pub and retrieved his torch. The publican rewarded Big Mull with a bottle of whisky.

Although Glasgow has a justifiably bad reputation for violence, not all the tearaways were thugs and layabouts. Many were 'earners' — villains who went after big money without doing violence to innocent people. But it sometimes happened that violence would erupt between the thugs and 'earners', usually because members of the thug element would use threats to extort money from an 'earner'. This could often lead to a serious confrontation and sometimes murder.

In the mid-1940's a thug named McLatchie from the Garngad area of Glasgow tried to extort money from a Gorbal's 'earner' named Andy. Although reluctant to get involved in violence, unless it was to a safe, Andy decided that something would have to be done. He sent word to McLatchie asking him to call at Milligan's pub in Caledonia Road and also sent word to a couple of members of the Bee Hive Gang letting them know about his trouble.

On the day arranged, McLatchie arrived at Milligan's pub but remained outside. Andy soon learned of his arrival but he was in no hurry. He remained in the pub calmly drinking in a convivial atmosphere until afternoon closing time at 2.30 then he and his pals strolled nonchalantly out into the daylight. At the sight of Andy, McLatchie walked forward and at that moment a shot rang out. McLatchie was dead within seconds of hitting the pavement.

It was an open secret in the Gorbals that Andy had put the finger on McLatchie but despite this the police arrested and charged another man with the murder, a man who had not even been in the area at the time of the shooting. But after a fortnight in custody he was released. The murder of McLatchie was never officially solved. There were, conveniently for Andy, no witnesses willing to testify.

Some years later a similar case of a thug trying to extort money from an 'earner' involved a heavy named Algy Airns from the Gallowgate and the 'earner' was a young man named Davy Barr, a barrow boy who supplemented his income from selling fruit with a little safeblowing. One day he was standing by his fruit barrow in Argyle Street when Algy Airns and one of his pals, with 'tram lines' on his face (razor scars), appeared on the scene. Algy demanded money from Davy as the price of protecting his fruit barrow from being vandalised.

"Who's going to vandalise my barrow?" asked Davy.

"I am!" replied Algy.

"Right!" said Davy. "If you want money from me then you can fight me for it!"

Algy weighed up Davy's slim build and smirkingly agreed. Leaving a boy in charge of his barrow, Davy accompanied Algy and his henchman to Glasgow Green. On the way Algy told Davy that when he had finished with him he would drag him into the bushes and leave him there until he regained consciousness and added, "That way you won't get picked up by the police as a drunk and incapable case."

"That's extremely considerate of you," observed Davy.

On reaching the Green they found a quiet spot and squared up, stripped to the waist. After five minutes of fists smacking on bone, gristle and muscle, it was obvious that Algy was in the process of getting the hiding of his life. At this point 'Tram Lines' decided to step in and help his mate but, at the end of another four ferocious minutes, both were soon lying unconscious on the grass with fractured jaws. Davy obligingly dragged them into the bushes before putting on his shirt and returning to his barrow. He was not bothered by them again after that.

In later years Davy had a certain notoriety in the city when he gave up his fruit business and concentrated full time on safe blowing. But after a couple of lengthy prison sentences he had the sense to get out of the game and become an honest citizen and a happily married man. As for Algy Airns, like so many Glasgow thugs who used violence just for the hell of it, he ended up on the human scrap heap and took to drinking meths, finishing in an unmarked grave.

Another character who was very much in the Glasgow criminal scene a number of years ago was Benny Davidson who believed in settling his differences by man to man combat on a Sunday morning, that day being chosen because the pubs were shut. He could have made his name in the boxing world (like fly-weight champion Benny Lynch) had he not been over fond of the bottle (also Lynch's downfall).

In the course of his pugnacious life Benny Davidson fought hundreds of fist fights, most of them for bets. In the latter half of his life, when he was past his prime, he got involved in a feud with two brothers who were themselves no mean fist fighters. On a Sunday morning in the mid-fifties Benny and his seconds rendezvoused with the brothers and their seconds on the banks of the Clyde. First Benny took on the elder of the brothers and after a gruelling fight which lasted half an hour Benny's opponent was out cold.

"Okay," said Benny to the younger brother. "You're next!"

The second fight lasted even longer than the first and was even more frenzied but the result was the same — Benny was the victor. But the two brothers were not prepared to accept defeat. A few weeks later they knocked on the door of a house where Benny was having a drink. On the door being opened the pair rushed in and attacked Benny: but the result was the same once more — at the end of the fray it was the brothers who suffered the most damage. As a result Benny ended up in court charged with serious assault. However, the brothers were even more determined to get their revenge. While Benny was on bail they waylaid him as he made his way home the worse for drink. The brothers nearly killed him up a darkened close that night and he was never the same man again.

A High Court Judge once said of Benny, shortly before his premature demise, "On a Sunday you go out into the park to indulge in stand up fighting the way other men go out for a game of golf!"

Violent folklore has always played its part in the city's sub culture and to this day the wildest donnybrook is treated in terms of humour, or even respectful admiration, rather than disgust. There is something intrinsically rough about the place and the toughest are often those most talked about admiringly.

One of the toughest was a character called 'Irish Gerry' who used to put on a show every Saturday night at Gorbals Cross (whenever he was out of prison that is). Doyle's Pub was his favourite watering hole, a place which made a Wild West saloon seem tame. Children of the district used to gather at the Cross to view his exploits after closing time. The door of Doyle's Pub would burst open and out would stagger 'Irish Gerry', one of the biggest men in the city. He would peel off his jacket, stand swaying in his vest, and shout "I'm ready — come and get me you bastards." Round the corner, as if on cue, would come a squad of six constables, truncheons at the ready. Bets would be placed among the gathering crowd as to how many 'Irish Gerry' could knock out as fists, boots, truncheons and helmets flew pell-mell through the night air. The toll of police casualties was usually between two and four before the writhing, swearing mass would tumble towards the open, waiting doors of the Black Maria. On one occasion Gerry actually battered his way through the partition separating the secured van from the cab, dumping the two surprised constables in the front seats onto the road as the Maria screeched to a halt against a lamp-post. Then Gerry would get his inevitable spell in jail for police assault and the neighbourhood would quieten down until the word went round "Gerry's out" and the children would converge once more to the door of Doyle's Pub of a Saturday night.

CHAPTER 21

On The Road

In the wee sma' hours of Sunday February 19th, 1969 two pretty girls stood in Glasgow's London Road trying to thumb a lift back south to their native Dumfries. They had spent Saturday shopping in the city and had then gone to the dancing at night. One of them was a lively 17-year-old brunette called Pat McAdam, the other her 19-year-old chum Hazel Campbell. A large articulated lorry drew up and the tidy, good looking driver grinned pleasantly and offered them a lift south to the border which the girls readily accepted. They stopped for a hot meal at an all night service station then continued on, laughing and joking, to Annan where Hazel was dropped. The lorry then doubled back towards Dumfries but stopped in a lonely lay-by where the driver, Thomas Ross Young, made love to Pat in the darkness of the cabin.

When the girl did not return to her parents council house the police were alerted, Hazel was contacted and a description of Young issued. He was eventually traced through the haulage firm he worked for and 'grilled' by detectives at Dumfries Police Station. He admitted he was the lorry driver but insisted he had dropped Pat off on the outskirts of the border town. Police tracker dogs, constables digging up newly disturbed ground, frogmen, helicopters, road checks, cottage to cottage inquiries — all the paraphernalia of a full scale search was concentrated on the woodland and moorland area between Dumfries and Annan, a stretch of twenty miles. A national newspaper even flew in a Dutch clairvoyant who had, with mixed results, helped detectives throughout the world in murder hunts, including the Boston Strangler Case. There was a flurry of excitement when he said there were girl's clothes buried beside a tree but Pat's mother said they were not her daughter's. The clairvoyant eventually said he felt water when he thought of her and believed the body had been washed away into the Solway Firth.

The objection to this — water nearly always yields up its dead somewhere — could be overlooked in regard to the Firth because it is notorious not only for its fast tidal currents but, more pertinently, for its deep quicksands. It is possible, if the clairvoyant was correct, that they will hide the solution to Pat's disappearance forever.

The missing girl's parents, knowing she had no intention of running away, appealed to Young the lorry driver, but he stuck to his story and was eventually grudgingly allowed to go. The search petered out and Pat was listed as missing.

Eight years later there were two incidents in an isolated lovers' lane in Glenboig, Lanarkshire, near Glasgow. A prostitute was raped by a lorry driver but managed to struggle free and in a state of collapse flag down a family in a car on a nearby road. Then only weeks later the decomposed, semi-naked and trussed up body of a woman, later identified as 37-year-old Miss Frances Barker from Maryhill, Glasgow, was found among trees in the lane. She had been brutally assaulted and had died of a combination of strangulation and suffocation, having her knickers rammed down her throat.

Detectives, looking for lorry driver Young in connection with the rape, raided his former wife's home in Glasgow and found him cowering in a makeshift hidey hole under the floorboards. They also found a powder compact which Young claimed he had bought for his teenage daughter Patsy at a shop round the corner, but when this was checked the shopkeeper said he did not sell compacts like that. Further checks revealed it was in fact one of a small consignment given to staff and special customers at Daly's store in Sauchiehall Street and one of the recipients had been none other than the murdered Miss Barker.

The forensic department now came into its own. Scientists went over Young's Scania Super 80 low-loader lorry with vacuum equipment. They discovered a hair that could have come from the dead woman and a hawthorn leaf which matched those in the lane. Blood on the hair was found to match Miss Barker's blood group. Even scratch marks on the roof of the lorry could have come from overhanging branches at the death copse and detectives spent several days driving a similar lorry around the lane to see if branches touched the roof, which they did.

Young, aged 43, was brought to trial and a picture gradually emerged of the most savage monster the West of Scotland had produced since Manuel.

Almost from birth, Young had a complex about women. He was born illegitimate and held this as a grudge from the day he realised what it meant. Not only that but his mother rejected him to such an extent that he had to be looked after by her parents. He never recovered from this rejection and perhaps as a result never had any real love or respect for women.

His career of crime started at the ripe old age of nine when he was admonished on a theft charge but that same year he was put on probation on three charges of housebreaking. Three years later he was sent to an approved school on charges of theft and indecent assault although he had not even reached puberty. Five years later while serving in the Army he was given 91 days detention for being absent without leave.

While working in an iron foundry in Kirkintilloch in 1955 he met his wife-to-be, Annie, whose mother, however, did not approve of her daughter's burly, good-looking boy friend so they eloped to Chesterfield and were married a year later. Young got his first job as a long distance lorry driver and the couple soon moved back north to Glasgow once Annie's mother had recovered from the news.

For a while the marriage went smoothly but then Young started to get moody and eventually violent towards his wife. She felt he was jealous of their baby son James and thought she was not giving enough attention to him. She also discovered that although Young was strong and had a powerful sex drive he was inadequate and unable to climax in the normal way. This used to infuriate him and he would punch the pillow in frustration.

He started roaming abroad on his own at nights, claiming he was going to the cinema which he always enjoyed, his favourite star being Doris Day. He did not smoke or drink to excess but after six months of his nocturnal jaunts Annie discovered he was unfaithful. He was seen with a girl in town who later came looking for him at his house and he received a Christmas present of a pullover signed 'Love from Margaret' which Annie threw on the fire, her reward being a severe beating.

He terrorised Annie over the years when he came back from trips and on one occasion he put her in a cupboard and nailed it up, but she escaped after an hour's screaming for help because he was afraid the police would be called. Plans for her divorce fell through because witnesses failed to turn up and she was so frightened of more batterings that she took him in once more, although they slept in separate beds. She was given a respite from his fists when he was jailed for three months for failing to maintain his children, three boys and a girl.

There was another shock for Annie when he was jailed for 18 months for raping a 19-year-old girl in Shropshire. Before he was sentenced he told her the girl was a prostitute and had been shouting for money which he had refused to give her.

When he came out of prison Young toured the length of Britain in his lorry taking sex from hitch-hikers or prostitutes whenever he felt like it. He boasted he had intercourse with more than 20 girls in his cab a month and that picking them up was easy. He was always plausible with smiling lies about his name, his home, his wife who had sadly "died". If his victims rejected his advances he went ahead anyway. Physically, he was hard to resist in the confines of his cab.

Although only five foot eight, he weighed 14 stone and used chest expanders and practised karate to keep in trim. He had large, staring hazel coloured eyes and a pallid complexion and when he started clenching and unclenching his fists in anger he could be a frightening spectacle. He had nude women tattooed on his arms, one with a snake curled round her, and the other squatting on a champagne glass with musical notes alongside. He claimed this denoted his lifestyle — wine, women and song.

At home he would spend hours in the bathroom sprucing himself up and he was always clean cut and immaculate. He would laze around watching television, reading war comics or going to the cinema.

Then in February 1970 the Law caught up with him at last and he was jailed for eight years for raping a 15-year-old schoolgirl in his lorry at Abington in Lanarkshire. This was the last straw for Annie who divorced him. When she told him the news in prison he glowered at her and said, "I'll kill you when I get out!"

When he was eventually released, after three years remission for good behaviour, he moved into a Glasgow flat of his own but frequently visited Annie's house to shower presents on his daughter Patsy. She also frequently visited him at his flat. But violence was never far away and after one fierce family argument he slashed his son Thomas across the throat with his lorry driver's clipboard and punched and slapped his two young daughters-in-law.

He returned to his old long distance habits and also as a 'hobby' would hire cars and stick a taxi sign on the roof so that he could pick up girls. He also took prostitutes to a multi-storey car park and beat them up if they refused to comply with his perverted requests.

The Glasgow of the time made it easier because it was rapidly becoming a motorway city. The crowded tenements had given way to ring roads, by-passes, long elevated concrete roads, a tunnel under the Clyde and a bridge over it so that a woman could be picked up on one side of the city and whisked across to the other within minutes. Using the high motorways it was possible to traverse straight through the city at high speed without ever entering it properly. The static city communities had been decimated, the inhuman, desanitised ring roads being the final strangling cords, and it was now very much a mobile population with people being picked up all the time. It made sex and murder on wheels very easy and Young took full advantage of this. To get to the outlying housing schemes it was preferable to have a car, especially late at night, and he was only too willing to oblige.

At his work Young was considered the best employee the haulage company ever had — punctual, tidy and uncomplaining. His colleagues could not believe this quiet, unassuming chap was a monster. However, the police knew all about him, so much so that a photo of him was flashed onto screens during lectures to senior detectives and they were warned "watch out for this man!"

It was partly his track record which led the police to Young but it was his present to Patsy, Miss Barker's compact, which finally nailed him.

The jury of eight women and seven men took only 57 minutes to find him guilty on a series of charges. Apart from killing Miss Barker, he was found guilty of raping the prostitute in the lovers' lane, guilty of raping a prostitute at knifepoint in a car park, guilty of holding a 16-year-old girl captive in his home for ten hours and committing indecent acts against her, guilty of assaulting a 65-year-old pensioner with a screwdriver after she had entered his 'taxi' and been taken to a lonely lane, guilty of attacking and attempting to murder a 20-year-old girl in a bus shelter and, last but not least, guilty of assaulting and intimidating Annie. Verdicts of not proven were returned to charges that he pushed a burning cigarette into another prostitute's face and assaulted her. Not guilty verdicts were returned in two other rape charges.

Young, dressed in a casual brown suit with a belted jacket, sat arms folded and showing no emotion as the jury returned their verdicts and Lord MacDonald told him, "You are a dangerous man and the public must be protected from you." He was sentenced to 30 years "which he must serve in full before being considered for remission" which is the longest term of imprisonment ever imposed in Scotland. Howard Wilson and Matthew Lygate only got 25 years and even Jimmy Boyle only got 15 years.

In Young's lair under the floorboards, where he retreated when he guessed the police were looking for him, were found, apart from the tell-tale compact, four different ladies buttons which had nothing to do with known victims.

Police forces throughout Britain were alerted about this. Files on scores of missing girls who could have been given lifts in lorries were reopened and samples of Young's blood were sent throughout the country. So many waifs and strays go missing yearly and are forgotten and there are so many good 'burial grounds' in the countryside that it would be impossible to calculate how many are dead. Young, who always carried a shovel in the back of his lorry, said it was easy to pick them up. Even Jack the Ripper and his later Yorkshire counterpart found it easy to get victims at the height of their reigns of terror.

During his trial Young had told detectives in Barlinnie that he would help them with other murders if he was allowed twenty minutes alone in a cell with his ex-wife's boyfriend and when told this was out of the question he replied, "My initials are T.R.Y. If you want to know about other murders — try and try again."

Within minutes of leaving the dock at Glasgow High Court he was confronted in a cell by two senior detectives from Dumfries who had interviewed him all those years ago. They asked for co-operation on the McAdam case but Young told them angrily to "F★ck-off!" Then he was driven away to the small solitary cell in Peterhead's top security wing, with the constantly burning light and the constantly checked judas hole, which will be his home until he is 73.

And Pat McAdam is still listed as missing.

CHAPTER 22

Underworld

At the beginning of November, 1977, Glasgow's Central Fire Station received an unusual call around midnight. A passing motorist said he thought the High Court was burning down. On arrival at the scene firemen found that the North Court was indeed engulfed in flames and sparks were spreading to the South Court. The sombre old building which had stood opposite Glasgow Green since last century was on the point of complete incineration.

A dozen fire engines converged on the blaze and sixty firemen using breathing apparatus and turntable ladders and utilising water from the nearby Clyde tackled the flames which lit up the night sky for miles around. After half an hour the fire was brought under control and the building, a symbol of continuing order, authority and justice to many Glaswegians, was saved, although the North Court was gutted.

Fire inspectors sifting through the charred wreckage later came to the conclusion that the blaze had been started by a deluge of petrol bombs flung through a shattered skylight on the roof.

That same day the trials were due to start of thirteen men charged with a series of robberies on banks, hospitals and post office vans. The fire raising incident was interpreted by detectives as an attempt to destroy the mass of articles to be used in evidence against the accused. If this were so, the attempt failed because the evidence was locked up in the basement and was undamaged.

However, the trials were postponed but only for a few days until the South Court, comparatively undamaged, was renovated enough to be utilised. The authorities were determined that these trials would go ahead regardless.

The trials lasted a total of sixteen days and during that time what remained intact of the High Court building was virtually turned into a fortress with armed police standing guard and swarming over adjacent premises. There were threats that witnesses would be shot if they spoke up and they had to be hidden away by armed detectives in secret addresses, being hustled in and out of the back door of the court into security vans when it came time to give evidence.

There were fears that the trial Judges, Lords Cowie and Kissen, as well as the four prosecuting counsel involved in the four trials, might be kidnapped and held hostage and they too had to be escorted and protected at their exclusive club in the city centre.

The public benches were cleared and anyone approaching the steps of the High Court had to identify themselves. Every morning and evening during the four mile journey between Barlinnie Prison and the court the accused were raced at high speeds through stopped traffic in a convoy of siren-wailing police vans and cars, an armed support unit taking up the rear.

All of this was a tribute to the fearsome power wielded by a dapper 49-year-old grandfather called Walter Norval who claimed Glasgow belonged to him and his big time crime syndicate.

He was a well-built, vain and ruthless thug who controlled his troops with a fist of iron. In and out of prison for assault and robbery since an early age, he had developed an animal cunning in matters criminal and, having eliminated potential rivals with knuckle dusters and coshes, he and his boys proceeded to amalgamate and organise the major gangs in the city into a cohesive force which struck with military precision.

Tens of thousands of pounds came in from the robberies he planned. Sometimes he took part in them himself just to keep his hand in and show he could use a bit of muscle when he had to. But more often he was the mastermind who used young thugs he recruited from the Milton and Govan areas of the city to do the violent work.

He paid well for information and once word of this got out it was easy for him to pick up on the grapevine when and where payrolls were being delivered, which banks were vulnerable and where vans could be hi-jacked. Before making a "strike" he would study the target for weeks, sometimes months, dressing his gang members in workmen's clothes to case buildings and driving over escape routes and pinpointing hideouts for getaway cars.

He had a secret arsenal in a garage where he kept shotguns, revolvers, axes, hammers, knives, swords, masks and gloves. He rehearsed his gangs on how to act and what to expect when they broke into a bank and illustrated how to get the best results quickly and brutally.

All this planning paid off and for three years the city's C.I.D. were baffled by a spate of seemingly unconnected but highly successful robberies on banks, post offices, security vans and wage offices.

And Norval led the sweet life, going about in flashy clothes with diamond accessories, driving fancy cars, smoking the best cigars and drinking the best champagne in the top night spots. He fancied himself as Glasgow's answer to Al Capone and in time the police began to hear of this flamboyant character with lots of money from nowhere.

On investigation, quietly and surreptitiously, they found he was married with seven children and six grandchildren. Despite his show, his family lived in a humdrum council house in Liddesdale Road, Milton. But he also had a glamourous, blonde mistress, Jean McKinnon, who he kept in a west end flat. He had a 15-year old son by her.

He had the effrontery to collect unemployment benefit, social security and family allowance each week. Meanwhile, he helped his elderly mother run a number of flats she owned, collecting rent for her and pocketing £225 for himself each week.

He was an inveterate gambler and each afternoon could be seen in his favourite bookie shops while of an evening he had a liking for casino life.

He was self-conscious about his looks and was a frequenter of sauna baths and health clubs. He could frequently be seen combing his hair in a certain way to ensure that his left ear, half bitten off in a prison brawl, remained hidden.

Gradually, detectives of the Serious Crime Squad built up a file on him and relying on whispers from the underworld concluded that he was the brains behind the robberies.

He almost slipped up after a breakfast-time raid on a van delivering wages to a hospital in which he took part. Detectives, realising it had all the hallmarks of the earlier robberies, converged on his house as soon as the alarm was raised. He had only arrived home minutes previously and just had time to disrobe, wrap a bath towel round himself and splash his face with water before answering the door. All wide-eyed and innocent, he denied all knowledge of the raid, swearing he had just got up — which his wife verified. The detectives left him to make other enquiries and when they returned discovered he had left for a fortnight's holiday in Teneriffe with his mistress, a holiday he had booked three months previously. His wife did not seem to mind, seeming to be glad to be rid of him.

When he returned, gang members met him at the airport with the news that his stepfather, Joe 'the Pole' Kotarba who was the boss of a west end vice ring, had been stabbed to death by a pimp trying to take over his racket and Norval was the beneficiary of £2,500 insurance money. Everything seemed to be coming up roses for Norval but his good times were running out.

After yet another successful robbery, the Serious Crime Squad armed themselves and descended again on Norval's house, where he was quietly watching racing on television, and hauled him in to a police station for questioning.

He was still nonchalant and protested his innocence. When asked about his luxury automatic Ford Granada car, he said he had bought it with gambling winnings. He even shrugged off the finding of a shotgun and ammunition in the car boot by telling detectives that someone must have put them there. However, possession of a firearm was enough to hold him and a team of detectives now proceeded to 'turn over' those criminals who were known to be in his gang.

In particular, they concentrated on an up-and-coming thug, 32-year-old Philip Henry, who they knew to be a weaker character than the rest. In tried, traditional but successful manner, they alternately cajoled and threatened him for hours in the interrogation room until under the glaring lights and the even more glaring eyes of the detectives he finally cracked as they knew he would. He took them to the Kilpatrick Hills and showed them where Norval had asked him to bury £3,000 and a sawn-off shotgun. It was all over for Norval as Henry now proceeded to 'sing like a canary'.

At the subsequent trials Henry had to be given special protection since Norval, furious and raging like a trapped animal, had put out a contract on the informer and ordered his execution.

Henry had been one of Norval's blue-eyed boys and the gang leader could not understand how he had misjudged his character. A special guard was put on Henry and he was kept in solitary confinement at Barlinnie but, despite this, another prisoner still managed to douse him with boiling water, causing painful scalding.

In spite of all the efforts to stop justice taking its course, Norval and his henchmen stood in the dock facing a list of charges and a mass of incriminating evidence — including Henry's which he gave in the witness box with downcast eyes.

If there had been an attempt to intimidate the jury, it too had proved unsuccessful because they returned guilty verdicts on all the accused. Norval was jailed for 14 years, which was less than some of his gang members who had taken part in more raids. The highest sentence of 21 years went to Norval's right hand man, John McDuff who was only 22, as was the next in line, Joe Polding, who was given 18 years.

As Norval and his boys, handcuffed together, left the court under the watchful eyes of dozens of police officers, they grinned and winked at press photographers as they piled into a Black Maria.

Possibly they were thinking of the 60% of the loot which is still unaccounted for and which is hidden around the city, being looked after by minders until the gang gets out.

Henry was given four years for his part in the robberies, a much reduced sentence because of his co-operation with the police. However, it also meant he would have to serve it in solitary confinement.

Three months later Norval's attractive, raven haired daughter walked free from the same court, cleared of plotting to disrupt her father's trial. She had been charged with conspiring to destroy the High Court Building. As she left the dock she kissed her husband who was given five years for telling a Crown witness he would be "filled full of holes" if he gave evidence against Norval.

The spate of armed robberies which had plagued Glasgow month by month came to an abrupt halt and no organised outfit has so far stepped in to fill the vacuum left by the departure of Norval and his boys.

Nor is it likely that there will be any heirs to the criminal throne. With the redevelopment of the inner city involving the lessening of the population by a third during the late sixties and seventies, with the destruction of close communities, the chances of another organised underworld network like the Norval system has been lessened.

There are still those men who claim to be big timers in crime, those fat, cigar smoking, richly coated, large shadows in the corners of pubs extending largesse to their thirsty vassals. They are often in the nefarious fringes of scrap metal business or restaurateurs or in the background of clubs and pubs but, despite the rumours they like to waft around them, the serious criminal danger of these bluffers is limited to the fear and grudging admiration of a comparatively small number of petty crooks.

While Norval was running his empire, the city still had the remnants of a cohesive underworld where organisations could be set up on an integrated basis. But now, with the break-up of the inner city areas, it has meant the police have scored a clinching victory and ended the danger of organised crime on a large scale. The old city, that giant industrial metropolis with its mixed communities, has gone. It's like will not be seen again. Ironically, there are now plenty of 'dear green' places once more, this time caused by slum clearance sites once again grassed over.

Epilogue

Crime, like so many other things, is not what it used to be. Advances in security have ended the days of the cracksman and the daring burglars. Advances in forensic science have meant the death knell for the poisoner. The gangs have been broken up along with their areas. And even simple developments like all pervasive television, allied to the closure of cinemas and dance halls, has entailed generations growing up without knowing the dubious delights of roaming the night streets restlessly looking for action.

Glasgow's 'best' years of crime coincided with the city's rise and fall. Like the city itself, the major crime was often cruel, vicious and heartless, but hardly ever dull. Now murder is commonplace, usually a sordid knifing or drunken domestic brawl of no interest to anyone outside the small family circle involved. As Sherlock Holmes was wont to sigh, "Oh, for the crimes of yesteryear!" Even more liberal regimes in prison has meant little trouble there. As in other walks of life, with easier conditions a lot of the characters have gone. They got their tough resilience and brassy humour battling against the odds and trying to forge their own personal life style.

The criminal has often been someone who makes up his own rules, society's outsider with his own tough code of living, his own black philosophy, his negative form of ambition.

The fact that there is presently concern over rising murder statistics proves that material well-being bears no correlation to the burgeoning problem of those with the mark of Cain. Society's values can be rejected equally by the poor or those with money or those who are simply bored.

In Glasgow in the mid-seventies the murder rate (an average of around 50 annually) was the highest since figures started to be recorded, proof that material comforts do not detract from crime.

At one time the problem was viewed very much in black and white terms: eradicate poverty and squalor and eliminate the money-seeking motive behind illegal acts. It is now obvious that the problem is much more complex than that.

To say criminals breed criminals is an over-simplification but there is no doubt that if a son has a natural admiration for his father and the father happens to be a villain then that is all to the bad. If the father's criminality leads to fighting in the family or the break-up of marriage, the tensions created plus the lack of love, concern or discipline result in the child becoming bitter, depressive, independent and unruly.

Alcohol also plays its part. Since the affluent society came into being those with a 'drouth' as well as a violent temperament have found it easier to buy more booze. Inhibitions dissolve more quickly and violence erupts. An unofficial survey among visitors to Barlinnie Prison recently revealed that 80% of those incarcerated for murder did not remember committing the deed.

Urban deprivation, that Government inspired euphemism for slums, has also played its inglorious part in the cause of crime. Those brought up, sometimes unemployed from leaving school, with no respect for their surroundings or the people who rule them will tend to have less compunction about taking a swipe at a society and an Establishment which has placed them bottom of the heap.

There are, of course, those psychopaths with a real blood lust. For them very little can be done and there is an argument in their case that they should be put down like vermin, although in what is still supposed to be a Christian country the belief that anyone, no matter how wicked, can be saved should theoretically come first.

Crime is the warped hybrid of social conditions and to concentrate on deterrents is to wallow in red herrings. There is only one deterrent to crime that works and that is to creat conditions where the criminal germ cannot fester. To change living conditions and the outlook of whole sections of the community takes time and there are no easy, overnight answers but the more the problem is shirked the worse it becomes.

Although punishment, which treats the symptoms and not the disease, is no cure, some reforms could still be introduced. The rules and regulations which govern penal institutions are calculated to strip a man of his dignity and even his identity. In the process it can be forgotten that the men who live out their existences in prison, although criminals, are human beings with the thoughts, feelings and reactions of free mortals. It is not likely that such men can be rehabilitated by subjecting them to a system that is geared to the creation of hatred and resentment.

To criticise is an easy matter. To advocate change is something else altogether. In Scotland the problem is somewhat different and in places more acute than elsewhere in Britain. A Scottish High Court Judge is on record as saying that crime in Glasgow has an undue preponderance of the vicious and the violent. One answer could be to institute an anti-violence campaign — in prisons. It is here that violence plays an important role in the maintenance of discipline. As well as being stripped of his identity, clothing and possessions, the rules take away the prisoner's self respect. This dehumanisation process, nothing less than a psychological assault on his character, does nothing except turn the inmate into a vegetable or implant ineradicable hatred.

To abolish the present system and replace it with one that would be much less expensive to run would be no easy task as it would have to tackle rehabilitation. One step in the right direction would be prison factories where the long term prisoner would be required to do a day's work. They could be run by civilians with prison staff in a security role. From any money earned the prisoner would be required to repay a victim or put it into a victims' fund, keeping a small amount for himself. In this way a prisoner would learn a trade, how to cope with responsibility and would also feel he was being treated as a human being.

Other changes could include a properly supervised six month hostel scheme for the newly released who feel at a loss in the outside world and revert to their criminal haunts and cronies — eventually returning again to prison. Such hostels should encourage the released man, among fellows with the same problem, to stand on his own two feet, face the harshness of reality outside and 'go straight'.

Recidivists should be treated in the same manner. It is difficult for a normal balanced person to understand the mentality of the institutionalised 'old lag'. The attractions of prison seem incomprehensible but to some desperate people they are there, nevertheless. For the destitute it provides a roof over their heads, regular nourishing food in their bellies and a warm bed at night. For the lonely it provides companionship and the comforting closeness of others who have lost their way and are in distress. For those who cannot face up to the pressures of life it takes away all decision making, all nerve wracking responsibility and the will which is necessary to act, replacing it with a mindless routine in which obedience means safety, peace and security of sorts. For the nihilistic, the self destructive, the masochistic, it satisfies all their black yearnings.

Alcoholics who end up inside because of their particular problem should be given proper medical treatment, detoxified and put in touch with an organisation which can help. The reputations of the so-called 'hard men' and troublemakers would collapse overnight if they were transferred to locked wards in state hospitals and labelled among the lags as simply 'loonies'.

The Special Unit in Barlinnie has shown in dramatic terms that the encouragement of an inmate's creative side can work wonders in reform and there should be more facilities available for prisoners to express their own individual personality — even if it is by keeping budgies or learning to play the banjo.

The 'batter squads' would have to disappear from the system. To achieve this it would be necessary to take the Official Secrets Act out of the Prison Administration. In this way those prison officers who are against the barbaric practice of beating up prisoners would be at liberty to report the activities of the 'batter squads' to the nearest police station. The majority of prison officers deplore the activities of the 'batter squads' but are reluctant to make complaints, especially where the prison governor has come up from the ranks and is steeped in the system's traditions. Those employed in the prison system, including church ministers and priests, should not be liable to prosecution for repeating anything heard or seen within prison walls.

The nether world inhabited by the twilight people — the fish-eyed killers, the pallid brawlers, the brassy whores and sleek pimps, the gun-toting robbers, the feline burglars, the slashing gangsters, the grinning heavies, the shadows at the corner — will always be with us, as much a part of life as that dark side of the moon in the all too human character. But there are some things to be improved and learned.

Original sin is not a fashionable concept any more but only by looking evil squarely in the eye, as well as accepting a basic goodness about much of humanity, can something be learned, perhaps only a little, but something relating to what it is all about. Compassion is not an easy virtue while ignorance is a cosy vice. It is advisable not to forget completely the forgotten people. They too once had their desires.

They too would have known Glasgow in its heyday with its swaying trams and jostling streets, its wide green parks and its close crowded pubs. They would have known the feverish excitement of a Friday night with all the long week-end to look forward to, the dressing up, the brushing of the hair in the mirror, the final jaunty adjustments.

They would have known Glasgow in its dancing years, the dark, perfume laden atmosphere, the loud, garish bands, the flowing, gyrating bodies. Possibly they too stood in a shipyard and watched the champagne bottle smash, the cheering crowds, the raging, dusty mountains of chains and the crackling clamour as the tall ship smoothly swept into the splashing, curving water.

They would have known the shop girls and the factory girls with their bright scarves fluttering as they bobbed and clicked home from work. They would have known the hawkers, the street vendors, the sellers of trinkets and jewellery, the barrow boys selling everything from baths to bongo drums.

Glasgow to them might have meant Sauchiehall Street of a Saturday night, waiting for the steamers at the Broomielaw or wending to an International football match at Hampden Park. It might have meant those yellow lighted windows in the twilight masonry and the tenements with their strange, savage beauty. It might have meant nothing more than feeding the ducks by a pond with a girl of a Saturday afternoon. Or kicking a ball about in the street.

Their memories may be of the long scarlet evenings of their youth. And memories are all they have to warm them in their cells tonight.